Enlightenment on the Eve of Revolution

ENLIGHTENMENT ON THE EVE OF REVOLUTION

The Egyptian and Syrian Debates

ELIZABETH SUZANNE KASSAB

COLUMBIA UNIVERSITY PRESS *NEW YORK CITY*

Columbia University Press
Publishers Since 1893
New York   Chichester, West Sussex
cup.columbia.edu
Copyright © 2019 Columbia University Press
All rights reserved

Cataloging-in-Publication Data is available from the Library of Congress.
ISBN 978-0-231-17632-3 (cloth)
ISBN 978-0-231-17633-0 (paper)
ISBN 978-0-231-54967-7 (ebook)

Cover design: Lisa Hamm
Cover image: Elias Zayyat, *Deluge: The Gods Abandon Palmyra: Study 01*, 2003.
Courtesy of the Atassi Foundation for Art and Culture.

Contents

[v]

CONTENTS

Acknowledgments

When my previous book, *Contemporary Arab Thought: Cultural Critique in Comparative Perspective*, came out in 2010, I had no idea that a momentous upheaval would shake much of the Arab world before the end of that year. Yet the book had laid bare an unmistakable alarm and discontent among intellectuals about how regimes and societies were faring in the Arab world. This discontent was largely about the failures of the postindependence states to secure a functional political life, healthy economic development, basic health care and education, freedom of expression, civil and human rights, and some hopeful future for its citizens. My analysis showed deep frustration at the enduring impossibility of change, but it could not foresee the large-scale outburst of that accumulated frustration and anger.

Like so many others who followed the massive protest movements that broke out in December 2010 in Tunisia and then spread to Egypt, Syria, Yemen, and Morocco during 2011, I became glued to my computer as I pursued the exhilarating albeit increasingly distressing developments across the Arab countries. My focus was on the intellectual debates that accompanied those developments and the attempts of Arab intellectuals and artists to make sense of what they were witnessing. I was also interested in situating those debates in contemporary Arab intellectual history, and in particular in the three decades that preceded the 2010–2011 upheavals.

This book is an attentive reading of two sets of debates on *tanwir* ("enlightenment" in Arabic) that took place in Cairo and Damascus in the

1990s and 2000s. My aim is to situate these debates in the Arab intellectual history of the second half of the twentieth century and leading up to the 2011 upheavals. I argue that these debates addressed the mounting failures of the postindependence states and that what they advocated under the name of tanwir was a form of political humanism. They called for the reconstruction of the human being in Arab societies, for the affirmation and protection of life and human dignity, for the assertion of people's right to political participation and civil mobilization, and for the invention of hope and faith in the human in the midst of despair. I also argue that by warning against the consequences of the state failures and asking for urgent change, they voiced demands that were to be heard a decade or two later in the streets of Cairo and Damascus.

Work on this book was generously supported over many years by German research centers. In spring and fall 2011, Gudrun Krämer hosted me as a fellow researcher at the Berlin Graduate School Muslim Cultures and Societies of the Free University. In weekly meetings organized with rigor and generosity by Professor Krämer, the school offered a lively and diverse forum for fellows to exchange research notes. It presented pleasant and optimal work conditions in the quiet and leafy Dahlem neighborhood of Berlin. It also allowed me to benefit from the rich network of academic centers across the Free University and beyond.

During the 2013–2014 academic year, I was offered a fellowship at the Käte Hamburger Center for Advanced Study in the Humanities in Bonn, an idyllic location and a haven for researchers. I thank Stefan Wild for recommending me to the center and for the many conversations we had during my stay in Bonn. The center's founding director, Werner Gephart, with his accomplished scholarly and artistic gifts, offered a welcoming setting in an atmosphere of conviviality, freedom, and intellectual erudition. The center's manager, Stefan Finger, and his team of young scholars and student assistants provided sustained, competent, and friendly support throughout my stay. And last but not least, the center's physical location on the majestic Rhine was a constant invitation for peaceful meditation and productive conversations, a most precious opportunity for those of us who hailed from the convulsive parts of the Arab world. For me, coming from Lebanon and working on the Arab world, it was a cherished safe setting at a comforting distance from the events unfolding in the east of the Mediterranean. After hours of following daily news and commentary on my office computer, I would lift my eyes and see from the window the tranquil flow of the Rhine, and I would ponder on how so much violence and serenity could coexist on the same planet. The contrast was unfathomable to me. I knew of the unspeakable horrors that had taken place on the banks of that clean and beautiful river, and I was often reminded of the barbaric propensity common to humanity. During my walks on the banks, I would pass by postwar Germany's old and modest house of parliament and think of the long and arduous journey of the new republic toward democracy. It is true that that journey was supported by foreign powers whose interest lay in bringing about a stable and pacified Germany, but it also involved the tremendous efforts of the Germans to pull themselves out of the moral, political, and economic ruins of their country. Public debates regarding this dramatic past continue to mark the country, and their intellectual, moral, and political quality remains a source of inspiration for me.

My stay in Bonn was extended by another semester when I was invited to be the Annemarie Schimmel Visiting Professor at the University of Bonn for spring 2015, during which I gave a seminar on the Arab *nahda* (or "renaissance"). I thank the students with whom I had interesting discussions about those past nahda debates, often in connection with the issues that were being raised by Arab thinkers as the uprisings were unfolding.

In fall and winter 2015–2016, I was a fellow at the Centre for Middle East Studies at the University of Marburg, in a program launched after the Arab revolutions entitled "Re-configurations: History, Remembrance and Transformation Processes in the Middle East and North Africa," with a hub of international scholars working on those "reconfigurations." The interaction with local and visiting scholars and the wonderful research facilities helped me progress with my manuscript. I thank Rachid Ouissa, head of the Re-configuration program, and its director, Achim Rohde, for hosting me. I was then invited to join the Leibniz Research Group "Figures of Thought-Turning Points: Cultural Practices and Social Change in the Arab World," headed by Friederike Pannewick at the University of Marburg. I thank Professor Pannewick for her warm support. During those two years, 2015 and 2016, the refugee flow from Syria, Iraq, Eritrea, and elsewhere in and around the Middle East reached unprecedented levels since World War II, with people desperately seeking safety and a glimmer of hope for their future. Exposing themselves to the murderous exploitation of traffickers and the hardships of the Mediterranean and Balkan routes, thousands of people lost their own lives or lost loved ones and precious belongings. Most of them wanted to reach Europe, and Germany in particular, and in so doing challenged the proclaimed values and unity of the continent, provoking a serious European crisis whose aftermath is still being felt today. I attentively followed the debates that ensued from this crisis in and outside Germany.

In fall 2016 I had the privilege of joining the new Doha Institute for Graduate Studies in Qatar as a member of its philosophy department. The institute offers students from across the Arab world graduate training in social sciences, media and cultural studies, development economics, and public administration, with a strong emphasis on humanities. My teaching and research in modern and contemporary Arab thought at the institute blended smoothly with the concluding phase of my manuscript. Being able to share and discuss the findings of my research both in writing and in teaching was a most rewarding experience.

The stations at which I completed the manuscript were in Aix-en-Provence and Vienna. In summer 2017 I was a fellow at the Maison méditerranéenne des sciences de l'homme, Université Aix-Marseille, in Aix-en-Provence, France, and in summer 2018 I was a guest fellow at the Institute for Human Sciences in Vienna. I thank Richard Jacquemond and Shalini Randeria, respectively, for their kind invitations.

Between the time I started working on this book (spring 2011) and the time I concluded it (summer 2018), dramatic changes took place across the Arab world, particularly in Egypt and Syria. The peaceful protests against tyranny, corruption, and injustice were brutally crushed. The initial and revitalizing moments of hope and pride were dissipated beneath the unrelenting pressure of increased tyranny and violence. The numerous critical voices were systematically marginalized and silenced. Ordinary Egyptians and Syrians were left exposed to the unbridled forces of repression amid the general indifference and at times even complicity of foreign governments. This led me to question the use and meaning of resistance acts in the face of such cruelty and lack of support. It also made me wonder whether documenting those intellectual debates could be in any practical sense meaningful or helpful when buffeted by so much criminality and impunity. Nevertheless, I remain convinced that efforts at analytical lucidity, as manifested in the tanwir debates, and the moral courage that they required under the most forbidding circumstances are vivid testimonies of life-affirming human intelligence and dignity. They need to be honored, acknowledged, and made available. They are, in my opinion, valuable sources of inspiration for the future struggles for decency and dignity that are bound to emerge again sooner or later.

I want to offer a big thanks to Wendy Lochner at Columbia University Press for having journeyed with me in the making of this book, both with patience and perseverance. I am grateful to her team in bringing the final product to light. I want to particularly thank Michael Simon for his careful copyediting of the manuscript. Last but not least, I wish to thank the four anonymous reviewers who read my manuscript and offered numerous helpful comments and suggestions.

Enlightenment on the Eve of Revolution

Introduction

THE TWO DECADES that preceded the 2011 revolutions in Egypt and Syria, especially the 1990s, witnessed animated debates on *tanwir* (enlightenment). During those decades, Egyptian and Syrian societies suffered the worsening impact of corrupt and autocratic regimes in almost every aspect of life. All efforts at protest and change had failed, leaving people with a deep sense of helplessness. State violence, repression, censorship, the absence of the rule of law, pauperization, and the collapse of health and education services had traumatized these countries and exhausted their people. Various sectors of society, including workers, students, women, peasants, and intellectuals, had tried to oppose, resist, and reform to no avail. The debates on tanwir emerged in the sociopolitical, economic, and cultural aftermath of these ominous developments, on the eve of the sweeping revolts of 2011. In both countries they addressed issues of human dignity, liberty, tolerance, reason, education, human rights, and democracy. What were the precise issues that the discussions focused on? How were those issues approached? What concerns, ideas, and values did the debates articulate? How did these, if at all, relate to earlier Arab contemporary intellectual debates? And finally, how did they connect, if at all, to the demands and concerns voiced in the 2011 popular revolts, particularly in Egypt and Syria?

The disenchantment with the independence era began with the stumbling of the postindependent nation-state building projects. It was caused by political instability, failed unions with neighboring Arab countries, the disaster of Palestine, wars with Israel (including the 1967 Arab defeat in the Six-Day War), military coups, thwarted economic development projects, social polarization, and national dissentions and conflicts leading in some cases to civil war. Arabs, particularly in the Levant, where these events had their epicenter, had to come to terms with these unhappy developments. A profound malaise came to dominate the second half of the twentieth century, leading to anxious soul-searching. This malaise was mostly articulated in the cultural sphere, under the headline of "cultural crisis." Clearly, the struggles for independence, liberation, and development had not achieved their goals, and self-examination was needed to offer explanations, for no longer could only external enemies be blamed. My reading of some of these Arab reflections on their cultural crisis shows two trends[1]: a strong inclination toward culturalism, meaning a tendency to explain sociopolitical and cultural phenomena through culture; and another, less prevalent turn to politics as the main cause of all the aborted projects of independence. The postindependent state, and the autocratic form that it had taken, became in this second line of thinking the major culprit. In the course of the second half of the twentieth century, one could observe the growth of this political reading of the situation.

The struggles for independence and the mobilization for nation-state building in its early phases were led by a quest for a sense of self, for the affirmation of a culture and identity of one's own, and for the establishment of an independent government. A few decades into independence, the concern had started to shift toward political participation. The quest for democracy had gradually overtaken that for identity. The demand had moved toward reclaiming people's critical faculties, as humans and as citizens. Agency and critical thinking were the concerns of numerous Arab critical thinkers. Ideologies such as nationalism, Baathism, Nasserism, Marxism, and even Islamism had started to lose their attraction. Many Arabs, including intellectuals, yearned for radicalizing critique and the empowerment of the people. At the same time, 'Ajz (impotence) had become another dominating feeling: the deep feeling of being unable to implement change in the face of repression, corruption, and neoliberalism.[2] The Cairo and Damascus tanwir debates of the 1990s and 2000s belong to and stem from this Arab fin-de-siècle mood.[3]

It is useful to start by saying what the tanwir debates were not. They were not studies of the Western Enlightenment, nor were they discussions of the place of Europe in a posited Arab enlightenment prior to the arrival of Europe with its armies. Indeed, the tanwir debates did not primarily aim at disseminating or discussing Western Enlightenment ideas, thinkers, histories, or literatures. This had been an important aspect of the *nahda* (renaissance), from Rifa'a al-Tahtawi (1801–1873) to Taha Husayn (1889–1973). Intellectual histories of the nahda, starting with Albert Hourani's *Arabic Thought in the Liberal Age, 1798–1939* and including recent reexaminations of the period,[4] have documented that endeavor and discussed its merits and shortcomings.[5] Systematic studies of the reception of the Western Enlightenment in modern Arab thought shed further light on the subject, though more needs to be done in the field.[6] In any case, it is clear that the Western Enlightenment legacy per se was not a focus of the tanwir debates. However, many of the ideas central to the Western Enlightenment, such as tolerance, secularism, rationality, human dignity, and freedom, were focuses of these debates. In the polemic between the Islamists and the secularists, the Islamists accused some of these ideas, such as secularism and freedom of worship, of being imported, alien, or polluting. Yet these ideas seem to have become established topics of the discourse, though defined and interpreted differently in each camp.

Moreover, the intellectual production of the nahda remains a highly significant component of contemporary Arab thought and continues to be evaluated in different ways: it is either appreciated—often with nostalgia, even when criticized—for the intellectual freedom, creativity, and productivity that it demonstrated; or it is condemned for being an aberration and a form of cultural alienation and for the intellectual corruption it visited upon Arab life in general.[7] Interestingly, many contemporary Arab thinkers, as we shall see, refer to the nahda as tanwir, using the terms interchangeably,[8] which shows that for many Arab thinkers the nahda represented some form of tanwir. Examining the pre-2011 tanwir debates will lay bare the sense in which that characterization is made.

The tanwir debates were also not concerned with the indigenous roots of the "nahda-tanwir" ideas in precolonial Arab-Islamic history. In fact, this was a theme of heated debates in the West, generated first by American historian Peter Gran's 1979 book *The Islamic Roots of Capitalism: Egypt, 1760–1840*, and later by a set of articles published in the 1990s by German historian Reinhard Schulze. In these contentious publications, the question was whether elements of enlightenment could be identified in the precolonial

Arab-Islamic eighteenth century. Gran's thesis was that between 1760 and 1840, elements of secular thought had emerged in Egyptian writings as a result of local capitalist socioeconomic developments not unconnected with global economic trends. A number of scholars found his economic data insufficient, and at times inaccurate, and believed that his arguments connecting the economic phenomena with the cultural were questionable. Nevertheless, many thought that his invitation to perceive the Egyptian and Arab eighteenth century differently from the established narrative of stagnancy was important.[9] Gran's book was translated into Arabic in 1993 but did not stir much discussion.[10] Schulze picked up on Gran's new historiographical orientation and hoped to improve on its conceptual and methodological aspects to corroborate the thesis of an indigenous enlightenment movement in eighteenth-century Egypt and the Arab world. His argument was based on testimonies of individual mystical experiences and rereadings of religious tradition that can be considered manifestations of enlightenment inclinations. His proposals were also vehemently attacked in the West without attracting much attention in the Arab world.[11]

However, Egyptian historiography gained some interest in Egypt in connection with the bicentennial commemoration of the 1798 Napoleonic invasion. On this occasion the French Ministries of Foreign Affairs and Culture and Communication and the Egyptian Ministry of Culture organized a number of commemorative events in the two countries. These events were numerous and spread across the country in France, less so in Egypt.[12] On the French side, the 1798 event was presented, sometimes with a sharp critical view, as an expedition that resulted in a cultural encounter and the cognitive exploration of a great civilization.[13] On the Egyptian side, however, a heated public debate arose about the appropriateness of commemorating this event and the nature of what was to be commemorated. According to the official state narrative, 1798 was the dawn of Egypt's modern era. Napoleon's arrival had ended the backward, tyrannical, and inefficient Ottoman-Mamluk rule (1517–1798) and paved the way for the modern Egyptian state under the leadership of Muhammad Ali Pasha. This narrative emphasized the transfer of Enlightenment ideas and values that supposedly took place with the Napoleonic invasion. Again, the pre-Napoleonic period, particularly the seventeenth and eighteenth centuries, were depicted as socially and intellectually stagnant.[14] But for many Egyptians, including thinkers and historians, the short Napoleonic period in Egypt (1798–1801) was mainly a time of invasion and occupation that did not deserve to be celebrated.[15] Unfortunately, apart from the polemics, the debate did not seem to give rise to new works in modern Egyptian historiography.

Instead of the question of indigenous elements of enlightenment and modernity, prior to and independent from European influence, and instead of the question of the Western European Enlightenment, the tanwir debates primarily address the respective contexts they stemmed from; namely, twentieth-century fin-de-siècle realities in Egypt and Syria. I will use the Arabic term *tanwir* in this study, instead of the English *enlightenment*, to focus on its meanings in the context of these debates. As mentioned earlier, the term and the debates that turned around it dealt with questions of human dignity, liberty, tolerance, reason, education, human rights, and democracy. In each country, the debates expressed different concerns and pointed to different targets. This book contrasts the debates in the two countries and examines the priorities and particularities of each, connected to the nature and history of the state, the image that the state was eager to project, the level of oppression and kind of state violence being practiced, the margin of openness to the outside world that was allowed, and the relation of intellectuals to the state.[16]

The Egyptian state is older and larger than the Syrian state and endowed with a more established set of state institutions. Founded by Muhammad Ali Pasha in 1805, it underwent various forms of administrative and economic modernization early on. Keen on strengthening his power vis-à-vis the Ottoman central power, Muhammad Ali built a modern army and several administrative, medical, and educational institutions that were to become the pillars of the modern Egyptian state. In this endeavor he mobilized and trained men for his service, forming in the process the nucleus of a state intelligentsia. This was the origin of the traditional organic bond between the Egyptian intellectual and the state. That bond would survive the vicissitudes of modern Egyptian history, from the British occupation of 1882 to independence in 1922, the fall of the monarchy through the 1952 Free Officers coup, the 1967 military defeat by Israel, the Anwar el-Sadat and Hosni Mubarak regimes, and beyond. Despite changing official ideologies and failures in delivering on promises, the state continued to be the central motor of modernization, stability, and security for most Egyptians and Egyptian intellectuals.

The intensification of the tanwir debate in the 1990s came as a reaction to the rise of the Islamists in Egypt from the 1980s onward. This rise took two forms: a violent Jihadist form with assassinations and attacks on Copts, tourists, Egyptian officials, and intellectuals; and a cultural-moral form, in which Islamist hegemony in the public sphere resulted from the tacit deal between the regime and the Islamists. Indeed, after being severely repressed by the Gamal Abdel Nasser regime, the Islamists were given a freer hand by Sadat to dismantle the Nasserite leftist forces in the economy and society, including on campuses, in labor unions, and elsewhere, with the understanding that the Islamists would stay away from politics. This power game between the regime and the Islamists continued under Mubarak, who offered wider spheres of influence to the Islamists. They in turn provided social services that the state could no longer ensure; they could increasingly impose themselves in questions of culture, morality, and religion; and they could run for parliamentary offices and gain a considerable number of seats, albeit as independent forces.[17] In reaction to rising Islamist power and aggression, secular intellectuals launched a tanwir campaign, criticizing bigotry, fanaticism, and terrorism, including intellectual terrorism. The state co-opted this campaign and sponsored a whole set of activities and publications on tanwir, without eschewing concessions to the Islamists when expedient. As a result of this expediency politics, the state often deprived the anti-Islamist intellectuals of much-needed backing. The Islamists in turn appropriated the tanwir discourse, on the one hand accusing the government of corruption and abuse of power, and hence of doing the opposite of what it preached under tanwir, and on the other hand accusing the secularist intellectuals of holding a westernized, imported, and inauthentic tanwir discourse. In place of that discourse the Islamists offered their own authentic, Islamic tanwir.

Thus the Egyptian tanwir debate was part and parcel of the power struggle between the Islamists and the regime, in which the secular intellectuals tried to defend their values. The debate was also characterized by the constraints, ambiguities, and paradoxes of the relationship between those intellectuals and the state. The debate was articulated in numerous monographs and journals and carried out in the media and at public events, such as commemorative conferences and the yearly Cairo International Book Fair. It was reported and commented upon and is thus fairly well documented, as we shall see in chapter 1. The sharp critique of this debate undertaken by critical Egyptian thinkers, however, is less well known. Chapter 2 sheds light on this critique, focusing on the deconstruction of the tanwir campaigns, both governmental and Islamist, and on analyses by Egyptian critical thinkers of the tanwir discourses, assumptions, approaches, and claims. The elitism of the tanwir intellectual will emerge as one of the salient topics of this deconstruction and will warrant a brief excursion into the topic of elitism in the European, and particularly German, Enlightenment at the end of chapter 2.

If the tanwir debate in Egypt revolved around the phenomenon of Islamic fundamentalism, the one in Syria was centered on the state's unbridled corruption and brutal oppression. The modern Syrian state was founded in 1920 under the French mandate. It gained its sovereignty as a republic in 1946. After an agitated period of military coups and brief intervals of liberal parliamentary rule, power was seized by Baath Party officers and monopolized in 1970 by Hafiz al-Assad, who ruled until his death in 2000. He was succeeded by his son Bashar. Both father and son ruled in an autocratic fashion, forbidding any semblance of political life and any attempt at opposition. All civil associations, whether religious, cultural, or social, including labor, youth, student, and women's associations, were put under strict state control. The circulation of goods, people, and ideas were severely restricted. The extensive corruption of the entire state apparatus and the unbridled abuse of power by the closely knit ruling circle did not lend much credibility to the state slogans of socialism, Arab unity, and progress. With secret police surveillance, paramilitary violence, and arbitrary arrests and torture, the state crushed all opposition, ranging from communists to Syrian nationalists, Iraqi Baathists, and especially Islamists. The Islamists were eliminated in the late 1970s and early 1980s, with the notorious destruction of Hama in 1982 and a broad repression campaign. Hence, compared to Egypt, Syria has had a much narrower space for open debates and political contest, if any, and its state and state institutions have had less legitimacy, as well as little moral or symbolic credibility for its population and independent thinkers. Moreover, no margin of freedom of thought or expression was left for co-opted intellectuals, thus creating a very different relationship between intellectuals and the state from that in Egypt.

Yet despite the repression, some critical thinkers were able to address the pressing issues of Syrian state and society and advocate tanwir, not primarily against political Islamism, but in an indirect way against the damage caused by the Assad dictatorship. Chapter 3 looks at a number of Syrian thinkers writing on tanwir in the 1990s, with special focus on Syrian playwright Saadallah Wannous and Palestinian literary critic and philosopher Faisal Darraj. Chapter 4 examines the themes discussed in the Syrian tanwir debates of the 1990s and those raised in the Damascus Spring of 2000–2001.

The 1990s tanwir debates in Egypt were primarily led by state-sponsored cultural institutions and secular, or more precisely non-Islamist, intellectuals who were more or less connected to the state. The 2000s discourses, on the other hand, were deconstructions of those earlier discourses and launched sharp criticisms against them. In the Syrian case, the 1990s and 2000s tanwir discourses stand in continuity with one another, with those of the later decade being associated with concrete public moves. I argue that despite this difference, both the Egyptian deconstructionists and the Syrian tanwir advocates of the two decades (I will call them the *tanwiris*) presented a view of enlightenment that I characterize as *political humanism*. This political humanism calls for the free and public practice of reason in view of producing knowledge that enlightens people about the realities they find themselves in and nurtures their yearning for a dignified and free existence. Its objective is the reconstruction of the Arab human being crushed by brutal regimes. Such a reconstruction requires, according to the tanwir critical thinkers, the reclaiming of the right to political participation. It necessitates the collective remobilization of people after their disenfranchisement by the regimes. Interestingly, this was also the aspiration of those who took to the streets a decade or two later in the cities of the Arab world, including Cairo and Damascus. My contention is not that the tanwir debates caused the popular movements to develop but that the tanwir critical thinkers were well tuned to the pulse of their societies, and that they and the movements expressed common yearnings for freedom and human dignity.[18]

PART I

Cairo

ONE

Secularist, Governmental, and Islamist Tanwir Debates in Egypt in the 1990s

AFTER THE ASSASSINATION of President Anwar el-Sadat, Islamist terrorist attacks multiplied in Egypt, targeting Copts in various parts of the country; tourists (e.g., in Ras Burqa in 1985, Luxor in 1997, Taba in 2004, Sharm el-Sheikh in 2005, and Dahab in 2006); politicians (e.g., the attempted assassinations of Interior Minister Hassan al-Alfi and Information Minister Safwat el-Sherif in 1993); and intellectuals (e.g., the assassination of prominent secularist Farag Fuda in 1992, and the knife attack on eighty-two-year-old Nobel laureate Naguib Mahfuz in 1994). Islamist cultural hegemony also manifested itself in the censorship of cultural products and the condemnation of individual thinkers like Nasr Hamid Abu Zayd, which became a cause célèbre and to which we will return in chapter 2. In the face of this mounting violence and hegemony, anti-Islamist thinkers organized a number of societies and activities. Among them was the Society for Enlightenment (Jam'iyyat al-Tanwir), founded in 1992, which published an irregular bulletin called *Al-tanwir* (The enlightenment). Its first issue contained articles by Saad Eddin Ibrahim, Rif'at al-Said, Yunan Labib Rizk, and Farag Fuda (a founding member who was assassinated shortly after establishing the society, when leaving its office). Its first president was the prominent Egyptian poet Abd el-Mu'ti al-Higazi. Moreover, the General Egyptian Book Organization (Al-Hay'a al-'Amma al-Misriyya li al-Kitab) launched a set of publications that included a series on modern Egyptian historical figures, such as Mustafa Kamil (*Ta'rikh al-misriyyin*); a series on the history of Egypt during the nahda period; and a series on the nahda itself, with reprints of landmark nahda books such as Abd al-Rahman al-Kawakibi's (1855–1902) famous 1902 book on despotism.[1] This last series, headed by Gaber Asfour, was called Al-Muwajaha (The confrontation), with Al-tanwir as subtitle. Its explicit aim was to confront and address the issues of extremism, Shari'a, and national unity. The 1990 Cairo International Book Fair was given the motto "Hundred years of tanwir."[2] A television program, Hiwar al-Tanwir (Enlightenment dialogue), was broadcast to present enlightened approaches to various societal and intellectual issues. In 1992 the al-Hilal magazine and publishing house commemorated its hundredth anniversary and "contribution to modernization and enlightenment" at the Cairo Opera in the presence of President Hosni Mubarak.[3] In 1993 two panel discussions were organized to mark the centennial of Ali Pasha Mubarak (1824–1893), who is called Abu al-ta'lim (the father of education) for having been the leading figure of educational reform during the nahda. In 1994 a three-day workshop was organized by the Committee on History and Thought (Lajnat al-Tarikh wa al-Fikr) of the Supreme Council of Culture (Al-Hay'a al-'Ulya li al-Thaqafa) and directed by its secretary, Gaber Asfour, to discuss the enlightenment movement of the nineteenth and twentieth centuries. In an essay entitled "De la renaissance aux Lumières: Autour de quelques productions historiques récentes," Ghislaine Alleaume reviewed the activities and publications of this tanwir campaign and made the following remarks: no real scholarly contributions were made, the move from nahda to tanwir was made in a fleeting way without ever clarifying the term tanwir, and Islamism dominated the discussions, as it dominated their reception in the press and the editorial work that ensued from it. She thought that the approach to the notion of tanwir was more political than conceptual.[4] As we will see, these criticisms were also articulated in the deconstruction of the 1990s Egyptian tanwir debates.

In 2002 the same council convened another three-day conference to celebrate the two-hundredth anniversary of the birth of Rifa'a al-Tahtawi (1801–1873), regarded as one of the nahda pioneers. Part of this enlightenment campaign was the revival of interest in the work of Ibn Rushd (Averroes) as an Arab-Islamic champion of rationality. In 1994 a conference on Averroes was organized by the Supreme Council of Culture, following the publication of a book on Averroes by the council in 1993, edited by Egyptian philosophy professor Atef al-Iraqi.[5] The Islamists rejected this enlightenment campaign, labeling it *"tanwir hukumi"* (governmental enlightenment), and proposed instead their own *"tanwir islami"* (Islamic enlightenment).[6]

Before moving to the critical deconstruction of these governmental and Islamic tanwir discourses, let us review, as a sample of these discourses, the ideas of Gaber Asfour for the secularist discourse and those of Muhammad Imarah for the Islamist one—both are spokesmen of their respective camps. Both men base their arguments on a solid grasp of the modern Egyptian history of ideas and are established experts in their respective fields of literary critique and Islamic studies. But before entering the polemics between these two figures and the currents they represent, it is important to note that a discourse on enlightenment already existed in the 1970s. It was initiated by Mourad Wahba (born 1926), professor emeritus of philosophy at Ain Shams University in Cairo. This third discourse was eventually drawn into the 1990s debates, as its intellectual concerns coincided with those of the debates, but it remained to a large extent independent from the two camps. A look into this independent discourse complements our picture of the late twentieth-century Egyptian debate on tanwir. Let us take one book from each of these prolific writers as an anchor point to present the gist of their arguments, referring to their other writings when relevant. For Gaber Asfour we will focus on *Hawamish 'ala daftar al-tanwir* (Marginalia on the notebook of tanwir) from 1994,[7] and for Muhammad Imarah we will choose *Al-Islam bayn al-tanwir wa al-tazwir* (Islam between tanwir and falsification) from 1995.[8] But we will start with Mourad Wahba's *Madkhal ila al-tanwir* (Introduction to tanwir), published in 1994.[9]

Mourad Wahba's Paradoxes

Underdevelopment in the third world in general and in the Islamic world in particular is one of the important reasons for Wahba's interest in the question of tanwir. The backwardness of these societies is, according to him, caused by a lack of critical reason due to cultural taboos. These taboos come from dogmatic, fundamentalist modes of thinking that stem in turn from fundamentalist and particularist approaches to tradition and religion. Third world intellectuals, he thinks, have not had the audacity to confront and change these approaches. The mission of tanwir is to unveil the nature of these taboos and to explain how they hinder creative thought and culture in view of overcoming those hindrances. A shift away from dogmatism and an opening to universal human civilization are urgently needed. This can only be secured by secularism. For Wahba, secularism is the necessary condition for the possibility of using critical reason, hence for tanwir. Religious fundamentalism, by imposing dogmatic certainties and forbidding critique, creates societies of absolutes in which critical thinking is made impossible, and as a result advancement is hampered. In his mind, the advancement achieved in European societies was owed to a large extent to the possibility of exercising critical reason. This possibility was gained through religious reform that liberated the mind from religious authorities and through the Enlightenment, which established human reason as the sole authority for the human mind—a reason, however, that was well aware of its limits and its inability to establish dogmatic certainties. A major contribution to these transformations was the philosophy of Averroes, which was neglected and fought in the East but welcomed and explored by the West—what Wahba calls the "paradox of Averroes."[10] Hence Wahba is committed to reviving the rationalist, hermeneutic philosophy of Averroes in contemporary Arab thought. That philosophy could serve additionally as common ground for the Arab-Islamic world and the West, since Averroes himself belonged to both cultures. Contemporary Arab-Islamic culture has been dominated, according to Wahba, by the literalist, conformist, and dogmatic spirit of Ibn Taymiyya (1263–1328). This spirit has shaped the prevalent Islamic fundamentalist currents. Countering this spirit is the necessary and difficult task of any present-day tanwir. Enlightenment, secularism, Averroes, and cultural dialogue have been the leitmotifs of Wahba's numerous writings, talks, interviews, regular press articles, frequent television appearances, academic conferences, and public debates.

Madkhal il al-tanwir is a collection of essays and conference papers written between 1975 and 1993 that document Wahba's journey, of which he gives an overview in the introduction to the book. The journey started with a 1975 talk in Lahore in which he expressed concern about cultural problems caused by the absence of secularism and critical thinking.[11] This visit eventually moved him to found the Afro-Asian Philosophy Association in 1978 to promote enlightenment. The association organized several conferences in collaboration with other associations and cultural centers, such as the 1989 Cairo conference Enlightenment and Culture, held in partnership with the

Goethe Institute and the British Council in Cairo. This conference was meant to be a joint Arab-European reflection on "enlightenment as a civilizational phenomenon" both in the Arab world and Europe, and more particularly on the challenges of enlightenment in the two regions.[12] Wahba ended his contribution to the conference by questioning the prevailing belief that Egypt has had a century of enlightenment, thus shedding doubt on the centennial claims made by the state.[13] *Madkhal ila al-tanwir* also contains a critique of the centennial republication of some of the major nahda writings, such as Farah Antun's (1874–1922) 1903 book on Averroes, *Ibn Rushd wa Falsafatuhu* (Ibn Rushd and his philosophy). The General Egyptian Council for Books published the book without the author's introduction, in which he had called for separating state from religion, and without his heated debated with Muhammad Abduh (1849–1905).[14] In this way, writes Wahba, the state aborted Antun's enlightenment efforts.[15] In 2012 Wahba wrote his own introduction and republished Antun's book in its integral form.[16]

Another misperception propagated by the state and maintained by public opinion, Wahba claims, is the characterization of Rifaʻa al-Tahtawi as a tanwir figure. In a paper presented at a 1976 Tahtawi conference, Wahba argues that in presenting his French Enlightenment readings, Tahtawi had not captured the main tenets of those readings; namely, the idea of a secular social contract and that of natural religion. Rather, Tahtawi had chosen to present the ideas related to these tenets as rational equivalents of the Shariʻa precepts.[17] It will be interesting to compare Wahba's view on Tahtawi with Imarah's, since Imarah also argues that Tahtawi remained committed to his Islam and did not advocate secularism, as secularist tanwiris claim. But Imarah's point, contrary to Wahba's, does not dispute Tahtawi's tanwiri character. Rather, it shows, as we shall see, that the nahda tanwir remained anchored in Islam and did not take a secularist form; in other words, that tanwir was Islamist.

The most recent article in *Madkhal* is "Mufaraqat Ibn Rushd" (The paradox of Ibn Rushd) from 1993. It is a reprint of his contribution to the volume on Averroes, published by the Committee on Philosophy and Sociology of the Supreme Council of Culture as part of the tanwir campaign. It was, as mentioned above, edited by a member of that committee, Atef al-Iraqi, professor of Arab philosophy at Cairo University and himself a prolific writer on tanwir.[18] It is after these Ibn Rushd publications and discussions that Mourad Wahba founded the Averroes Forum (Muntada Ibn Rushd) in 1994 and convened an international conference in Cairo on Averroes and the Enlightenment.[19]

Among the articles included in *Madkhal* is a 1991 piece, "Al-tanwir wa rajul al-shari'" (Enlightenment and the man on the street). Back in 1983 Wahba had organized a conference on philosophy and the man on the street, which was strongly criticized by the press and some fellow philosophers, such as Zaki Naguib Mahmud, who thought that exposing philosophy to the "man on the street" was putting it in peril. Wahba remained convinced that philosophy, critical thinking, and creative culture had to be disseminated to the general public. In this piece Wahba saw the age of technology as a chance for disseminating enlightened modes of thinking to the masses, contrary to the pessimistic views of Charles-Marie Gustave Le Bon, José Ortega y Gasset, Martin Heidegger, and Wilhelm Reich on the masses. Wahba did acknowledge the dangers of manipulating the masses against enlightenment, as was the case in ancient Athens, when, as he describes it, public opinion about Socrates was influenced by charges of atheism and corrupt moral influence. Wahba believed modern technology could offer a chance to propagate a culture of creativity instead of conformist, rote-learning culture.[20] Finally, *Madkhal ila al-tanwir* contains a survey of European Enlightenment figures and ideas. This period remains for Wahba the epitome of modern enlightenment without being limited to Europe geographically, ethnically, or culturally. Its ideals are for him universal, stemming from the human yearning for freedom and progress.[21]

For Wahba, tanwir as the autonomous use of critical reason is but one of the constituents of democracy. The other three are liberalism, social contract theory, and most important, secularism. Liberalism for him is the valuing of individual liberties, and social contract theory is the understanding of the body politic as based on a secular agreement among humans, not on divine rule. Secularism is the cornerstone of democracy, he insists. Secularism is first and foremost a mode of thinking that excludes absolutes (*mutlaqat*) and works with the relative as relative (*al-nisbi bima huwa nisbi*). It is the worldly, and thus inevitably, changing and relative approach to the world. It is also a principle that takes critical reason as its reference.[22] When advised to use the word "rational" (*'aqlani*) instead of "secular" (*'almani*) to avoid criticism, Wahba retorts that he prefers "secular" because rationalism runs the danger of absolutism, since it is the natural tendency of reason to be tempted by absolute truth when not reined in by critique. As often stated in secularism debates in Egypt, the term *secularism* has a bad reputation because it is associated with atheism—anathema to Islam and society. People opt for the more cautious term *civil* (*madani*). Islamists use it to claim that they do not aim for theocratic rule and so avoid the accusation of fundamentalist extremism, and non-Islamists use it to avoid accusations of atheism—an accusation that can have fatal consequences, as shown by the assassination of committed secularists like Farag Fuda. Wahba thinks intellectuals have lacked the courage to be clear about their beliefs and have preferred to avoid confrontation with the Islamized public and religious authorities dominated by fundamentalists, thus blurring the central cause of secularism. He has consistently refused to make such compromises and remained clear in his secularist advocacy. He is the founder and head of the secular Egypt movement (Harakat Misr al-'almaniyya), whose an online magazine, *Majallat harakat misr al-'almaniyya*, publishes most of Wahba's articles in addition to essays, book reviews, and interviews by others.[23]

As an outspoken secularist and an uncompromising critic of all forms of fundamentalism, Wahba has remained consistent in his positions.[24] He has also kept a critical distance from the state, despite his having been a professor at a state university and a member of several Supreme Council of Culture committees. He has maintained contact with foreign colleagues around the world and served for fifteen years on the executive committee of the International Federation of Philosophy Societies (1988–2003)—the only Arab to serve on that committee, as he often states with pride and sadness. For all this, he has been attacked and accused of propagating Western ideas and serving foreign agendas.[25] Yet he has kept his tanwir and secularist campaign, advocating it in academic writings, regular newspaper articles (e.g., in *Al-masri al-Yaoum* and *al-Ahram*), and in frequent public appearances. Since the 2011 revolution his public statements have connected the recent events with his decades-long analysis of Egyptian intellectual and cultural realities.[26]

Indeed, Wahba saluted the youth movement behind the popular uprising and its use of technology to raise awareness, mobilize, and organize. But if the revolution was stalled, it was, according to him, because the masses were not supported by intellectuals, who could offer them a vision for the future. People revolted against the actual situation (*al-wad' al-qa'im*) but could not formulate a future situation (*al-wad' al-qadim*). The conception of that future is incumbent upon philosophers, whose views need to be transmitted to the people by intellectuals. Philosophy is absent because there is no philosophical activity in the country. There are philosophy departments in which courses are taught in a rote-learning manner, but there is no teaching of true philosophizing. Intellectuals and academics have been busy with their individual struggles and ambitions. Many have focused their attention on the shortcomings of the ruling party, instead of focusing on the main problem (al-asl), of which the ruling party is but a branch (fir'i); namely, Islamic fundamentalism propagated by the Muslim Brotherhood. The Brotherhood, which has spread its destructive influence everywhere in society, including universities, state institutions, and ministries, is the source of the evil that needs to be combatted. In this sense, intellectuals have been for Wahba the most traitorous group in the nation.[27]

Muslim Brotherhood rule lasted barely a year, writes Wahba, because it went against the natural law of civilization, which is change, and which calls for relative critical thinking, not stultifying absolutes. By wanting to impose fixed and absolute dogmas on society, the Muslim Brotherhood put social dynamics in danger, and so people rejected it. But for Wahba this does not mean mentalities that have been shaped and influenced by the Brotherhood for so long have changed. In the absence of the necessary work of philosophers and intellectuals, only the army was capable of protecting the youth. It did so when the Brotherhood hijacked the revolution from the youth in its early phase, and then again when the youth rose against the Brotherhood's short-lived rule. Wahba appreciates Field Marshal Abdel Fatah el-Sisi's audacity in undertaking this salutary action, as well as his creativity in fighting terrorism by undertaking bold projects such as the opening of the new Suez Canal under difficult circumstances.[28]

By focusing his attention primarily on the fundamentalism propagated by the Islamists, Wahba exonerates the autocratic, and inevitably corrupt, state from the far-reaching damage it caused to Egyptian society in the areas of education, health care, public discourse, security, and not least politics. He also overlooks the state's responsibility in encouraging the rise of the Islamists, especially under Sadat. That the state was infiltrated by fundamentalists and in the end became dominated by fundamentalism was not the result of some natural spread of Islamism, but the outcome of a calculated state policy under Sadat meant to crush leftist opposition forces. It was also supported and financed by petrodollars. By treating the ruling party as a branch of the problem and not its root, he disregards the heavy-handed, self-serving power politics of the state that consistently played social and cultural actors against one another, including the fundamentalists and their opponents. The close examination of this politics by Egyptian literary critic Samia Mehrez, as we shall see, lays bare the devastating impact of such politics on the cultural, academic, and intellectual fields, and also on secular thought, freedom of expression, and democracy. Moreover, despite his criticism of what he calls the "pharaonism" of the Egyptians—that is, their alleged endemic misperception of the ruler as divine, and so beyond criticism—Wahba gives Sisi unconditional support without holding him accountable on the basis of clear principles. The urgency of halting the Muslim Brotherhood's control seems for Wahba to justify all means. After all the harm caused to the country by successive autocratic rulers over decades, often in the name of protecting the nation from obscurantist and barbaric Islamism, Wahba does not see the need to warn against renewed, or rather continued, autocracy, nor against the unbridled violence used by the state to combat the Muslim Brotherhood and terrorism. This combat justifies for him, at least implicitly, all measures of autocracy and state violence. He expresses no fear that such measures might thwart any move toward peace, liberty, and democracy. He often states that the only organized political and cultural body in the country is the Muslim Brotherhood, and that individual liberals, secularists, and democrats have failed to form popular currents capable of facing the Islamists. Therefore, he thinks that only the national army is able to stop the Islamist takeover of the state. Such domination, he fears, would lead to the end of the Egyptian nation-state, since the Brotherhood's real allegiance is to the larger Islamic *umma* and not the Egyptian state, and its ultimate goal the domination of the entire world. Given this perception of an existential threat to the Egyptian state, he thinks that all means of protection are justified. Furthermore, he thinks President Sisi not only ensures the persistence of the Egyptian state but also protects civilization as such from the threats of Islamism. In a television interview Wahba stated that Sisi and Donald Trump are God-sent protectors of civilization, after Barack Obama's lenient attitude toward the Muslim Brotherhood.[29] He fails to note that it is the absence of real political life under despotic regimes that has prevented any organizing against the Brotherhood and any alternative, non-Islamist opposition from coming into being.

So in the final analysis, has there been a shortage of non-Islamist philosophical vision, as Wahba claims, or has it been impossible to translate that vision into political action? In other words, has it been the absence of ideas or the absence of politics? Wahba is not the only Egyptian intellectual to have taken this position, which I call the "Wahba paradox": the paradox of strongly defending freedom, critical thought, and democracy while giving uncondi-tional support to the absolutist state against the Islamist-terrorist peril, without any caution against the perils of an unchecked state power that has proved extremely dangerous to life, freedom, and dignity. This paradox stems from a perceived stark choice between an autocratic state and reli-gious despotism, a choice that perpetuates itself because both systems for-bid the development of a third alternative; namely, peaceful democracy. It is remarkable that the momentous upheaval of January 2011 could not bring even a courageous thinker like Wahba to break from this choice and state loudly and clearly the need for a different way of opposing religious despotism, one that firmly upholds human rights and genuine constitu-tional rule. Some intellectuals and academics, mostly of a younger genera-tion, did maintain that third option. They warned early on against the return of the autocratic state and condemned it when it started to manifest itself. Wahba seems not to have heard their voices or shared their wisdom. Furthermore, he failed to acknowledge the significant work of politico-moral reflection, conceptual articulation, and dissemination that numer-ous Egyptian intellectuals and academics undertook in accompanying the revolutionaries in their yearning for security, freedom, and dignity. For many years he had deplored the absence of such contributions from intel-lectuals and academics. Sadly, these contributions almost came to a stand-still with Sisi's clampdown on free expression and political life when he came to power in July 2013. Sisi was the leader whom Wahba, and others, cheered as the only force capable of stopping Islamist obscurantism, while the intellectuals and academics who were doing the antifundamentalist enlightenment work that Wahba advocated were thrown in jail, intimi-dated, and forced into exile, and their media and publication outlets were censored or silenced.[30] Their work still waits to be documented.[31]

Gaber Asfour: The Antidote?

Egyptian literary critic Gaber Asfour (born 1944) is, in my opinion, a good embodiment of Wahba's paradox. Professor of Arabic literature at the

University of Cairo since 1966, director of the National Centre for Translation (2007–2011), general secretary of the Supreme Council of Culture (1993–2007), and vice minister to the most state-loyal and long-serving minister of culture, Farouk Hosni (1987–2011), Asfour has been an outspoken advocate of tanwir, a strong detractor of religious fundamentalism, and a constant critic of political despotism, while at the same time being a faithful civil servant of the Mubarak state. He has headed a number of book series publications and organized numerous conferences in the tanwir campaign under the auspices of the Ministry of Culture. He has also been a prolific writer of serious works of literary critique and a regular commentator on Egyptian and Arab affairs in the press, especially in *al-Ahram* and *al-Hayat*. He has twice been appointed minister of culture, serving in the last Mubarak government for only nine days, after which he resigned (January 31–February 8, 2011), and then for less than a year in the first Sisi government (June 2014–March 2015).

His becoming minister in the dramatic early days of the revolution drew sharp criticisms from fellow intellectuals.[32] He resigned nine days later "for health reasons." A few days after his resignation, he justified his acceptance of the appointment in television interviews and press articles,[33] saying that he had thought he would be part of a coalition government that would lead the country into safety during that critical phase. He had decided to resign the moment he discovered that this was not to be the case and that the government was still in the hands of the old ruling party. He expressed his sympathy with the youth and admitted that they were ahead of him in their belief in the possibility of change, and that they helped him overcome his profound despair, on the eve of the revolution, of seeing things improve in Egypt.[34] Furthermore, he affirmed his belief that the youth, who gave Egypt new faith in a better future, should lead the country toward that future, and that the older generation should limit itself to giving advice.

This did not prevent him from accepting another appointment, this time as minister of culture in Sisi's government, whose rule opened, according to Asfour, a new era in which he believed he could implement his cultural vision for Egypt.[35] To implement this vision, he asked Egyptian sociologist Sayyid Yasin (born 1919) to draw up a strategy. He then explained that Yasin had a strategy paper that could be discussed and implemented by the youth. With this, he again attracted strong criticism.[36] But the graver criticism came for his serving a regime that distinguished itself through repression and human rights violations at a scale even bigger than Mubarak's. With a restrictive demonstration law that made any free opposition demonstrators liable to large-scale arrests and extreme punishment, swift death sentences for hundreds of defendants, large numbers of disappearances, severe restrictions on freedom of expression, and near-total control of the media, Sisi's regime left no room for opposition.[37]

In his numerous analyses of the dismal state of affairs in Egypt, Asfour had always underlined the destructive effects of political repression and state despotism. And yet he had agreed to serve the Mubarak and Sisi regimes, believing, as he said, that he was bringing solutions to their shortcomings, or even serving as an "antidote" to those bad systems. In some interviews regarding his two ministerial appointments, he was pushed to account for this paradox. About six months after his first short-lived tenure as minister of culture, he was asked whether he had difficulties reconciling his positions as a critical writer with those of a state employee expected to serve state policies, whether his exchanging the university chair of Taha Husayn (1889–1973) with that of a Mubarak ministerial chair was a betrayal of his principles as an intellectual, and whether his connections to key figures of the regime, like the president's wife, were not opportunistic. He rejected all these allegations and asserted that he always knew that he would give up any official function were it to compromise his principles.[38] As proof of his steadfast commitment to critique, he pointed to his writings, both his monographs and his regular press articles, directed against political despotism and state policies. He held the latter responsible to a great extent for the dismal state of Egyptian culture.[39] When asked if he was part of that culture and that catastrophe, he denied it, saying that he saw his work as part of the efforts to come out of the prevailing predicament. Those efforts aimed at disseminating an enlightening mass culture (*thaqafa jamahiriyya mustanira*) and combatting a powerful fundamentalist influence. This influence, as mentioned earlier, was sometimes encouraged, often tolerated, but always kept politically under control by the same state that also advocated tanwir. When asked how he, as a thinker, could not see that by joining the Mubarak government he had bestowed legitimacy on an illegitimate regime, he answered that he honestly had not expected the fall of the regime and had thought he was helping to salvage what could still be salvaged for the sake of Egypt, until he saw the real face of that regime. The interviewer wondered how he had missed seeing that face until then. At some point in the interview

Asfour stated that Mubarak and his wife had multiple facets, good ones and corrupt ones, but that he had gotten to know mainly the good ones. He appreciated the fact that Mubarak had sent him to the best doctors in France when he suffered a stroke. Finally, he thought that in the last years Mubarak was not really ruling, that the man really in power was his son Gamal, together with his clique of corrupt businessmen. This association of power with wealth was, in his opinion, one of the disasters of the late Mubarak regime.

In June 2014, at the beginning of his second tenure as minister of culture, Asfour was interviewed by prominent anchor and journalist Hamdi Rizk.[40] In it he justified his acceptance of a second appointment by saying that it was made on the basis of a comprehensive vision for the development of the Egyptian cultural system, articulated in a paper published a week before his appointment and approved by the prime minister and the president.[41] This vision involved at least four ministries: those of culture, education, media, and religious affairs (*Awqaf*). He added that his understanding was that this government, though meant to last only until the parliamentary elections,[42] was to lay the foundations for a wide-ranging reform of the country, including its cultural life. These reforms were to be undertaken within the parameters of the January 25 and June 30 revolutions, which demanded bread, freedom, social justice (of which culture was an important aspect), and human dignity. Unlike some who separated the two revolutions and looked at the January 25 one as an American conspiracy, Asfour asserted that he saw the two movements as complementing each other and again expressed his admiration for the youth who started the movement. He admitted that he had anticipated a revolution of the hungry, but not one of middle-class, educated youth. Rizk then asked him about the whereabouts and fate of that youth at present. Asfour said that they went in different directions: some participated in the Council of Fifty (Majlis al-khamsin), which worked toward the new constitution, some went to support different presidential campaigns, and some organized the rebellion (*tamarrod*) to oust Islamist president Mohamed Morsi. When pressed to comment on news of large-scale arrests of revolutionary youth, Asfour affirmed that he was against arbitrary arrests but said that one should differentiate between revolutionaries and thugs (*baltagiyya*). However, he added, the lists of arrested people needed to be revised, as some of those arrests might have happened in the heat of volatile situations. Moreover, he insisted that he was against accusing people of treason until charges were proved in court, and this included, for him, accusations against one of the most active revolutionary youth groups, the April 6 Movement, banned under Sisi. Then the interviewer asked him to comment on the restrictive demonstration law, promulgated by a regime that came to power on the back of mass demonstrations. Asfour again referred to the distinction between anarchy and revolution. Furthermore, as to whether he would have preferred to see a younger person filling his position as minister of culture, Asfour asserted that he would have indeed, but that he hoped that that would happen after his tenure, once he had laid down the foundations for the future. He promised to draw on the positive youth energy he had come to know since January 25.

Finally, when asked about the right way to deal with the Muslim Brotherhood, Asfour emphasized that freedom of thought should be upheld, and that people should not be persecuted for their beliefs. But he thought that those who put the security and the existence of the Egyptian state in danger should be stopped from further harming the country. About the tolerance of the new regime toward the Salafis, perhaps for their political quietism and docility toward the ruler, Asfour thought that they were a cultural problem to be addressed. At the end, when invited to share his impression of President Sisi, Asfour said that he believed he could do a lot for Egypt. He denied all fears of a military or police state being reinforced in the country, stating that after the revolution Egyptians had changed and become less tolerant of governmental failure, and that the constitution had shifted power from the president to the parliament. These two factors reassured him that no such shift could affect the country.

The third and last interview I would like to present is the one Asfour did in June 2015 after leaving the ministry.[43] The main topic of this conversation was Sisi's call in early January 2015 for religious institutions to reform and renew the religious discourse. Invited to comment on this call and on the fact that it came from the head of state and not from intellectuals, Asfour welcomed it, saying that someone like Sisi was needed to initiate this renewal, because religious thought had become a matter of national security. Pushing the youth toward extremism, religious fundamentalist discourse nurtured violent groups like the Islamic State of Iraq and the Levant (ISIL, or Daesh in Arabic) and endangered the security of the Egyptian state and society. Like Mourad Wahba, Asfour stated that Ibn Taymiyya needed to be replaced by Ibn Rushd. Asked about the possibility of accomplishing such a shift amid a deep cultural crisis, with a population plagued with high levels of illiteracy and poverty, Asfour thought that it was vital to face this challenge. He also added that a *Rushdiyya* reform would not be that far from the moderate Ash'arite Islam of the majority of the people. In addition, reform and renewal had always been a majority effort resisted by the forces of conservatism and traditionalism. Furthermore, he emphasized the fact that in his opinion, religious discourse was part of a larger cultural discourse. The former could not be reformed and renewed without a comprehensive change in the latter. This should be a general Arab development project. It required democracy, a civic modern state, a genuine notion of citizenship, and the combatting of patriarchy.

How Asfour could believe that such requirements could be fulfilled under Sisi's rule remains a puzzle—one that I subsume under "Wahba's paradox." That Wahba, Asfour, and like-minded intellectuals and fellow Egyptians felt relieved to see a strong political power stand up to the Muslim Brotherhood takeover of the state is understandable, and that they welcomed that power is perhaps comprehensible. But that they explicitly or implicitly accepted that this fight against the total Islamization of state and society should be undertaken at any price, even that of sacrificing human life, human rights, and freedom, is bewildering. At the ousting of President Morsi, the expectation was that elections would bring a new democratically elected president to replace him. Thus, many felt betrayed when Sisi established himself as the leader of an indefinite transitional phase. The violent confrontations—especially the massacres at Rab'a and Nahda in August 2013, in which the state killed hundreds of Muslim Brotherhood partisans in a single day—are certainly telling, if not founding events, for the Sisi era. That critical thinkers such as Wahba, Asfour, and others had nothing to say to warn against the return of a ruthless autocracy is perplexing. But some intellectuals did speak up against the murderous course of action the new regime had embarked upon, intellectuals whom the Wahbas and Asfours failed to acknowledge. Again their work waits to be documented.

The paradox that characterizes Asfour's political judgments and career choices does not appear in his writings, which are consistent and outspoken criticisms of political despotism and religious fundamentalism. His views on tanwir will be represented here by one of his numerous books on the topic, his 1994 *Hawamish 'ala daftar al-tanwir* (Marginalia on the notebook of tanwir). The book is a collection of articles on tradition, modernity, despotism, religious discourse, culture, and major nahda figures. The need for this book, he writes in the introduction, stems from the painful realization that what was taken for granted and considered established by many regarding the values of tanwir, including reason, knowledge, and progress, turned out to be marginalized and weakened, if not nonexistent.[44] It also arises from the sad observation that while we thought we lived or aspired to live in a modern civil society, we found ourselves living in intellectual and political despotism, dominated by sociopolitical and religious patriarchy, that sanctifies the principle of consensus (ijma') and practices discrimination toward anyone who does not conform to that principle. This despotic, patriarchal, and intolerant culture is so pervasive that it has become imperative to recall that another culture existed in Egypt not so long ago, one that upheld tanwir values. To reminisce about that culture and the set of ideas that constituted it is vital to helping us overcome the culture that has engulfed us in recent decades. Hence the need to write marginalia on the notebook of tanwir and nahda. For our purposes I will focus on three articles published earlier in the state magazine al-Ibda', in April, May, and June 1992.

In the first article, "Min al-tanwir ila al-idhlam" (From enlightening to obscuring), Asfour compares the recent times with earlier ones, measuring the shrinking space of free public intellectual debate.[45] He gives as examples the exchange between Ismail Adham, Mohammad Farid Wagdi, and Ahmad Zaki Abu Shadi and the one between Farah Antun and Muhammad Abduh. Both cases would be unthinkable in the present day, writes Asfour. The first exchange was initiated by Ismail Adham's (1911–1940) 1937 essay "Limadha ana mulhid?" (Why am I an atheist?), published in the Egyptian magazine al-Imam. It was followed by a response essay entitled "Limadha hua mulhid?" (Why is he an atheist?) by Mohammad Farid Wagdi (1878–1954), published in al-Azhar, and another response by Ahmad Zaki Abu Shadi (1892–1955) in the next issue of al-Imam, called "Limadha ana mu'min?" (Why am I a believer?). What is remarkable, writes Asfour, is that the exchange occurred without accusations of heresy and consisted of arguments and counterarguments.[46] The same applies to Antun's 1903 call for separating state from religion and the heated debate that it started with Muhammad Abduh. Obviously, there prevailed at the time a certain ethos of debate and a certain margin of tolerance for new and nonconformist ideas. This margin and this ethos withered away under the pressure of the growing Islamist influence, encouraged at first by Sadat, and then spread to state institutions, including universities, the media, and the judiciary.

In his May article entitled "Limadha yantakis al-tanwir?" (Why does tanwir suffer setbacks?), Asfour offers an analysis of the main causes for the failure of the nahda tanwir efforts.[47] He identifies three main obstacles. The first one lies in the nahda conciliatory strategy toward change; that is, the attempt at harmonizing the new Western cultural and political modernization with the old classical tradition. He admits that in the first phase of the nahda, this strategy did facilitate the acceptance of new ideas and avoid painful confrontations; in other words, it did have some positive effects. But ultimately, because those tough options were never faced and clear choices between modernity and tradition were never made, matters remained hanging, tempting thinkers to lean back toward tradition, encouraged by the inclination toward conservatism and inertia. For many, this conciliatory strategy amounted to an intellectual forgery (talfiq) that ultimately thwarted the critical change it was supposed to "smuggle" in. [48] In fact, young Egyptian political scientist Ibrahim el-Houdaiby thinks that this talfiqiyya is one of the main characteristics of Egyptian religious thought since the mid-nineteenth century, allowing for confusion, dishonesty, and inconsistency. The ambiguity of this religious thinking has served both modernist and conservative discourses, like those of the state and political Islam respectively. One of the best articulations of this confusing and misleading strategy is found, according to el-Houdaiby, in the work of Muhammad Abduh, celebrated by Islamists, non-Islamists, and the Egyptian state, as a major reference of tanwir. Indeed, the forty-sixth Cairo International Book Fair in 2015 was dedicated to Abduh, with Saudi Arabia as its guest of honor. It is interesting to note that el-Houdaiby comes from a family of prominent leaders in the Muslim Brotherhood. His great grandfather and his grandfather both headed the organization for a number of years. El-Houdaiby distanced himself from it and developed an independent perspective in matters of politics and religion.[49]

For Asfour, the establishment of tradition as the ultimate reference for the validity of any change became the second obstacle to the development of tanwir. Tradition and conformity to tradition became ends in themselves. This referencing mechanism (al-aliyya al-marji'iyya) became a stultifying factor for any movement forward, especially when tradition became associated with religion and took on a sacral character. The third obstacle has to do with the historical circumstances that did not encourage tanwir ideas to grow and take root in Egyptian society. These ideas suffered often from the absence of political freedom, social justice, and national independence, which hindered the blossoming of critical thinking.

In his June article, "Mihnat al-tanwir" (The crisis of tanwir), Asfour elaborates on those historical circumstances.[50] According to him, tanwir benefited from periods of relative political freedom and economic prosperity, especially in the first half of the twentieth century. That freedom and prosperity shrank considerably and withered away after the military coup that inaugurated the second half of the century. The authoritarian, voluntaristic state project launched by Gamal Abdel Nasser started the systematic practices of repression. This included the politicization of the judiciary and the police; the use of political violence; the arrests of nonconformist intellectuals and artists; the waves of university purges of independent and liberal professors in 1954, 1959, and 1966; the dissolution of political parties; and control of the media. All of these measures erased the margins of dissent, pluralism, and debate. These practices continued under Abdel Nasser's successors, Sadat and Mubarak, with the additional support of the Islamists, whom they hoped to keep under control.[51] Sadat was in the end assassinated by them, and Mubarak manipulated them to conduct his own repressive policies. This combination of political despotism and religious fundamentalism led to the acute crisis of tanwir, writes Asfour. Its predicament was aggravated by the growth of illiteracy and pauperization, the deterioration of all state services, the increase in fanaticism and intercommunal tensions (between Copts and Muslims), and pervasive religious bigotry. Under such circumstances, it became almost impossible to practice free thought and to further develop the project of the nahda. Younger generations were severed from the nahda tradition, and the challenge now was to protect that tradition from oblivion. Literary fiction was able to some extent to get around the repression and intolerance by resorting to symbolism, but analytic writing could not, because by its nature it needed to use clear and explicit language.

Baha' Taher's 1993 novel *Abna' Rifa'a: Al-thaqafa wa al-huriyya* (The sons of Rifa'a: Culture and freedom) was a significant statement in this regard.[52] Taher, a prominent Egyptian novelist (born 1935), wanted to assert his filial connection to one of the pioneers of the nahda, Rifa'a al-Tahtawi. For him, it was a way of reestablishing a genealogy that had been damaged, if not severed, by political fiat. For Taher, Tahtawi and his fellow nahda tanwiris worked toward a culture of freedom that was rooted in the lived realities of the Egyptian people. It is through political choices and decisions, he believed, that such tanwiris were replaced with obscurantists. He underlined the fact that the tanwiris were closely related to their people's emancipation struggles, such as the 1882 and 1919 uprisings against the British occupation. By then Tahtawi's ideas of citizenship, liberty, equality, and fraternity had spread, and popular journalists like Abdallah al-Nadim (1843–1896) had advocated knowledge for all. Nadim had participated in the 1882 revolt. What would have happened, wondered Taher, if Abdel Nasser had appointed Taha Husayn as minister of education, instead of marginalizing him politely and making him an "honorary" intellectual. Wouldn't he too have worked toward the consolidation of a culture of freedom? Unfortunately, intellectuals kept on being marginalized, especially under Sadat. Their reputations were intentionally smeared; they were ostracized and silenced, and so the government could domesticate the people, deprive them of proper education, and leave their minds in the hands of mediocre, enslaved scribes. The result was the total flattening of public awareness (*tastih kamil li al-wa'i al-'am*), which could then be the suitable ground for obscurantist ideas and projects. These projects benefited from funding, including petrodollars, to spread Islamist hegemony in education, culture, and social services. Free intellectuals were replaced with religious preachers, and intelligent, critical media with loyal and subservient ones. The government could then coerce people by presenting the prospect of a religious state as the only alternative to itself. Free intellectuals were disconnected from their public, and all traces of that culture of freedom started by Tahtawi and his like were erased.

For Asfour, the first step out of this predicament is resistance to repression and rejection of the monopoly on knowledge claimed by Islamists and other bigots. His June 1992 article coincided with the assassination, on June 8, of one of the most defiant thinkers against fundamentalism and bigotry, Farag Fuda. Asfour consistently wrote against specific attacks on the freedom of thought and expression, such as those against Nasr Hamid Abu Zayd, Hassan Hanafi, and Sayyid Qimni in Egypt, Ahmad al-Baghdadi in Kuwait, Marcel Khalifeh in Lebanon, and others across the Arab world.[53] But as we saw, these writings and ideas did not prevent him from participating in and serving the state that actively undermined the principles of and possibilities for freedom and enlightened culture.

Muhammad Imarah: The Mistakes and Betrayals of Secular Tanwir

In the preface to *Al-Islam bayn al-tanwir wa al-tazwir* (Islam between tanwir and falsification), Islamist scholar Muhammad Imarah states that his book aims to engage the advocates of secular tanwir in a constructive—that is, patient, objective, and genuine—dialogue.[54] He writes that the unprecedented polarization regarding the identity of the intellectual reference (*huwiyyat al-marji'iyya al-fikriyya*) for the much-desired renaissance project necessitates such a dialogue. Never before in recent or ancient history, he adds, has this polarization been so exacerbated, threatening all parties involved. It has become, according to him, some kind of cultural sectarianism (*ta'ifiyya thaqafiyya*) that calls for self-examination (*waqfa ma' al-dhat*) on the national, pan-Arab, and Islamic levels. This sectarianism developed during the rise of the Islamic revival and the waning of other ideologies, mostly those imported from and supported by the West since colonialism and the period of Western hegemony after independence. In reaction to the growing number of people committed to Islam as a doctrine, a law (Shari'a), and a method (*nahj*) in all aspects of human civilization, the proponents of secular thought have launched a confrontational campaign under the heading of tanwir.[55] Instead of a confrontation (*muwajaha*) Imarah proposes a dialogue (*hiwar*) on all three levels, the national, the pan-Arab, and the Islamic. Such a dialogue would create common ground and establish some shared bases for agreement and disagreement. The first step in this direction is, according to him, the unpacking and clarifying of the central notion of tanwir and its uses. This is what he wants to achieve in this book. But the arguments he makes in it do not leave much room for common ground, as they impute to his secular tanwiri addressees either wrong information, bad influences, traitorous intentions, or all of the above. In fact, Imarah makes three main arguments: first, that the notion of tanwir arises from and applies to European cultural history, and that it is a mistake to think it can be applied to Arab-Islamic history; second, that the characteristics associated with tanwir do not pertain to those thinkers the secular tanwiris consider to be the pioneers of Arab tanwir, such as Tahtawi, Jamal el-Din al-Afghani, Muhammad Abduh, Ali Abdel Raziq, Taha Husayn, and Salama Moussa; and third, that the Qur'an itself is the ultimate reference for light and reason, and hence for genuine tanwir. It is important to note that in the 1970s Imarah had edited the complete works of many of the nahda figures, among them Afghani (1979), al-Kawakibi (1975), Tahtawi (1973), and Ali Mubarak (1979) and later Abduh (1993). At the time, Imarah had emphasized the modernist, rationalist, or nationalist, even leftist, character of these works.

In *Al-Islam bayn al-tanwir wa al-tazwir* Imarah starts by clarifying the intellectual genealogy (*al-nasab al-fikri*) of the term *tanwir*: clearly it belongs to European cultural history. Even the Arabic Language Academy confirms it (*majma' al-lugha al-arabiyya*).[56] European culture, writes Imarah, has since the times of the Greeks been predominantly materialist. When it was Christianized, it had to accommodate a religion that was fundamentally otherworldly. For centuries the church authorities imposed Christianity's otherworldly beliefs on Europe, causing the emergence of the Dark Ages. Tanwir, or enlightenment, came as a reaction against those dark ages and against the incongruities between an otherworldly religion and a materialist culture, between a religion that believed in miracles that break the laws of nature, scientific truths, and social rules and a knowledge that was constantly growing thanks to science. Ultimately, the Enlightenment was a critical and oppositional reaction to religion.[57] This opposition between religion and culture was never the case in Islam, because Islam's "comprehensive moderation" (*wasatiyya jami'a*)[58] could not give rise to absolute binaries such as faith and reason, faith and science, state and religion, individual and collective, self and other, soul and matter, and so on. Western Enlightenment, he adds, came as a reaction to those binaries. By adopting this Western Enlightenment, secular tanwiris mistake Islam for Western culture and religion and advocate a tanwir that is not called for in Islam. Their eagerness to imitate the West and to identify with it has prevented them from acknowledging the specificities of Islamic religion and culture, in which reason (*'aql*), experience (*tajruba*), conscience (*wujdan*), and tradition (*naql*) do not clash with one another.[59] When Mourad Wahba calls for taking reason as the absolute authority, and Gaber Asfour claims that only experimentation can accompany reason, not tradition (*naql*), writes Imarah, they only show their poor understanding of Islam. Moreover, they think that the whole issue of identity should not be dwelled upon, so how can their tanwir be considered Arabic?[60] This is one of the main theses of Imarah's book; namely, that the idea of tanwir, in the sense of the European Enlightenment, is specific to European cultural history and thus a foreign import that cannot be applied to the Arab-Islamic world.

His second thesis is that understanding the work of the nahda pioneers (including Tahtawi, Afghani, and Abduh) and the generation after them (including Abdel Raziq, Husayn, and Moussa) as embodiments of that European tanwir is another gross mistake committed by the secular tanwiris.[61] An honest examination of those works shows that their authors did not pursue the goals of European tanwir, as claimed by the secular tanwiris, and in fact their efforts were of a quite different nature. He starts by examining the works of Abdel Raziq, Husayn, and Moussa.

In 1925 Egyptian Islamic scholar Ali Abdel Raziq (1887–1966) published *Al-Islam wa usul al-hukm* (Islam and the principles of governance),[62] which stirred a heated controversy and cost him his position as a religious teacher and judge. The book was banned, and Abdel Raziq was forbidden to teach until he was reinstated in the 1940s. In the book he argued that contrary to widespread assumptions, the caliphate was not a religious dogma but rather a historical phenomenon that came wrongly to be perceived as a pillar of Islam. Neither the life of the Prophet nor the text of the Qur'an implied that Islam stipulated a specific form of government. Political government and state power were not among the end goals of the Islamic revelation, which was primarily a spiritual message. Moreover, given how corrupt, despotic, and inefficient the caliphate had been, it was important to turn away from it and explore alternative forms of government drawn from universal human experience. The book was part of a larger debate on the caliphate in the aftermath of its abolition by republican Turkey in 1924.[63]

Imarah looks at this abolition as a service to the triumphant Western powers, a historical turn that had to be justified by some theory. As this could not be done in Islamic terms, Western secular tanwir had to be invoked and presented as a required step toward progress and modernization. So it was argued that it was good and necessary "to isolate the religion of Islam from the world of the Muslims."[64] Imarah criticizes Abdel Raziq's position by contesting the arguments of the book and by examining the authenticity of its authorship. Imarah draws on a whole host of elements from the Prophet's biography and his sayings to prove that, contrary to what Abdel Raziq claimed, political governance was very much part of his mission and message. But the type of governance that the Prophet advocated and to some extent practiced was not that of the Christian states under the pope, and it is a mistake, Imarah thinks, to portray them as equivalent. Unlike the Christian states, the Islamic state, embodied later in the caliphate, combined a representation of the *umma* with Shari'a law, and historically Islamic states flourished when they were associated with religion.[65] Imarah believes that there are enough indications from statements and conversations that Abdel Raziq renounced his views and refused to republish the book during his lifetime.[66]

Imarah next examines the rumors regarding the authorship of the book. According to those rumors, which he does not find very convincing, the book was commissioned by British intelligence to prevent any reconstitution of the caliphate, and Abdel Raziq was lured into translating it into Arabic and putting his name to it. Imarah thinks it is more plausible that the book was written by Taha Husayn or at least conceived under his influence, as Husayn was close to Abdel Raziq and defended similar positions in his own work. But Imarah admits that short of strong evidence, this can only be plausible speculation, the closest one could get to truth, as he puts it, but not a certainty.[67]

Like Abdel Raziq, Taha Husayn (1889–1973) refused to republish his own 1938 *Mustaqbal al-thaqafa fi Misr* (The future of culture in Egypt) during his lifetime.[68] This shows, according to Imarah, that Husayn too retracted the views he expounded in this book regarding Egyptian cultural identity. In it Husayn had presented Egypt as being European and part of a Mediterranean culture shaped by Hellenistic, Roman, Christian, Islamic, and modern European components. He did not acknowledge, according to Imarah, the specificity of Islam as a religion and culture. Before that, in fact only a year after Abdel Raziq's *Al-Islam wa usul al-hukm*, Husayn had published *Fi al-shi'r al-jahili* (On Jahili poetry),[69] which had also stirred controversy. In this book Husayn had approached some of the alleged pre-Islamic poetry and some of the Qur'anic legends with a Cartesian methodic doubt. This book was also banned, Husayn was tried, and he had to retract his views. It was only later that the book, including the trial documents, was published in its entirety in Cairo. It is Imarah's belief that Husayn's retraction shows his good intentions and his ultimate commitment to Islam. In both Husayn and Abdel Raziq, Imarah finds scholars who applied themselves to new approaches to their religion and culture, erred in certain respects, and then repented. But their efforts, according to him, were in good faith and not directed against Islam, unlike the efforts of Salama Moussa, a Christian Egyptian.

Salama Moussa (1889–1973) was indeed a strong advocate of large-scale Europeanization, and he also looked at Egypt as being part of a Mediterranean culture. His early formulations of this viewpoint came in his 1928 *Al-yawm wa al-ghad* (Today and tomorrow).[70] But contrary to the other two thinkers of his generation, writes Imarah, Moussa did not modify his views with time and remained consistent with his project of cultural alienation and "intellectual civilizational agency" (*al-'amala al-hadariyya*).[71] According to Imarah, Moussa wanted to historicize and naturalize religion by presenting it as a primitive human product; he called for a secular Europeanized education system and government, for the abolishment of the communal religious bond, and for making religion a personal matter; he thought that patriotism and nationalism could not be upheld on the basis of Islam; he hated the East and advocated a total identification with Europe; he rejected the classical Arabic language and wanted to replace it with the Egyptian colloquial; he despised things Arabic and supported instead a return to the Pharaonic heritage; and finally, he refused to acknowledge any contribution that Arabs had made to European culture.[72] Given all this, Imarah finds it outrageous that present-day secular tanwiris should republish Moussa's works and present them as an enlightenment reference for Arab Muslims. Imarah adds a cautionary remark, saying that Moussa's positions should not be understood as representative of those of Egyptian Copts. In fact, he thinks that Moussa is the exception to the rule, Copts having in general shown patriotic allegiance to Egypt and its Muslim cultural heritage.[73] Moussa represents for Imarah the ill-intended traitor of this culture and heritage and not one of its enlightening figures, as the tanwir campaign claims.

In 1994 a Palestinian Marxist historian living in Damascus, Maher Charif, wrote a rebuttal of Imarah's views on Salama Moussa. In his rebuttal, "Musahama fi al-jadal al-rahin hawl al-tanwir / Salama Moussa namudhajan" (A contribution to the current discussion on tanwir / Salama Moussa as an example),[74] Charif accused Imarah of reducing Moussa's thought to one book, *Al-yawm wa al-ghad*, of imputing false claims to him, and of using double standards in evaluating his positions. Moussa, writes Charif, wrote some forty books and one hundred articles, and his ideas kept developing and changing with the circumstances. Any assessment that would not take this into consideration would fail to do justice to Moussa's ideas. Contrary to what Imarah claims, adds Charif, Moussa never called for atheism; in fact, he expressed admiration for the work of Abduh and Afghani. The East that Moussa called to reject was that of underdevelopment, and the West he called to adopt was that of the philosophical, political, and economic revolutions, without the colonial side of the West, which he clearly rejected. On the other hand, he appreciated the achievements of India, particularly those of Mahatma Gandhi and Jawaharlal Nehru. Moreover, and contrary to Imarah's accusation, Moussa did not reject or vilify the Arabic language but called for its modernization. He was not against Arab or Islamic civilization but was primarily an Egyptian nationalist, like many others of his time, including Ahmed Lutfi al-Sayyid (1872–1963), whose positions Imarah has no problem with. Furthermore, Moussa shared many of al-Kawakibi's ideas, although the two men came from different backgrounds. They both advocated tanwir values—namely, the use of reason; the securing of liberties, especially intellectual and political liberties; the call for development; openness to the West and borrowing from its culture, particularly the concept of citizenship; constitutional and parliamentary rule; and the separation of state and religion. Their differences came from their different backgrounds. Al-Kawakibi, writes Charif, came from a place (Aleppo) that witnessed the birth of Arab nationalism; he was raised in a religious Islamic fashion, which made him inclined to combine Arabism with Islam; and his knowledge of Western ideas came from translations. Moussa, on the other hand, grew up in a Coptic family and became acquainted with the West in his youth in Paris and London, he adopted socialism but remained attracted to liberalism, and he conceived of Egyptian nationalism in isolation from Arab nationalism. What Imarah accepts in al-Kawakibi's case he condemns in Moussa's, showing a clear bias against the latter.

The point, concludes Charif, is not to advocate a "back to Moussa" call or a "back to the ancients" call, in this case the ancients of the nahda tanwir. Moussa himself would have rejected such a call. Rather, the point is to reactivate Moussa's mode of thinking, which was free from ideological constraints, and also his interest in combining socialism with liberalism. Some might find this eclectic, Charif adds, but it might not be a bad thing if it can help shape a critical and comprehensive emancipatory thought (*nuzu' naqdi yatatalla' ila ufuq tahriri shamil*).[75] In fact, Charif starts by noting the renewed interest in the "pioneers of Arab tanwir," as he calls them, especially in critical Arab intellectual currents, and particularly in the Marxist one. He explains this through five phenomena: first, the identity crisis of Arab Marxism after the recent intellectual and political changes, including the fall of the Soviet Union, and hence its need to reconnect with another intellectual legacy as a reference; second, the growing awareness of the important role that the liberal current played in shaping the tanwir project, and of the loss that critical Arab thought suffered when Arab Marxism and tanwir liberalism were disconnected; third, the growing realization of the importance of religious reform in the nahda tanwir, especially with regard to the rampant Islamist current; fourth, the feeling that many of the nahda tanwir issues are still with us today, and that the nahda texts still have important things to offer, especially their openness and freedom from ideological constraints; and fifth, the emergence among Arab Marxists of a need for critical Arab currents to open up to one another and work out a common intellectual construct of emancipation (*sabika fikriyya jadida*) instead of remaining confined to narrow ideological systems.[76] Charif is not the only Arab Marxist to have encouraged such an orientation. As we shall see, prominent Syrian Marxist thinker Sadeq Jalal al-Azm (1934–2016) and Abdulrazzaq Eid will argue likewise.[77]

But the claims of the tanwir campaign according to Imarah are flawed not only regarding Abdel Raziq, Husayn, and Moussa but even more so when it comes to the nahda pioneers Tahtawi, Afghani, and Abduh. These pioneers worked for an Islamic renewal (*tajdid islami*) and not for a westernized enlightenment (*tanwir gharbi*). Both Islamic revival and Western Enlightenment aim at civilizational revival but with opposite means: the former through a religious renewal, the latter through a distancing from religion.[78] Present-day tanwiris such as Gaber Asfour, writes Imarah, miss this crucial difference.[79]Tahtawi was indeed for reason and experimentation, but he was not for secularism. He did not call for the exclusion of the divine law, and when he translated the French constitution, it was not to apply it to Muslim lands. Moreover, he did not regard Europe to be primarily a Christian culture.[80] So regarding him as a pioneer of tanwir distorts the facts (*tazwir*).[81] Similarly, Afghani (1838–1897) stood against Western modernization: what Westerners saw as the remedy for civilizational downfall—namely, the exclusion of religion—he saw as the cause of the downfall.[82] Finally, for Imarah it is an equally incongruous error to label Abduh a figure of Western tanwir, when the man regarded Islam as a comprehensive moderate whole that served faith, reason, and civilization in the most ideal way. Not only are his works reprinted within the Muwajaha tanwir series, writes Imarah with indignation, but they are reprinted in a truncated manner, whereby his statements on Christianity and its differences with Islam are simply omitted. So in Abduh's case, the distortion is double.[83]

For Imarah the whole tanwir campaign is, in a nutshell, a fraud in which Egyptian, Arab, and Muslim intellectual history is distorted and misrepresented to fit an anti-Islamic agenda that fails to understand the enlightenment message of Islam. Interestingly, Imarah himself was accused by a more conservative Islamist, Muhammad Ibrahim Mabruk, of being too lenient with the secularists, of shying away from advocating a religious Islamic state, and of using terms adopted by them such as "civil state" (*dawla madaniyya*). However, Mabruk agrees with Imarah's theses concerning the falsification of the nahda legacy by secularists.[84]

Clearly the nahda, its nature, and its identity occupy a central place in all three discourses on tanwir. The state and the secularist ones want to recall its main enlightening ideas and impulses to support their present tanwir advocacy. The Islamists want to insist on its religious character. Religion, religious fundamentalism, and secularism constitute the second major headline of these Egyptian 1990s tanwir discussions. The role of the state in defining and managing the place of religion and the project of tanwir is the third headline. Indeed, the state's role and the position of the intellectuals in it with respect to the tanwir project are particularly intricate issues in the Egyptian case, as we shall see in the following chapter. Non-Islamist Egyptian intellectuals seem, on the one hand, to bet on the state's defense of liberties against religious fundamentalism and its robust protection of nationalism against the Islamists' universalist challenge. On the other hand, they complain about the state's autocratic policies and its occasional leniency with the Islamists. Moreover, Egyptian intellectuals criticize the inflated weight of the state while at the same time fearing it will wither away under Islamist influence. Critics of the state and secularist discourses on tanwir have pointed out these contradictions, as we shall see in the next chapter.

TWO

The Deconstruction of the 1990s Egyptian Tanwir Debates by Egyptian Critics at the Turn of the Millennium

THE GOVERNMENTAL AND Islamist tanwir discourses came under severe attack from a number of angles. I will examine here three attacks: from sociologist Mona Abaza, Islam scholar Nasr Hamid Abu Zayd, and historian Sherif Younis. All three thinkers denounced the hypocritical, superficial, and even cynical abuse of the idea of tanwir and analyzed the sociohistorical background of the intellectuals involved in the two respective campaigns. They found the discourses hypocritical, because their proponents were in reality conservative conformists uninterested in the emancipatory ideas of tanwir. They thought that the discourses were superficial, produced in haste in the face of the Islamist threat, without any earnest analysis of the situation that gave rise to that threat, and without any conceptual elaboration of the tanwir ideas. Finally, they showed that the discourses were cynically used in a power game to manipulate or grab power and certainly not to spread tanwir values. The authors of the discourses were trapped, either willingly or unwillingly, in this power game, speaking down to the masses that remained alien to them. The subservience of the tanwiris vis-à-vis the state, especially the anti-Islamist ones, and their elitism vis-à-vis the masses came, according to the critics, from the history of the Egyptian intelligentsia dating back to the origins of the modern Egyptian state. This subservience and elitism were and remained for these critics a predicament that weighed on the Egyptian intellectual debates, including the one on tanwir.

These three critics of the secularist and Islamist tanwir discourses suggested a different practice of tanwir, one that involved substantial autonomous critique of existing realities, based on a solid sociohistorical knowledge of the society and animated by a clear commitment to values of emancipation. Abaza and Younis actually put this other tanwir into practice at the outbreak of the revolution, together with a host of other Egyptian critical thinkers.[1] Abu Zayd unfortunately did not witness the revolution, passing away a few months before its outbreak.

Mona Abaza: Tanwir as the Site of an Intellectual and Political Struggle

A professor at the American University of Cairo and an Egyptian sociologist, Mona Abaza has been a keen observer of Egypt's intellectual and cultural scenes.[2] She has also been a perceptive and critical supporter of the revolution.[3] She has devoted part of her studies to analyzing the tanwir debate in Egypt in the 1990s and 2000s. In two seminal articles she has shown how the notion of tanwir has become the site of a bitter intellectual and political struggle between the secularist intellectuals, the state, and the Islamists: "Tanwir and Islamization: Rethinking the Struggle Over Intellectual Inclusion in Egypt," from 2000, and "Trafficking with Tanwir (Enlightenment)" from 2010.[4]

In the first article, she reviews the writings of prominent Islamists, including Muhammad Imarah (born 1931) and Tariq al-Bishri (born 1933),[5] who respond to the secularists and the state on tanwir. Among those writings is the journal *al-Manar al-jadid* (The new lighthouse), launched in 1998 and edited by Imarah. The journal celebrated the centennial of another journal, *al-Manar* (The lighthouse), edited by Rashid Rida (1865–1935). Rida was the disciple of the Egyptian Islamic reformer Muhammad Abduh (1849–1905). Through his writings and the journal, Rida contributed to the dissemination of Abduh's complex reform thought, which tried to reconcile Islamic doctrines with modernity, science, reason, and civilization.[6] *Al-Manar*, which appeared from 1896 to 1936, expressed, on the one hand, alarm over the danger of Western domination and, on the other, concern over the weakness of the Muslim world. However, at the same time it expressed faith in the possibility of overcoming this weakness and working out a constructive interaction between the West and the Muslim world. Despite its affirmed alignment with the orientations of this older journal, *al-Manar al-jadid* emphasized instead the Western-Muslim divide and articulated a more defensive and self-sufficient view of Islamic thought. Abaza quotes Imarah's statement from his opening article of the first issue: "*Al-Manar al-jadid . . .* is an Arab-Islamic forum, an authentic enlightened work that does not wear the masque of enlightenment to trade with culture."[7]

Clearly, a distinction is made here between an "authentic" Arab-Islamic enlightenment and a fake one that conceals westernization, alienation, and betrayal of identity and Islam. Yet despite this clearly oppositional stand vis-à-vis secularist tanwir, the Islamist tanwir discourse, writes Abaza, in fact mirrors the issues and ideas of that "inauthentic" enlightenment, giving them an Islamic twist. Enlightenment calls to reform as well as values such as reason are recuperated and redefined. Figures, writings, and ideas associated with tanwir, whether from the nahda or the older classical heritage, are represented as Islamic, or at least as not being un-Islamic and belonging instead to a general Islamic whole. In other words, the tanwir legacy promoted by the secularists is reclaimed by the Islamists and put at the service of cultural and political directions opposed to those of the secularists: "*Al-Manar al-jadid* shows that the 'Islamic liberals' have started to use language identical to that of the secularists, although with different meanings and with different practical political implications."[8] Not only are Islamists eager to reclaim Egyptian intellectual history, they are also keen on imposing themselves as apt players on the intellectual scene and on demanding recognition accordingly: "It would seem that what worries the writers of *al-Manar al-jadid* is that they are not being identified as intellectuals and elites (*al-nukhba*) by their opponents, the secularists, although they curse them. In fact, they advocate calling themselves 'the Muslim intellectuals' and claim that their intellectualism is as legitimate as that of the secularists."[9]

This ambition on the part of Islamists to compete for intellectual authority is older than the dispute regarding tanwir. It dates back to the faltering authority of secular and traditional religious intellectuals after the 1967 Arab defeat by Israel in the Six-Day War and the end of the Nasser era. French political scientist Gilles Kepel gives a cogent history of the competition for intellectual authority in modern Egyptian history between traditional religious clerics (the ulemas), secular intellectuals (the intelligentsia), and

Islamists.[10] Kepel employs Edward Schils's definition of the function of the intellectual to examine the performance of those three competing groups. According to this definition, intellectuals offer a worldview that reflects the central values of society and interprets the real in view of changing it. The oldest among those groups, the ulemas, have fulfilled, according to Kepel, the double poles of religious work, following Pierre Bourdieu's analysis of the religious field. Their task has been, on the one hand, to legitimize the social order and on the other hand to check the power of the ruler.[11] In Islam this has indeed been the ideal role of the religious authorities. In history, however, they have rarely fulfilled that role and have usually sided with those in power. Yet despite their customary closeness to power, the ulemas have preserved some margin of autonomy through their independent wealth, ensured through the Awqaf (religious charity endowments) and through control of clerical training institutions, primarily the Azhar. Only in the late 1950s, under the rule of Gamal Abdel Nasser, did they lose both sources of independence. Abdel Nasser transferred their assets to the agrarian reform program and imposed far-reaching modifications on the Azhar, ultimately bringing the latter under his control. On the other hand, he supported the secular intelligentsia to replace the religious one, though only within the parameters of his political agenda. While the ulemas legitimized the social order by referring to the transcendental order, the secular intellectuals did that with reference to a "translated," "transmediterranean," "trans-Atlantic," or even "trans-Siberian" order, as Kepel calls it. In other words, the authority to which the intelligentsia appealed was that of overseas modernity, primarily Western modernity. This had been the case since modern Egypt's formation under Muhammad Ali Pasha. The challenge to indigenize this "translated" order persisted until it espoused Egyptian nationalism and served the struggle against British colonialism between the two world wars. But even then, writes Kepel, it was still not able to monopolize or even dominate Egyptian society. Having brought the ulemas and the intelligentsia under his control, Abdel Nasser was left with one oppositional current, that of the Muslim Brotherhood. He repressed it ruthlessly.

But with Abdel Nasser's fall and the defeat of 1967, both intellectual groups, the ulemas and the intelligentsia, were severely discredited. A new group claimed the mission of calling for societal change in the name of the transcendental order, this time in the form of jihad; it also undertook the mission of censuring the ruler in the name of the same order. This ascending group was the Islamists. The two older groups disputed its authority and competence in assuming its double mission. The ulemas, some more than others, agreed with the Islamists about the need for societal reform, but they stated that the Islamists lacked the right training to speak authoritatively in the name of the transcendental. The intelligentsia, on the other hand, challenged the Islamists' understanding of the modern world as well as their ability to articulate the tensions between society and the "translated" order and those between society and the ruler. The Islamists' response to these challenges and doubts translated into a determination to prove their competence on the level of both religious authority and interpreting and acting in the modern world.[12]

To illustrate the Islamists' will to recuperate modern Egyptian intellectual history, Abaza refers to an article from the first issue of *al-Manar al-jadid* written by moderate Islamist legal scholar Tariq al-Bishri, in which the author compares *al-Manar* to another journal of the time, *al-Hilal*, founded by Jurgi Zaydan (1861–1914) in 1892. By making this comparison, Abaza argues, al-Bishri highlights the two components of modern Egyptian thought, secularism and Islam, and affirms the more significant presence of the latter in modern Egyptian intellectual, cultural, and political history. In fact, as mentioned earlier, in 1992 the Egyptian government had celebrated the hundredth anniversary of *al-Hilal* as part of its "One Hundred Years of Enlightenment" campaign.[13]

Abaza points out the notable turn that the prolific intellectual careers of al-Bishri and Imarah have taken: after being rather progressive thinkers, with left-leaning orientations, they have both become conservative Islamists, advocating in the latter part of their careers the opposite of what they had supported earlier. Known as a serious scholar and jurist, appreciated as a sensible debate partner, and respected for his moderate discourse regarding a wide range of issues, such as his conciliatory approach to Copt-Muslim relations, al-Bishri seems to have given up on the possibility of a secular-Islamist dialogue and increasingly keen on demonstrating the "Islamicity" of the Ottoman epoch and the persistence of that Islamic character throughout the modernization process.[14] Imarah, on the other hand, had edited some of the major works of the Arab rationalist and reformist legacy in the early part of his career, including Ibn Rushd's *Fasl al-maqal* (The decisive treatise) and the writings of Jamal el-Din al-Afghani and Muhammad

Abduh. He also wrote extensively on the Mu'tazilites (the rationalist school of theology in the Middle Ages) and on a number of nahda figures, such as Rifa'a al-Tahtawi, Abd al-Rahman al-Kawakibi, and Ali Abdel Raziq.[15] After having celebrated their rationalist and secularist ideas, he later on criticized and even denied those ideas, insisting instead on the Islamic and anti-Western character of their work. As we saw in the previous chapter, by reprinting those nahda works as part of its tanwir campaign, the government was, according to Imarah, misrepresenting those works as advocating secularism. In reality, he says, most of those thinkers either did not propose secularist ideas at all and remained attached to their Muslim worldview or were for a while under the influence of westernized and alienated figures such as Taha Husayn, whom he calls the "Imam of westernizers and imitators of the West" (*imam al-mughtaribin wa muqallidi al-gharb*).[16] Interestingly, in the fall of 2014 Imarah published a book on Taha Husayn entitled *Taha Husayn: min al-inbihar bi al-gharb ila al-intisar li al-islam* (Taha Husayn: From infatuation with the West to championing Islam).[17] In it he stated that his aim was to be fair to Husayn and to acknowledge the different phases of his thought. Imarah asserted that the last phase—namely, the return to Islam and Arabhood—was the most important. This thesis was immediately debunked by Mahmud Dab''s *Taha Husayn . . . laghu al-sayf wa jadd al-shita'* (Taha Husayn . . . The summer play and the winter earnestness),[18] which emphasized the seriousness of Husayn's modernism. Once again the opposite views on a tanwir-nahda figure, if not the most prominent one, gave rise to a heated debate.[19]

Clearly, in the eyes of these Islamists, the tanwir discourses of the secular intellectuals and especially of the government are neither fruitful nor honest; they are at best misleading. The tone of the exchange between the parties is harsh, uncompromising, and mutually intolerant. Some of the Islamists have accused the secularists of being extremists in their "irreligiosity" and collaborators with an unjust government. Abaza writes: "The Islamic camp wants to show that there is a close relationship between the government and the 'irreligious' intellectuals. It is a notion that is not altogether invalid, given the fact that there is a tacit coalition between secular intellectuals and the state."[20] Indeed, this coalition between the secular intellectuals and a government that did not practice any of the tanwir precepts could only damage the intellectual, moral, and political integrity of those intellectuals and discredit the cause of tanwir. The practices of the Egyptian government during its tanwir campaign constitute the backdrop of Abaza's discussion of the tanwir debate in her second essay, published in 2010, on the eve of the revolution of January 25, 2011. In "Trafficking with Tanwir (Enlightenment)" she reviews those practices and depicts the context in which the tanwir debate was carried out:

> Precisely when the government has been trying to sell for the Western "democratic" and free world an image of a civilized, "enlightened" government, combating its "dark" opponents, it has itself reinvented practices from the Middle Ages, such as publicly stripping and raping female demonstrators, acts that were committed in May 2005 by thugs paid by the regime. The launching of campaigns of enlightenment in official and literati circles for more than a decade has run parallel with the regime's mounting of highly barbaric practices in its attempt at harshly disciplining the unruly. These practices have included handcuffing in hospitals the seriously wounded workers who demonstrated against inadequate salaries and the country's worsening economic conditions in El Mahalla El Kubra in April 2008; witch-hunting homosexuals and charging them with "debauchery," imposing anal inspections on those charged, torturing them, and handcuffing them to hospital beds before sentencing them for homosexuality; jailing en masse the Islamists as the regime's number one public enemy: and torturing citizens to death in police stations. Witch-hunting has extended to courageous bloggers, to poor innocent citizens, and to stray street children, who are tortured routinely, raped, and, as evidenced by some reports, killed by mafias with the consent of the police.[21]

These grave violations of basic human rights were made more public with the outbreak of the revolution, as faltering state censorship allowed increasingly outspoken denunciations of these practices. Unfortunately, with the onset of the counterrevolution after July 2013, perpetrators of those practices seem to have regained impunity. Committing such violations on the one hand and preaching enlightenment on the other, the government and its agents couldn't help but reveal the hypocrisy of what Islamist opponents called the "*tanwir hukumi*" (governmental enlightenment) and embarrass secularist intellectuals associated with tanwir or the government or, as was often the case, with both. Adding cynicism to hypocrisy, the government allowed the increasing Islamization of public morality by Islamists, in particular when it came to culture and women. Abaza discusses two incidents from the early and mid-2000s that illustrate this hypocrisy and cynicism most conspicuously, both dealing with statements and actions by the minister of culture, Farouk Hosni. The first incident deals with censorship and the second with women's issues.

Hosni was appointed minister of culture in 1987 and stayed in office, despite numerous controversies, until the outbreak of the revolution in 2011. During all those years, he loyally served the regime and was a close collaborator of President Hosni Mubarak's wife, Suzanne Mubarak, on projects meant to support enlightened culture and learning. Always introducing himself as *"al-fannan Farouk Hosni, wazir al-thaqafa"* (the artist Farouk Hosni, minister of culture), Hosni considered himself a champion of the liberal arts. In early 2001 he faced a testing moment when a Muslim Brotherhood parliamentarian objected to the publication of three novels by the General Organization for Cultural Palaces (GOCP), denouncing them as pornographic. One of them, *Walima li a'shab al-bahr* (A banquet for seaweed), by prominent Syrian writer Haydar Haydar, had been published in 1983, with several subsequent reprints, without any objection. A vilification campaign ensued against the Ministry of Culture, under whose auspices such allegedly immoral works were published. After a brief investigation requested by Hosni, several GOCP officials were sacked. Hosni justified the punitive measure by affirming that social moral values needed to be respected. Several Egyptian intellectuals protested against the minister's stand, among them the late prominent Egyptian novelist Gamal al-Ghitani (1945–2015). A few weeks later, at the Cairo International Book Fair, President Mubarak supported his minister and asserted that "traditions, morality, and religious considerations" would prevail. Obviously, despite its claims to enlightenment and its tanwir campaigns, the regime found it expedient to please the Islamist camp and the public influenced by it, and to acquiesce to the alleged "values of society," betraying a core value of the enlightenment and its anti-Islamist intellectual supporters. These intellectuals deplored this blow to the freedom of expression. Commenting on the incident, and recalling the history of the relationship between Egyptian intellectuals and the state, professor of Arabic literature at the American University of Cairo Samia Mehrez writes: "For Egyptian cultural figures, this history has meant that the cultural is the handmaiden of the political and must always abide by its rules. . . . So long as the political field remains obsessed with its own power to the detriment of its own development, the cultural players will continue to be reminded—should they forget—that the cultural is political. This is the name of the game."[22]

The other incident was triggered by a remark Hosni made in 2006 about his dislike of the veil as a sign of backwardness and a marker of Muslim-Christian difference. The remark was met with fierce attacks and insults against him. But once again he was able to weather them with the support of the regime. Abaza recalls that just a few weeks before this incident, women in downtown Cairo had been sexually harassed, and this had not been mentioned by the official press or in the ruling circles. Once again the contrast between official progressive politics regarding women and the brutalization of the public sphere, including increasing systematic sexual harassment, undermined the credibility of that politics. Suzanne Mubarak had supported the enactment of progressive family laws improving the rights of women in divorce and custody, which came to be known as the "Suzanne Mubarak laws," thus spreading discredit by association to feminism in Egypt. Abaza writes that oppositional groups such as Kifaya agreed with the Muslim Brotherhood in condemning the mendacity and corruption of the government.[23] She quotes from a comment by Khaled Hamza Salam, the founder and editor in chief of a Muslim Brotherhood website, responding to the minister's antiveil remarks:

> Many observers of the cultural affairs in Egypt know that the Culture Minister is not a secularist, according to the Western concept, as he is closer to a technocrat who has [been] serving in the Egyptian tyrannical government for more than 20 years; also, he isn't a liberal, according to the Western concept, as he is a member of a repressive regime that rigs the elections, fights civil society institutions, violates humans rights, drags Kifaya Movement's female members in the streets, arrests bloggers; he is a member of a regime that violates intellectual and cultural freedoms in public, turns a blind eye to sexual harassment against women in the streets.[24]

Abaza concludes her piece with four observations: that attacks against secularism stem partly from its association with the corrupt regime, that most political actors see the need to compromise with the dominant Islamist moral and cultural worldview, that a witch-hunting atmosphere has come to prevail under this worldview, and that the regime's appeasement of religious institutions, primarily the Azhar, has increased the power of those institutions and led to their encroaching influence on the Ministry of Culture.

Clearly, such conditions cannot be favorable to genuine tanwir endeavors, therefore articulate and lucid analyses, such as Mona Abaza's, that depict and denounce these conditions are all the more important. These conditions and the attempts to challenge them remain part of the Egyptian reality to date.

With Nasr Hamid Abu Zayd and Sherif Younis, the focus of critique shifts from the overall sociopolitical context of the tanwir discourses to their contents. The two men deplore the elitism of the tanwir proponents and their subservient dependency on the state. They criticize the discourses' lack of credibility and the poverty of their content, which consists of shallow sloganeering. Finally, they both call for an authentic tanwir, defined as a free, concrete, and uncompromising critique that engages people in their real-life situations. Recognized for the solidity of their scholarship and their independent opinions, both have closely studied contemporary Islamic religious discourses, Abu Zayd having focused on the history of Islamic religious thought and Younis on the history of Egyptian ideological thought. Moreover, both have followed the political tensions of the second half of the twentieth century, with Abu Zayd being directly implicated in a conflict with the Islamists. Both have been committed secularists, Abu Zayd defending secularism from a faith-based position and Younis defending it regardless of faith.

Nasr Hamid Abu Zayd: The Dismal Failure of Governmental Tanwir

Nasr Hamid Abu Zayd (1943–2010) was a renowned Egyptian scholar of Islamic thought, who distinguished himself in writings on hermeneutics and exegesis, as well as studies of past and contemporary religious discourses. He advocated a historicist reading of the Qur'an that would employ human sciences to read and interpret the holy book in light of its revelatory context, especially its cultural and linguistic contexts. He believed that such a reading enabled the receiver to better grasp the revealed divine message. This did not mean reducing the sacred text to a mere historical text and so losing its divine character, which his opponents accused him of doing. Rather, it meant better access to the meanings conveyed by the sacred text to the contemporary reader. Moreover, he wanted to distinguish the sacred text from the rest of the religious intellectual tradition, which was produced in different historical epochs. Finally, he drew attention to the power struggles that shaped religious discourses throughout the ages and up to contemporary Egypt.

In 1993 he became a victim of those power games when he denounced the various abuses of the Islamists, including their financial frauds. He was denied promotion at Cairo University by an Islamist who sat on his committee. After that he was accused of apostasy and then required by court order to divorce his wife, because as a non-Muslim he could no longer be married to a Muslim woman. He eventually fled the country with his wife, and his case became a cause célèbre. However, he remained a close observer of his country and continued to speak his mind until his death in 2010.

In 2001 he addressed the issue of governmental tanwir in "Wizarat al-thaqafa: I'lan fashal al-tanwir al-bragmati, hal hunak tariq akhar? Al-tathwir la al-tanwir" (The ministry of culture: Declaration of the failure of pragmatic tanwir: Is there another way? Revolutionizing not enlightening). A few years later the piece was republished as "Suqut al-tanwir al-hukumi" (The fall of governmental tanwir).[25] As the second title indicates, the piece is a damning assessment of the regime's attempts to use tanwir discourse against the Islamists.

Tanwir, he writes, has become the slogan of the epoch (shi'ar al-marhala) and its adored idol (sanamaha al-ma'bud). It is the slogan that the regime raised against the Islamists after it failed to defeat them with its security apparatus. He adds that the government ignored pleas by him and others for a concept of security based on the security of the citizen. But as long as the terror attacks (before and after the 1981 assassination of Anwar el-Sadat) targeted ordinary people, especially Copts in Upper Egypt, the government did not care. However, when the attacks were aimed at government officials and prominent personalities of the intelligentsia in the heart of Cairo, the government decided to react, because it was interested in the security of the regime, not of society. It reacted first, writes Abu Zayd, by negotiating with the Islamists and allowing them greater control over culture and society, following a trend of Islamization of culture and society that had been going on since Sadat's rule. This trend suited the regime because it gave it religious legitimacy at a time when it lacked every other kind of legitimacy; in addition, cultural and societal Islamization distracted people's attention away from the regime's corrupt practices with endless discussions about authenticity and identity. The government's second response was to launch a discursive campaign for tanwir, spreading slogans of tolerance against bigotry, openness against fanaticism, creativity instead of blind imitation, reason against tradition, and so on. It started republishing nahda works, including those of Taha Husayn, Ali Abdel Raziq, Mohammed Abduh, and Salama Moussa, in a claimed effort to disseminate tanwir ideas and confront the obscurantist ideas of the Islamists. For this task it appointed new editors in chief for major newspapers and new managers in its Ministry of Culture, and it mobilized intellectuals, even leftists who were previously reluctant to work with the government but now felt directly targeted by the Islamist threat.

The problem with this campaign, writes Abu Zayd, is that it lacked both credibility and depth. The tanwiris employed in it did not have time to develop any serious critical analysis of the situation or understanding of the roots of violence in general, and Islamist violence in particular, or time to lay bare the connection between this violence and the ruthless practices of the regime. As a result, the tanwiris could not produce reliable knowledge that could enlighten people on the origins, nature, and workings of fundamentalism and extremism in their society. They cheered for tanwir but did not make it (al-hutaf li al-tanwir la sina'atuhu). They could only draw slogans from other times and other situations, those of the classical age or the nahda, thus becoming revivalists like the Islamists, who drew slogans from past times without adapting them creatively to the present. The confrontation was between two sets of slogans, two sets of absolutes and idols, that did not produce any serious reflection or knowledge.

Moreover, tanwir became associated with the regime itself, a regime that many saw as corrupt and unjust. In the absence of a genuine critique of the Egyptian realities of the day, including those of the regime and the Islamists, the governmental tanwir discourse could not offer an alternative sociopolitical vision that would overcome the either-or of the regime and the Islamists. On the contrary, intellectuals repeated that "the military boots on the head were better than the turbans of those claiming Islam" ("Hidha' al-'askar 'ala al-ra's afdal min 'amamat al-muta'aslimin") and that "the hell of the despotic military regimes was more merciful than the paradise of the preachers of the Islamic state" ("Nar al-nudhum al-'askariyya al-mustabidda arham min jannat du'at al-dawla al-islamiyya"):[26] clearly not very emancipatory statements!

Indeed, by joining this governmental tanwir campaign, Egyptian intellectuals aligned themselves with a regime that embodied the opposite of tanwiri ideas, believing that it was at least better than the Islamist evil. Despite its ills, the regime was seen as a bulwark against the Islamist peril, which for the intellectuals threatened the survival of the Egyptian state. This alignment with the state had existed, in Abu Zayd's view, since the foundation of modern Egypt, particularly since the nahda, when the major projects of cultural modernization were undertaken. Already then, intellectuals believed that change could only come from state power, in a top-down fashion. And since then reform projects led by Egyptian intellectuals have in general been elitist, catering to the middle class and the higher echelons of the state, and geographically limited to the major urban spaces, primarily Cairo and Alexandria. The intellectuals have been patronizing to the larger population and have never really been interested in closing the gap between the elite and the masses. Sometimes they believed that they could bend the state to serve their own reform goals, but they did not realize how difficult it was to do so given the nature of state power, inherently and exclusively geared toward its own interests.

The behavior of Farouk Hosni is a case in point, according to Abu Zayd. In the final analysis, all intellectuals involved realized that they were merely, or in the first place, employees of the state, forced to abide by its self-serving policies. Sometimes people point to Taha Husayn as an example of a free and enlightened thinker who served as a civil servant, took on public offices, and even became minister of education (1950–1952). The difference is that before the Nasser period, there was still a distinction between the state and the regime, unlike later, when the Nasser, Sadat, and Mubarak regimes usurped the state. Under such conditions, an alliance with the government could only turn the intellectuals into guard dogs (*kilab hirasa*) and prevent them from being the guardians of values (*hurras al-qiyam*) they should be.[27]

Instead of this shallow and unconvincing "tanwir," writes Abu Zayd, what we need is to revolutionize (*tathwir*) thought; that is, challenge taboos and break into areas of the "unthought," referring to Mohammad Arkoun's (1928–2010) work:[28]

And the revolutionizing of thought that we need requires an effort to move minds by challenging and entering into forbidden areas, domains of the unthought as defined by Mohammad Arkoun, and by opening a debate around issues. And most importantly, it is imperative to get rid of that long standing separation wall between the "masses" [al-ʿamma] and the "elite" [al-khassa]; those calls that recur every now and then to restrict the discussion of certain religious issues to the "people of knowledge" [ahl al-ʿilm], in order not to confuse or corrupt the beliefs of the masses, are in their appearance calls for mercy and righteousness, but are in reality calls for evil. How is it possible in a time of open skies that transport the world to the bedrooms, and in an age in which the information revolution invades all borders,. . . to call for the protection of the "masses" from the danger of scientific thought in the gravest issues that touch their lives. It is unfortunately the logic of "patronization" that takes the name of "protection" to practice an intellectual and mental dictatorship that is no less dangerous than the political dictatorship in our societies.[29]

Abu Zayd elaborates further on this elite-masses divide as well as on the relation between the intellectual and power in "Ishkaliyyat al-muthaqqaf wa al-dawla/al-sulta: al-zawaj al-kathuliki bayn al-muthaqqaf wa al-sulta, istibʿad al-ʿamma" (The problematic of the intellectual and the state/power: The Catholic marriage between the intellectual and power, the exclusion of the masses).[30] In this piece Abu Zayd affirms his belief, contrary to many of his fellow intellectuals, that lasting change can only come from the base, not the summit. Moreover, he thinks one of the biggest challenges is to connect with the people by producing a profound and at the same time intelligible discourse regarding matters of common concern, a discourse that is respectful of people's feelings without being populist. He thinks no real tanwir can happen without overcoming the elite-masses divide that is so entrenched in the long Arab intellectual legacy:

And the question now: How does the intellectual communicate with a wider public? And how does he produce a discourse that is deep and intelligible at the same time? I don't have a ready recipe to solve this problem, which I consider to be a true challenge to every intellectual of the Third World, when "education" is a chronic crisis. It is not about producing a populist discourse that pleases the feelings and instincts of the masses. The media do that with a crushing success, I mean a success that crushes all the discourses of the intellectuals. What is needed is a critical discourse that respects people's feelings, without trying to outbid them. It is certain that what people don't make themselves cannot sink into their cultural conscience. And the distortion that happened to modernity and its values in the course of "modernization" in the Arab world was not caused by the people, but by the modernizing authorities in their collaboration with the modernist intellectual, who remained hanging between tradition and modernity and was unable to produce any scientific knowledge of either. It is not possible to achieve modernity from the top while preserving the traditional structure at the bottom for whatever reason.[31]

Similarly, no real tanwir can take place without independent intellectuals able to keep a distance from the powers that be, political, social, or religious, and who are not bound to them by some kind of "Catholic marriage." This independence does not mean the destruction of these powers, but their critique, separation, and limitation. Only with such autonomy can intellectuals be effective in their society and not become apologists for these powers. The nahda tanwir projects that people miss today were severely challenged and eventually stifled because of that "marriage."

Political, social, and religious powers have found in religious texts convenient tools to serve their own interests. Hiding behind the assumed sacred authority of those texts, they have justified their despotism and corruption and imposed a rigid conservatism. What we need, Abu Zayd writes, is liberation from the authority of the texts (sultat al-nusus). That authority (sulta) is acquired through interpretations in different historical circumstances under the influence of sociopolitical and economic interests: one epoch's consecrated doctrine becoming anathema in another epoch. Power groups have presented certain interpretations as replacing the sacred texts themselves and taken them as tools for their self-serving ambitions. In an essay entitled "Ishakaliyyat al-'ilaqa bayna al-'aql wa al-wahi" (The problematic between reason and revelation),[32] Abu Zayd affirms that no liberation and no rationality is possible without appreciating the interpretative component of religious textual traditions:

It is not possible to found rationality without the call for emancipation from the power/authority of the texts, the dominating power/authority of the past behind which hide dictatorship and despotism and under whose umbrella prospers corruption. The liberation from the authority of the texts is not the elimination of those texts or a call to get rid of them. Rather, it is a call to shed the light of reason on them, and to read them in a contextual way in the light of their history and the history of those agents who produced them. The religious texts—the Qur'an and prophetic Hadiths—have a context that cannot be ignored either, and these religious texts do not acquire their authority by themselves or in themselves. Rather, that authority is given to them by humans through their faith.[33]

He adds that authority is also bestowed upon those texts by different interpreters in different ways at different times. The only protection from the possible abuse of these interpretations by political, social, or religious powers is faith free from the authority of mediators: "Free 'faith' remains the only true protection, I mean, the faith that is the 'covenant' [al-ʿaqd]—and hence the word doctrine [ʿaqida]—between the individual or the community and their sacred texts, without the mediation of any authority, including that of the intellectual or the interpreter."[34] It is the task of the state to protect the unavoidable plurality of ways of understanding sacred texts and the multiple forms of religiosity that result; to do that the state should not be based on a specific interpretation or even a specific religion. In other words, the state should be the protector of citizens and citizenship. It is ridiculous to assume that a state can have a religion: a state doesn't go to the mosque or pray. The state should be separated from religion. This is the meaning of secularism. It does not imply that society should be separated from religion. Rather, it entails that the state should guarantee the freedom of all, believers and nonbelievers, Muslims and non-Muslims alike. Moreover, to claim that secularism is not an issue in Islam because it has no institutional religious authority equivalent to the church in Christianity is deceitful, he adds, when one knows the immense power of the numerous Muslim religious authorities. In fact, he thinks that there is a proliferation of authorities that monopolize not only religious meaning but also social, cultural, political, moral, and spiritual meanings.

But for secularism to be consolidated, a serious religious reform should be undertaken, and this has not taken place yet in the Muslim world. In his essay "Al-fazaʿ min al-ʿalmaniyya: fasl al-Din ʿan al-dawla" (The fear from secularism: The separation of religion and state),[35] Abu Zayd affirms that secularism is extremely important in the Arab and Muslim worlds, where one sees the tragic consequences of the abuse of religion, not only by radical groups or Islamists, but also by states, since the middle of the twentieth century:

> It is "secularism"—which separates the state and its political regime from religion—only that is capable of opening the horizons of freedom and rationality and plurality of meanings. Religion concerns the religious, and the task of the state is to guarantee the freedom of all, and to protect some from the oppression of some others in the name of religion, or this meaning or that specific religion. But secularism cannot be founded without religious reform, a reform that hasn't yet been achieved in our region. It was achieved in Europe in the sixteenth century. No philosophical revolution took place here as it did in Europe at the hands of European philosophers—that revolution upon which was achieved the socio-political revolution, which in turn established the notion of "citizen," to replace that of "subject." The latter still governs our societies, despite the rhetoric of the constitutions that emphasize the notion of "citizenship." After the liberation of the human from the chains of political despotism and from the ecclesial view of the world, thanks to all the aforementioned, i.e. the religious reform and the philosophical revolution and secularism, the scientific revolution was achieved.[36]

This statement shows an intellectualistic reading of the modernization processes in Europe, with philosophy leading the way to changes in religion, science, society, and politics. We know that those processes were complex, involving long-term economic, scientific, social, and political transformations. Abu Zayd elsewhere offers a more nuanced understanding of European Enlightenment history by emphasizing the role of the public dissemination and discussion of new scientific ideas, such as Darwin's evolutionary theory.[37] Here he expresses his belief in the necessity of freedom, and its only guarantee, secularism, for the sake of the historical deconstruction of religious interpretations and discourses. Only deconstruction could open the way to new seminal readings of the revealed message and prevent the abuse and manipulation of religious meanings, whether by "moderate" or "extremist" trends. He was critical of both and skeptical about the distinction between the two.[38]

The tanwir Abu Zayd conceived of and labored for was a work of enlightening theological, exegetic, and hermeneutic innovation, which contributes to a new understanding of religious discourse that is critical of ahistorical interpretation and abuse of power. He showed the human component in transmitting and receiving the revealed message, thus allowing for an ever-renewed, responsible, autonomous, and intelligent faith in every epoch. In one of his books he declared, "I think, therefore I am Muslim"; a Muslim who is theologically, morally, and politically enlightened.[39]

How would he have reacted to the momentous upheavals that Egypt witnessed shortly after his passing? What would the shaking of that corrupt and repressive political power that he held responsible for distorting everything, including religious thought and discourse, have meant for him? What new possibilities of conceptual and institutional reform would those changes have opened for him? Having lost him before the upheavals, we cannot know the answers to these questions. But we know that the margin for change did not last long, and the counterrevolution brought back renewed repression, banning the main Islamist groups and resuming an open war on terror, and by so doing failing to open the doors for the reform that Abu Zayd called for. But it was the rise of the so-called Islamic State of Iraq and the Levant (Daesh), in spring 2013 that brought new urgency to the issues raised by Abu Zayd, and also by Younis, as we will see shortly: the importance of secularism and the place of religion in politics, the urgency of a radical religious reform not confined to an elite sphere but translated into educational and cultural reform, the questioning of the assumed difference between "moderate" and "extremist" Islam, the serious understanding of the phenomenon of religious as well as nonreligious violence, and the need to take clear stands on questions of moral and human values in Muslim societies.

In the meantime, the old tanwir debate in Egypt continues. A contemporary of Abu Zayd, a former student of his, and a fellow colleague in Islamic studies, professor emeritus of the University of Cairo Hassan Hanafi (born 1935) discussed tanwir in several articles published in 2014 in the Egyptian and Arab press. I will refer here quickly to three pieces published in the Egyptian daily al-Masry al-yawm and five pieces printed in the Emirati daily al-Ittihad. In the first three pieces Hanafi distinguishes between tanwir, tathwir (revolutionizing) and tazwir (faking). In "Al-tanwir am al-tathwir?" (Enlightenment or revolutionizing?),[40] he notes, like Abu Zayd, how the term tanwir has been used by the regime to defend itself against the Islamist opposition without distinguishing between the various Islamist trends and without contextualizing the different sources of tanwir legacies, mainly Western, classical Islamic, and Arab nahda. For him what is crucial about genuine tanwir is its effort "to minimize the prevailing of the religious right over the religious left, to move from doctrine to revolution, from translation to innovation, from text to reality, from the ephemeral to the lasting, and from imitation to reason. And this is revolutionizing. Tanwir is no longer sufficient without revolutionizing."[41] This is in line with what he purported to do in his own oeuvre, especially in his efforts to create what he called an "Islamic left" by combining the justice-oriented revolutionizing values of Islam with Marxism. I have argued elsewhere that he has had difficulties abiding by these guidelines and has often limited himself to the confines of the textual analysis of tradition.[42]

In "Al-salafiyya wa al-'almaniyya . . . hal yakhtalifan?" (Salafism and secularism . . . do they differ?),[43] he underlines the similarities between the Salafis and the secularists, like Abu Zayd did, by underlining their appeal to heteronomous authorities—the ancient conservative religious thinkers for the Salafis and the Western Enlightenment figures or the ancient Muslim rationalists for the secularists—instead of producing creative thoughts of their own. Both the Salafis and the secularists, in Hanafi's opinion, are products of their times, bound to face their respective limitations and to realize the importance of reconciling their positions, eventually leading the way to a national reconciliation. Finally, in "Tanwir aw Tazwir?" (Enlightening or faking?),[44] Hanafi affirms that genuine tanwir has historically meant the use of reason to challenge past knowledge, miracles, and religious and political despotism. In this sense, tanwir cannot apologize for a regime's power while standing against its religious and political opponents. Another abuse of tanwir is to deny the enlightenment component of enlightened religion.

In 2014 Hanafi published a series of five articles, each devoted to the five aspects of tanwir: reason, freedom, the human, nature, and society.[45] He believes it is important to underline these aspects and understand them properly if one is to support the cause of tanwir. Despite the many failures of his generation, he thinks that it is still a cause his generation is ready to work for. He defines this cause as facing tradition with reason, holding onto freedom of thought and action, and demanding a democratic regime based on freedom and equality.

Finally, the postrevolutionary and counterrevolutionary Sisi regime seems to have found its own tanwiri apologists. In August 2014 young Egyptian political scientist Shady Louis denounced the claims of those he calls the "new tanwiris" or the "late tanwiris" in an article entitled "Dhulumat

al-tanwir al-masri" (The manifold darkness of Egyptian tanwir).[46] The majority of these new tanwiris, he writes, are from the secular right, and some
are from the secular left. They hold a condescending attitude toward the
Egyptian people, whom they find immature and backward, especially compared to European societies. The two-centuries-old tanwir efforts of modern Egypt are absent in their accounts, and so no attempts are made to
understand the causes of the failure of those efforts. All hopes are put in the
institutions of the "new" state, and hence once again a tanwir discourse
becomes a ready-made recipe for repression in the name of individualism,
rationalism, and freedom. Still more recently, in April 2015, a young Egyptian political scientist, Ahmed Abd Rabou, addressed the need for tanwir in
Arab countries and the failure of Egyptian and Arab tanwiris to bring it
about in an article entitled "'An asatir al-tanwir" (On the myths of tanwir).[47]
Abd Rabou asserts the need of tanwir in societies dominated by myth and
superstition, even among the educated and the elites, and ruled by authoritarian clergies, whether religious or political (al-kahanutat al-sultawiyya
diniyya kanet aw siyasiyya). These authoritarian powers pursue their own
narrow interests and abort all hopes for emancipation, democracy, development, and progress. He sees six reasons why tanwir has remained a myth in
Egypt and the Arab world, and why tanwiris, including the serious ones,
have failed to push forward the much needed tanwir: Proponents of tanwir
conflate tanwir with westernization, and as a result people resist it. Most of
those proponents are elitists who look at their tanwir ideas as a way of con-
solidating and flaunting their elitism rather than a way of liberating the
masses. Being authoritarian themselves, they oppose all revolutionary
impulses that are inevitably contained in any tanwir, in so far as it challenges established authorities, whether cognitive or real. Tanwir gets discredited because it is used as a means in the conflict with the Islamists
rather than for emancipation, becoming a way of disparaging things considered sacred, and without any real critical substance. Tanwir fails not
only because its spokespeople associate themselves with the authoritarian
structures of their countries but also because the authoritarian state apparatus, including its religious institutions, claims to undertake religious
reform and to represent "moderate Islam"; that is, to revolt against itself.
And finally, the tanwiris need to be moderate in how they present their
ideas and goals if they want to engage the public, instead of aggravating an
already polarized situation. So long as these causes of failure do not

change, Arab societies will fail to have the much-needed tanwir, Abd Rabou concludes.

Sherif Younis: The Authoritarian, Elitist, and Statist Character of the Modern Tanwir Discourse

Egyptian historian Sherif Younis addressed questions of contemporary Egyptian tanwir in a series of articles published in the mid-1990s. A prolific scholar and translator, Younis is professor of history at Helwan Cairo University. He has been a critical supporter of the Egyptian revolution up until Abdel Fatah el-Sisi came to power.[48] In his scholarship he has examined the developments of the two major modern Egyptian ideological currents, Nasserism and the Muslim Brotherhood, both in terms of their ideological content and their popular support. His writings before the 2011 revolution did not provoke much discussion, despite their pressing topics. Some of his 1990s articles appeared in a journal edited by Egyptian poet Hisham Qishtah, *al-Kitaba al-ukhra* (Other writing), which was launched as a defiant response to the state-sponsored, elitist journal *Ibda'* (Creativity), edited by another poet, Abd el-Mu'ti al-Higazi (who later became the first president of the Society for Enlightenment, as mentioned in chapter 1). *Al-Kitaba al-ukhra* was meant to offer an alternative and freer writing platform.[49] In 2013 and 2014 Younis found himself writing a bimonthly column for *al-Ahram*, one of the major dailies of the Egyptian press, when it decided to include more critical voices after the revolution—for a short while, until the Sisi "Gleichschaltung" (the "bringing into line") was imposed on most of the Egyptian media. By then Younis had become one of the major critical historians and intellectuals of contemporary Egypt. A staunch opponent of the Muslim Brotherhood and its rule, he welcomed the ousting of Mohamed Morsi and turned into an outright adversary of the revolutionaries.

Some of Younis's articles were collected in *Su'al al-huwiyya: Al-huwiyya wa sultat al-muthaqqaf fi ma ba'd al-hadatha* (The question of identity: Identity and the power of the intellectual in postmodernity).[50] His master's thesis on Sayyed Qutb was first published in 2005, then again in 2014. His first book on Nasserism, *al-Zahf al-Muqaddas: Mudhaharat al-tanahhi wa tashakkul 'ibadat Nasser* (The holy march: The demonstrations of the resignation and the formation of Nasser worship), also came out in 2005 and was then republished in 2012.[51] His second book, *Nida' al-sha'b: Tarikh naqdi li al-idiyolojiyya al-nasiriyya* (The call of the people: A critical history of the Nasserite ideology), appeared in 2012.[52] His most recent book, *al-Bahth 'an al-khalas: Azamat al-dawla wa al-islam wa al-hadatha fi misr* (The search for salvation: The crisis of the state, Islam, and modernity in Egypt), came out in 2014 and won the prize for best political book at the forty-sixth Cairo International Book Fair.[53]

Al-Zahf al-Muqaddas focused on the largely spontaneous popular demonstrations of June 9 and 10, 1967, that took place in Cairo and elsewhere in Egypt in reaction to the resignation speech of Gamal Abdel Nasser, in the wake of the 1967 defeat against Israel. Younis sets out to analyze what he sees as the rather peculiar reaction of a people bitterly disappointed by its charismatic and promising leader: they asked Abdel Nasser to withdraw his resignation and continue to lead the nation, despite the humiliating defeat. For Younis, the explanation of this reaction lies in how the Nasser regime shaped the ideological formation of people's minds during its fifteen-year rule. In his second book on Nasserite ideology, *Nida' al-sha'b*—a voluminous monograph of over seven hundred pages—he digs further into that formation, analyzing the extensive discourse that the regime produced about itself, including Abdel Nasser's numerous speeches , press articles, and the various other writings of the regime's many apologists. For Younis, this discourse was a performative act that produced perceptions of reality that became actual facts on the ground. His purpose, as he explains in his preface, is to critique this discourse in a Kantian sense, looking into the conditions of its possibilities, into its nature and limits. The discourse and the policies it justified were made in the name of the people (*al-sha'ab*): a hypostatized identitarian entity that Younis wants to demystify in his writings. According to him, the Nasserites as well as the Muslim Brotherhood based their respective discourses and policies on this alleged identitarian entity, defined by the first as the Egyptian-Arab nation and by the second as the Muslim nation, the *umma*. Younis's book is dedicated to his sons, and to the martyrs and heroes of the January 25 revolution who revealed, according to him, the shallowness of that "people's name." His latest book, *al-Bahth 'an al-khalas* (The search for salvation), is a further deconstruction of what he calls the conflict focus (*al-bu'ra al-sira'iyya*) of the last century in Egypt; namely identity or "the people."

The book on Sayyed Qutb, the main theoretician of the Muslim Brotherhood, was written originally as Younis's master's thesis in the history department at 'Ain Shams University in Cairo. In the 1994 preface to the first edition of *Sayyed Qutb wa al-usuliyya al-islamiyya* (Sayyed Qutb and Islamic fundamentalism),[54] Younis states the urgency for human sciences in Egypt to address the phenomenon of Islamic fundamentalism in order to understand and successfully oppose it. Should Islamic fundamentalism manage to take hold of the means of power, he writes, it would impose itself and its modes of thinking, and in the process eliminate the possibilities of rational thinking. The basic modality of fundamentalist thinking consists in a jurisprudential exegesis of given religious texts regarding all matters of life, including the social, economic, and political. The meanings produced by this exercise are then imposed on all in society. Hence, for Younis intellectual terrorism lies at the very heart of Islamic fundamentalism. The only way to resist and ultimately overcome this threat is to actually exercise rational thinking, and not wave the flag of reason as an abstract counterprinciple. In fact, he thinks that Islamic fundamentalism has been fought to date in two ineffective ways: either by advocating a larger scope of rational interpretation of religious texts or by accusing Islamism of being antirational. Both are doomed to fail, according to him, because in the first case the debate is kept in the religious universe of discourse and limited to religious texts, thus reinforcing the power and authority of those texts; and in the second case an abstract principle, reason, is held up—a principle that can easily be rejected by the fundamentalists and replaced by their own principle, sacred textual authority. Instead of these two failed strategies, Younis thinks it is imperative to practice a rational approach to the intellectual, social, and political components of Islamic fundamentalism. And this is, as we shall see, what governmental claims of tanwir fail to do. He sees his book as one contribution to such an examination. It looks at the life and thought of one of Islamic fundamentalism's main theoreticians, Sayyed Qutb (1906–1966), and puts them in the larger context of Egyptian intellectual history.

In his study of the biography and writings of Qutb, Younis underlines Qutb's close connections to some of the major liberal thinkers of modern Egypt, such as Taha Husayn (1889–1973) and Abbas Mahmud al-'Aqqad (1889–1964). He also sheds light on the persistent modernist, reformist, and leftist elements in Qutb's thought before and after his turn to fundamentalist radicalism. Younis sees the intellectual roots of Qutb's radicalism in his essentialist view of identity: a view of the self as an unchanging entity determined to express itself in the world, and as the absolute measure of the good and the right that it is bound to impose on the world. This entity bears within it the explanation for, and the solution to, everything. It is the Islamic nation, the *umma*. Younis notes that this essentialist identitarian mode of thinking also characterizes the thinking of the rival camp, the secular nationalists, except that for them the identity is not the Islamic nation but the Egyptian one, or what they also refer to as "the people." But this is not the only commonality Younis finds between the Egyptian fundamentalist and secularist modes of thinking. The other significant commonality is the elitism and authoritarianism of Egyptian modernist thought. In both camps one finds an elite that considers itself the select, enlightened circle burdened with the task of leading the ignorant masses forward. Younis ends his preface by calling upon the secularist/rationalist camp to abandon its futile battles, to give up on its conservative, opportunistic inclinations toward power, and to merit its "rationalist" designation by actually using reason to understand real phenomena, such as Islamic fundamentalism, instead of confining itself to the towers of abstract wisdom.

Eighteen years later, in the 2012 preface to the second edition,[55] Younis expresses an even sterner opinion of the so-called secularist/rationalist camp. He writes that at the time of the first preface, he still considered himself a member of that camp and believed it was capable of improving its performance and becoming truer to its principles. So many years later, he sees the need to radicalize his criticism and denounce the dismal failures of that camp. In the new preface he also reflects on the poor reception his book received from the rationalists as well as from the Islamists. He notes that both seemed reluctant to acknowledge the commonalities that the book showed. Each camp expected an exclusive condemnation of the other. For the rationalists, the book was not "othering" enough of the fundamentalists. The idea that Islamic fundamentalism was the indigenous son of the Egyptian modern intelligentsia, and not the alleged import of a desert Wahhabism or an aberration of moderate Islam, did not please them. Whereas Islamists did not like the charges of elitism, essentialism, and authoritarianism directed against them. Younis hopes that in the wake of the January 25 revolution, the theses of the book will be better acknowledged and debated. He also hopes that the book's demystification of secular-Islamist polarization can contribute to the formation of a genuine democratic free thought, robustly opposed to the bankrupt authoritarian and identity-focused ideologies. It is from within this general critique of modern Egyptian thought that Younis undertakes his deconstruction of millennial tanwir discourse in Egypt.

I focus here on three articles he published first in 1995 and 1996: "Awham an-tanwir" (The myths of tanwir), "Ma'zaq al-tanwir ma bayn al-sulta wa al-usuliyya al-islamiyya" (The deadlock of tanwir between power and Islamic fundamentalism[56]), and "Al-wida' al-akhir li al-haras al-qadim: Azamat al-intelligentsia al-masriyya wa idiyolojiyyat al-huwwiya" (The last farewell of the old guard: The crisis of the Egyptian intelligentsia and the ideology of identity).[57] They were republished in his 1999 book Su'al al-huwwiyya: Al-huwwiyya wa sultat al-muthaqqaf fi 'asr ma ba'd al-hadatha (The question of identity: Identity and the power of the intellectual in the postmodern era).[58] They were later republished again in the online journal al-Hiwar al-Mutamaddin (The civilized dialogue).[59]

A sharp critic of the modern Egyptian tanwir debate, Younis deconstructs its numerous claims, assumptions, and beliefs. In "Awham al-tanwir" he starts with the recurring question about the alleged failure of the tanwir project. He notes that this question makes at least three assumptions: first, that there was a clearly defined tanwir project with well-known criteria and values; second, that the supporters of this project strove to realize it; and third, that it failed. The need to investigate these assumptions arises, he writes, from his doubts regarding the claims this tanwir makes about itself; namely, those of struggling for democracy and reason, combatting myths, and enlightening society. To what extent, he asks, are these claims justified by the actual history of those who make them?

The political and intellectual history of modern Egypt shows, according to Younis, that what the participants of the tanwir debate have associated with tanwir has been the power and will of a centralized state to lead the country toward progress and modernization. In this sense, their project of tanwir has been a state project that does not stem from the will and freedom of the people, but from those who are in power. It has not been a project for freedom of thought and worship, a project of critiquing reality, or for that matter a project of democracy. Proponents of what came to be known as governmental tanwir, or secular tanwir, have claimed the values of freedom, reason, and democracy as theirs to advance a state project that, by its authoritarian, coercive, and elitist nature, could not uphold those values. On the other hand, the Islamists who challenged them with an Islamist tanwir wanted to adopt those same values to advance their own state project. Each camp defined the state with its own conception of identity—Egyptian for the one and Islamic for the other—and each tried to impose it on the other and on the country. In this struggle the will and interests of the people were sidelined. He summarizes his description of secular, pro-state tanwir in the following way:

> Thus is the state of Egyptian tanwir: instead of practising freedom of worship and critique of myth, it talks about the importance of secularism. . . . And instead of applying reason to the study of real phenomena, including that of political Islam itself, it talks about the importance of reason. . . . And instead of practicing historical analysis it makes of the latter a hermeneutic [*fiqhi*] principle that is to be defended. And of course, when reason ceases to be an applied practice, it becomes an idol to be worshipped and an object of belonging and loyalty. . . . It loses every critical character, i.e. rational character, in the tanwiri sense of reason.
>
> And tanwir in this form becomes nothing but a power [*sulta*] . . . because it presents itself as a sacred principle. . . . And so it wouldn't be surprising that it uses all the terror weapons against its opponents, because it becomes a matter of war: a power [*sulta*] facing another, and a sacred principle facing another.[60]

Moreover, the struggle for tanwir became a war between two elites: one claiming to defend the homeland and democracy and another claiming to defend God. The first elite is closely tied to the state apparatus, while the other seeks to replace it in that same function. The secularist elite demands freedom of thought, enlightening reason, and democracy for itself, but not so much for the people, and certainly not for its adversaries. As for the people's causes, for instance the rights of workers and victims of police brutality, they have never been the concern of the secularist elite.

Understood as the project of building a centralized authoritarian and modernizing state, the tanwir project has indeed been successful. Younis argues that it is in this success that tanwir for reason, freedom, and democracy has failed. The Nasser regime was the embodiment of that state project: it rested on the belief in the necessity of a strong state that intervened in all domains of public life to achieve development, modernization, and justice at the expense of political life, political pluralism, and individual liberties. This bargain of promised development and justice in exchange for liberties and political life has been perceived by secularist modernists to be ultimately beneficial, making them apologists of repression and despotism in the name of tanwir. This is a fundamental paradox that persists among secular intellectuals today—even among those who stood with the revolution but then sided with Sisi's military takeover.[61] The Islamists challenged this tanwir state project for the sake of their religious ideology but with the same conception of, and interest in, a coercive centralized state. All participants of the present tanwir debate remain, for Younis, captive to this state ideology and oblivious to the will and interests of the people.

The only possible real tanwir under the circumstances, he adds, is the denunciation of these tanwir discourses and the practice of modest critique that is engaging and respectful of people, that deals with concrete issues of social reality, and that steps outside the confines of an elite and liberates itself from state bondage:

> The only possible tanwir now is the one that critiques this tanwir, that leaves the camp of power, and rejects the elitist tendency to worship itself by worshipping reason in order to justify a regime that is in the final analysis despotic and repressive. There is an urgent need for a modest tanwir, that "bows down" from its height to social reality in order to learn from it; a tanwir that does not claim wise leadership, does not monopolize reason, nor speak in the name of higher beings, such as nation, people and renaissance. . . . A tanwir that looks for reason in the real social practices in their simplest forms . . . and discovers itself through them, as part of a wider reality.
>
> Modern tanwir won't be one tanwir . . . but a hundred thousand tanwir, that starts from various locations in society, from the fragmental, the real, the concrete, and so liberates itself from the absolute connection to the state and the whole problematic of the "relation of the intellectual to power" that has become one of the main problematics of the agonizing and stultified tanwir.[62]

My claim is that a whole host of Egyptian scholars, academics, journalists, writers, and artists have practiced this kind of concrete tanwir critique before and after the Egyptian uprising. I have in mind Khaled Fahmy, Hoda Elsadda, Ezzedine Choukri, Reem Saad, Belal Fadl, Ahdaf Soueif, Wael Gamal, Rabab el Mahdi, Mohammad Shoair, Huda Lutfi, and Ahmed Abd Rabou, to name but a few. In a forthcoming study I hope to corroborate this claim by looking at some of their writings since the beginning of the revolts, particularly from summer 2013. I hope to show how their participation in the vibrant public debates corresponded to the conception of tanwir advocated by Younis and Abu Zayd before him.

In his second article, "Ma'zaq al-tanwir ma bayn al-sulta wa al-usuliyya al-islamiyya" (The deadlock of tanwir between power and Islamic fundamentalism), Younis attacks what he considers to be the two main failures of Egyptian secular tanwir: the failure to defend freedom, in particular freedom of worship, and the failure to trust and relate to people.

Secular tanwiris raised their voices against the Islamists, he writes, when President Sadat encouraged the latter and supported them to defeat the leftists, and when he waved the flag of Islam to pass his neoliberal policies. Secular tanwiris became even more vocal when individuals of their own camp became targets of Islamist terrorist attacks, including Farag Fuda, who was assassinated in 1992; literature Nobel prize–winner Naguib Mahfuz, who was the victim of armed aggression in 1994; and Abu Zayd, against whom charges of apostasy were brought in 1993. Secular tanwiris protested against these Islamist aggressions and defended the victims—not in the name of the freedom of expression, worship, and thought but by arguing that the victims were "good" Muslims who did not deserve such aggression. In other words, they failed to champion the core value of their tanwir cause, freedom in its various facets, and to support the secularism that goes with it. Secularism, writes Younis, is the opposite of the "Hakimiyya" (rule of God) doctrine upheld by official Islam and represented by the institution of the Azhar, as well as by the various shades of political Islam. According to this doctrine, the rule of God should govern individual and communal life, and its principles are found in the holy book and interpreted in the narrowest sense. For Younis, this amounts to the denial of individual freedom and is bound to privilege hypocritical faith over free inner faith and to create a hypocritical community, in which external conformity is given priority.

In opposition to this understanding of faith, liberal interpretations of Islam are to be encouraged by the tanwiris, he writes, but not in the name of "true" Islam. By using this line of defense, tanwiris let themselves be drawn into their opponents' value system and end up parading as scholars and exegetes of Islam, which often they are not. Their defense of liberal Islam should instead be in the name of freedom and liberation—values that are supposed to be their primary concerns. But Egyptian tanwiris have shunned such a defense, fearing accusations of atheism and the consequences thereof, lacking conviction, or both, and betraying in all cases the cause of secularism that is at the heart of tanwir. Liberal interpretations of Islam cannot just be the abstract mental products of certain thinkers, he adds, but must respond to the expectations of a society in which freedom and critique of religion are real practices. Here Younis distinguishes tanwir from religious reform: tanwir cannot be reduced to reform, since it is a necessary condition for it.

Secular tanwiris have failed to defend freedom and secularism not only because of their lack of courage and commitment but also because of their doubt that those values will appeal to the masses, who are, in their eyes, fundamentally conservative and religious, uninterested in liberation ideas, and more receptive of Islamist proposals. And so these tanwiris find themselves beleaguered, on the one hand, by an increasingly aggressive Islamist camp and, on the other, a public that misunderstands and fails to appreciate their tanwiri ideals. Herein lies for Younis the second major failing of the secular tanwiris: their inability to reach out to people and connect to their actual liberation practices, be they religious, sexual, or political.

As is well known, he adds, popular religiosity has been more inclined toward mythical, Sufi, ritualistic, and even magical practices and less interested in rigid doctrinal and legalistic matters. Official Islam, carried by the middle classes, has had difficulties imposing its constraining guidelines on the larger population. In sexual matters too, people have been far less conformist than what the official moral rules prescribe; for instance, in matters of premarital sex. Moreover, workers and peasants have been protesting regularly against socioeconomic and political injustices imposed on them by those in power. All this shows that people in general have not lacked protest and liberation impulses. It also shows that official and political Islam have had practices that come closer to those of a centralized political power, geared toward the privileges and interests of the few, than to the interests and sensibilities of the masses. Instead of encouraging, supporting, and working with people's liberation impulses, Egyptian tanwiris have ignored, denigrated, and feared people. And so they have turned into a defensive, conservative, and defeatist elite:

> And so, as it does not propose a clear secularist ideological vision in the face of fundamentalism, tanwir does not propose values in the face of the sexual taboo regarding women. And as it dreads the accusation of atheism, it trembles from

the accusation of obscenity. And instead of courageously defending the values of social liberation as positive values that allow for deeper and more authentic and frank human relations, based on real human communication, it reduces the liberties of women to the right to work and education.[63]

Their distrust of the public has rendered the tanwiris profoundly antidemocratic. They would rather side with military coups, as in the Algerian case (and in the Egyptian case with Sisi), than with the aspirations of the people, however complex these might be. By so doing, they grant the Muslim Brotherhood the honor of opposing the corrupt and brutal government. Younis summarizes his damning assessment of the Egyptian tanwir in the following way:

> In general and in a nutshell, the present tanwir has one single political project to offer, that of reinforcing the existing state. It does not present a radical critique of fundamentalism, nor a radical critique of the existing state. It does not have a project to propose to the masses that could connect the interests of the latter with secularism as an indivisible liberational cause. The contemporary Egyptian tanwir is not oppositional; it is dependent, objectively loyal to the regime, forced thus to accommodate its principles according to the needs of the regime—a regime that does not demand real tanwir, but only cries outrage against political Islam, but not against fundamentalism, in the name of the nation or "true" Islam or freedom, or any other nice slogan . . . those cries, which justify then the intervention of the state as an arbiter and defender of freedom of thought.[64]

In his third piece, "Al-wida' al-akhir li al-haras al-qadim: Azamat al-intelligentsia al-masriyya wa idiyolojiyyat al-huwwiya" (The last farewell of the old guard: The crisis of the Egyptian intelligentsia and the ideology of identity), Younis adds a historical dimension to his analysis of the tanwiris' estrangement from the people and their ties to the state. According to him, these characteristics come from the origins of the modern Egyptian state, founded in 1805 by Muhammad Ali, an Albanian officer appointed by the Ottoman authorities to rule Egypt for them. This foreigner, who did not speak Arabic, aimed to build a state that would serve his power ambitions and aspirations for autonomy from the Ottomans. He conscripted Egyptians into an army and established an administration to run the country. For this administration he recruited and educated men, including local Egyptians, who would then become civil servants of the state and constitute, according to Younis, the origins of the Egyptian intelligentsia. Younis defines *intelligentsia* as the sector of society that earns its living through mental work, thanks to education, and includes lawyers, physicians, engineers, accountants, and university students.[65] Intellectuals, on the other hand, are those among the intelligentsia who produce, develop, and disseminate ideas. They include writers, journalists, artists, media people, and preachers.[66] The role of this educated elite was to support the interests of the ruling military class and to put the population at the service of these interests. This was to be done in the name of a state ideology, defined as national identity. But this elite also had to struggle for its own interests, especially vis-à-vis the Turkish elite, and later the British colonial rulers, who put limits on its ambitions in terms of administrative positions and benefits. In this struggle the Egyptian intelligentsia co-opted the demands of the people and claimed to speak in their name. But it never really represented them and did not relate to them.[67] Moreover, the state ideology of national identity did not stem from the people but from the state, which was created neither by nor for the people. Hence from the very beginning the educated elite, created by the state for the service of the state, was a stranger to the people's needs and aspirations; its task was to provide the state with ideological constructs centered around national identity and to incorporate in them worldviews that could serve the state, including Marxism, liberalism, enlightenment, and *Hakimiyya*, depending on the circumstances of the day. At no time was reason or critique part of its mandate. This explains, for Younis, why intellectual debates in Egypt were so heavily constrained by identity ideology.[68] Like Abu Zayd, he believes that even the nahda projects were conceived as top-down projects, for which the people were the means but never initiators or even partners:

> And here enter the ideas of national or Islamic "nahda," understood as a calculated mental operation based precisely on the aloofness and loyalty of the elite that leads the state in the name of identity; nahda as a political work that the state creates and then directs people to engage in. . . . This is what has characterized the numerous Egyptian nahda projects: intelligence and loyalty to identity, in isolation from the inhabitants, who become the sheer matter of the nahda planned by the state.

And so all the different nahda projects of the intelligentsia turn around the concept of the strong interventionist state, which exercises power over the inhabitants, whose role in turn is limited to being the matter of the nahda, and it might even be said that they are to be the goal of those projects. . . . But they are neither its makers nor the deciders in it.[69]

This historical formation of the Egyptian intelligentsia explains, for Younis, its estrangement from the people, its fixation on issues of identity, and its close ties with the state. This formation was to reach its apex under the Nasser state, which expanded the public sector and employed journalists, scholars, and writers in various media outlets as well as cultural and educational institutions. But by that time the Nasser regime had co-opted most of those outlets and institutions, dominated the public space, and imposed the main lines of the state ideology, which did not leave much room for opposition and dissent for the intellectual elite.[70] This was the price the elite paid for the employment security and benefits it obtained from the state, but also for its belief in the legitimacy and feasibility of the enlightening role of the state. In this tacit agreement, intellectuals put themselves, or were put, in a subservient position from which they could not challenge state repression, mismanagement, or corruption. They had tied their destiny to the state's and were among the losers when it fell in 1967. Ironically, the only real survivor of the 1967 disaster, according to Younis, was the army, especially with the mitigated "victory" of 1973. Under the Sadat regime and its neoliberal, Islam-friendly policies, the Egyptian intelligentsia became redundant, a burden to the state and the economy. Many members of the intelligentsia migrated to the private sector for jobs created by globalization or to the emerging Arabian Gulf countries. Others became Islamists in protest against a state that was no longer interested in their services. With the assassination of Sadat and the growth of Islamist terrorism, many intellectuals returned to the state, blaming it for its religious turn and tolerance of fundamentalists. Under Mubarak, intellectuals started serving the new mainstream state ideology, one less inimical to imperialism and Israel but friendly to the business class and to "moderate Islam." One of their main tasks now was to combat fundamentalist ideologies. But even when charged with such a crucial task, they kept on being reminded of their redundancy. Younis describes the sad state of the intelligentsia from the 1950s onward in the following way: "In this deal, the intelligentsia accepted the repression of liberties, the spread of terrorism, the robbing of the rural provinces, while it got enthusiastic about the theses of Arabism and Socialism, and tied itself totally to the regime. When the latter fell and got reconstituted, it fell with it and became superfluous, an impediment to development and made responsible with its slogans of Arabism and Socialism for the ruin."[71]

The late French-Egyptian scholar of the Arab world and Egypt specialist Alain Roussillon (1952–2007) identified three major crises for Egyptian secular intellectuals in the twentieth century.[72] All three crises originated in the tensions between intellectuals, the state, and society. The first crisis arose with the authoritarianism of the Nasser regime, when the state coerced intellectuals into serving its agendas. This crisis, writes Roussillon, was not an ideological one, because the state did not impose an official intellectual or aesthetic orientation, but it demanded that intellectual efforts be instrumentalized for the service of the "raison d'état." Despite waves of arrests targeting intellectuals, most of them believed that the state worked for the same ideals they themselves upheld; namely progress, liberation, and social justice. They deplored the loss of freedom but identified with the ultimate goals of the regime and found in the state a generous employer who ensured their livelihood and allowed them to carry out their endeavors, as long as they stayed in line with state orthodoxy. The most famous debate on the attitude of the intellectuals toward the Free Officers revolution took place in 1961 in the pages of the *al-Ahram* newspaper. Among the participants were Lutfi el-Kholy, Ismail Mazhar, Zaki Naguib Mahmoud, Abbas al-Aqqad, Louis Awad, Magdi Wahba, Clovis Maqsoud, Abdel-Razeq Hassan, Abdel-Malek Auda, Salah Dessouki, and and Mohamed Hassanein Heikal, editor in chief of the newspaper, ideologue, and spokesperson for the Nasser regime.[73] The proregime writers, Heikal first among them, deplored the intellectuals' lack of commitment to the revolution: even when they were collaborating with the regime, they were not putting their hearts and minds into the revolution's goal; namely, socialism and national liberation from foreign hegemony. They were expected to elaborate a comprehensive theory of revolution. Others pleaded for freedom of thought and offered various explanations for the lack of trust between the intellectuals and the regime. Among the most famous commentators on this debate was the late Egyptian thinker Anouar Abdel Malek (1924–2012), whose contribution was "La 'crise des intellectuels,'" a chapter in his 1962 *Égypte: Société militaire.*[74]

A nationalist Marxist, he resented Abdel Nasser's crackdown on, and internment of, intellectuals and leftists. He himself had had to flee in 1959 to France, where he spent the rest of his life as a researcher. In his comments on the debate, he deplored the Free Officers' relinquishing of humanist values, including the leftist ones, and their narrow conception of knowledge, reduced to instrumental, technological knowledge. He also deplored the purging of competent, humanist faculty from the universities.[75] What he saw in the regime's call to the intellectuals was the demand for a narrow nationalism, combined with a supposedly modernist Islam impoverished of its humanist dimension.

The second and more ideological crisis, according to Roussillon, happened in the early 1970s, when many if not most of the intellectuals disagreed with the new orientations of the state under Sadat, especially regarding Israel and economic policies concerning liberalization. On both counts intellectuals found themselves at odds with the major state goals. But ideological estrangement was not their only problem with the state. With the liberalization policies, the state relinquished its previous financial support of cultural institutions, depriving intellectuals of their ensured employment. Yet the state continued to expect their alignment with state ideology and incarcerated those who did not comply, as in the 1981 wave of arrests a few weeks before the assassination of Sadat. The third crisis, according to Roussillon, came after that, when the withdrawing state gave way to foreign research funders. The withdrawal of the state liberated intellectuals and scholars from the dictates of the state, but it also deprived them of the means to channel their work toward society. Egyptian scholars then had the choice of emigrating, mostly to the Arabian Gulf countries, or working on research agendas set by foreign donors, primarily American ones. Roussillon elaborated on the repercussions of this new condition of knowledge production for sociology.[76] According to him, it ultimately led to delinking Egyptian social scientific work from society and reintroducing the foreign other in determining and evaluating that work. Moreover, social scientific production was no longer relevant to any state societal project, as the state had lost interest in such projects. According to "Description de l'Egypte American-Style: A Call for the Exposure of Dangerous Particulars," a feature article published in fall 1982 in *al-Ahram al-iqtisadi*, this foreign-funded and foreign-guided social research produced an "American description of Egypt," analogous to the famous French "description de l'Égypte" initiated by the

Napoleonic occupation of 1798.[77] The article provoked a heated public debate, leading President Mubarak to ask a ministerial committee to ensure that all research projects served national interests. From this political, social, and cultural estrangement arose, writes Roussillon, what came to be known as the "crisis of the Arab social sciences." One attempt at resolving this crisis was the call for "Arab" or "Islamic" social sciences; that is, native social sciences not dependent on foreign funders and decision makers and not intellectually and practically alienated from local social realities and cultures. This nativist, identitarian response brought in turn its well-known essentialist problems of particularism.[78]

The Mubarak regime (1981–2011) intended to reconcile the intellectuals with the state and reintegrate them back into state cultural institutions under the "leadership" of its minister of culture, Farouk Hosni. Mustapha al-Ahnaf, an Egyptian scholar residing in France, reviews the Egyptian intellectual scene under Mubarak at the beginning of the 2011 revolution and characterizes it as a juxtaposition of various actors and currents, in which apparent debates are in reality isolated monologues. He notes the proliferation of think tanks and NGOs and much talk about "democracy," "human rights," and "citizenship." Despite the cacophony and logomachy, he sees the growth of organized associations for protest and change, and the search for an "Egyptian description of Egypt."[79]

In an analysis of the impact of political authoritarianism on Egyptian and Arab intellectuals, published on the eve of the revolutions in 2010, Egyptian sociologist Hazem Kandil has a rather somber account to offer.[80] According to him, Arab intellectuals from the major schools of thought—nationalism, liberalism, the Left, and Islamism—had either accommodated the prevailing policies of their states or turned away from politics, focusing instead on the cultural. This resulted in a dearth of political thought in the Arab world and the absence of political vision for an exit from repressive authoritarianism. Liberals, he writes, ended up espousing the neoliberalism of their governments, maintaining that the economic liberties that would allegedly come with neoliberalism would eventually lead to political liberties; pan-Arab nationalists abandoned political Arab unity and limited their unification ambitions to cultural unity; Leftists turned away from concrete socioeconomic criticisms and entered more general and abstract global struggles; and Islamists shifted their efforts to the sociocultural field, claiming that the political would naturally follow once society was converted to the right ways of Islam. I think that Kandil depicts a correct picture of the Arab intellectual scene, albeit an incomplete one. My own exploration of this scene shows that a number of uncompromising Arab thinkers stated quite early on, starting in the late sixties, that the root cause of the Arab malaise was political and not cultural. Theirs was, admittedly, a minority report. However, they did raise their voices, at great risk, and condemned the illegitimate, corrupt, and violent power of their governments, articulating a lucid analysis of a reality they knew they could not change on their own. They were at least honest and courageous witnesses of their times. I think of Saadallah Wannous from Syria; Abu Zayd from Egypt; Abdel Rahman Munif from Saudi Arabia, Iraq, Jordan, and Syria; and Faysal Darraj from Palestine, to name but a few. Moreover, the turn to culturalism was certainly influenced by the interdiction on politics imposed by the rulers, but it was also the result of soul-searching provoked by the trauma of 1967 and its aftermath. These were some of the major findings of my book *Contemporary Arab Thought.*[81]

In the final analysis, what do these deconstructions of the 1990s Egyptian tanwir debates enlighten us about? In fact, they show that the debates were in reality disguised struggles over political and intellectual power, and that in this sense the tanwir discourse was an authoritarian and elitist discourse of power. The deconstructions unveiled and denounced the mendacity of the debates and their lack of credibility or substance, and they decried the contrast between the ever-recurring slogans of freedom, reason, and tolerance and the brutal and corrupt practices of the government. The deconstructions also condemned the contrast between those slogans and the attitude and behavior of a conservative, elitist, and often co-opted intelligentsia. In the face of violence and fanaticism that they were supposed to counter, the debates had failed to produce a serious understanding of the root causes of that violence and fanaticism. Moreover, the government had never shied away from manipulating religion and supporting bigotry against freedom whenever it suited its purposes.

Furthermore, these deconstructive criticisms pointed out the centrality of the intellectuals' bond and subservience to the state, and the need for some modicum of independence for free and rational thinking. The criticisms condemned the betrayal of freedom and democracy by intellectuals who claimed to champion those values. These alleged democrats were shown to have never trusted the people or respectfully engaged them in concrete emancipatory projects. Our three deconstructionists advocated a tanwir that takes the values of freedom and reason seriously, by practicing them in concrete instances and by engaging people, including their interlocutors, with respect and modesty. As I mentioned earlier, my thesis is that the revolutionary rattling of the governing system opened new spaces for more intellectual enlightenment work of the kind advocated by the deconstructionists, until the counterrevolutionary clampdown hit back. More on that enlightenment work will be available in my next book.

Finally, given the centrality of the elite-masses divide in these tanwir debates, it is worth opening a parenthesis here to look briefly at the presence of this divide in another enlightenment debate, one from eighteenth-century Germany.

Parenthesis: Elitism and Enlightenment in Eighteenth-Century Germany

One of the most famous texts of the German *Aufklärung* is Immanuel Kant's 1784 essay "What Is Enlightenment?," considered the classic statement on enlightenment, which it defines as the ability and willingness to use one's reason in an autonomous way, without tutelage. The essay makes a distinction between "private" reason and "public" reason, private reasoning being what one does as the holder of an office or function, such as a judge, priest, or civil servant; and public reasoning being that articulated for, and shared with, the reading public—admittedly, a somewhat counterintuitive distinction. While private reason is beholden to the prevailing authority, public reason enjoys full freedom and obeys only its own authority. Contrary to its content, the circumstances of this essay are not that well known. The essay is read as part of Kant's highly abstract philosophy, disconnected from the Prussian political and cultural realities of the second half of the eighteenth century. In Arab tanwir circles, Kant's essay is often referred to, but without putting it in the Prussian context. In fact, for most Arab participants in the tanwir debate, the Enlightenment refers to France's religious-secular antagonism. The specific character of the French Enlightenment and the multiplicity of European Enlightenment currents are often not taken into consideration.

Kant's famous essay was published in the *Berlinische Monatsschrift* in response to the journal's call to address the question "What is enlightenment?" The journal was closely linked to the Berlinische Mittwochsgesellschaft (the Berlin Wednesday Society), known as the Friends of the Enlightenment. The society was one of the many secret societies that proliferated under the enlightened despotic rule of Frederick the Great (1740–1786) and offered free intellectual gatherings. In an absolute monarchy, no matter how "enlightened," and in a hierarchical administration, these gatherings were a substitute for real political gatherings and activities. The Berlinische Mittwochsgesellschaft included jurists, men of letters, pastors, and civil servants eager to discuss enlightenment ideas in connection with their social and political givens. In 1783 one of the society's members, theologian and educational reformer Johann Friedrich Zöllner, invited colleagues and concerned thinkers to elaborate a clear understanding of the widely used concept of enlightenment. The responses as well as the debates they generated stemmed from, and reflected on, the cultural and political realities of that tumultuous period in German and European history, which was marked by a century of political upheavals, starting with the English Glorious Revolution of 1688 and ending with the French Revolution of 1789. Among the major participants in the debate were C. F. Bahrdt, J. G. Fichte, J. G. Hamann, F. H. Jacobi, I. Kant, M. Mendelssohn, J. K. W. Möhsen, K. F. von Moser, H. S. Reimarus, K. L. Reinhold, A. Riem, C. M. Wieland, and J. F. Zöllner.[82] Its major questions were as follows: Should enlightenment involve all men or only citizens? (Both Moses Mendelssohn and Kant made this distinction.) How much enlightenment of the citizenry is possible or desirable? What kind of knowledge dissemination does it necessitate? How many of the beliefs and values of people can be questioned by an enlightened reason without undermining the foundations of social and political life? To what extent can such questioning be pushed without falling into nihilism and moral corruption? How much freedom of thought and expression is advisable? Should there be limits to the liberalization of censorship regulations? Is it advisable to have purely civil marriage ceremonies? Do the exigencies of society conflict with those of enlightenment? What is enlightenment in the first place? Are the assumptions it makes about the primacy of reason tenable? What about emotions, instincts, and bodily drives? Can reason alone be a realistic or trustworthy guide? Can enlighteners in the name of reason become new oppressors? Proponents and opponents of enlightenment exchanged opinions about these questions in debates that were closely followed by the monarch and at times more or less sanctioned by him. The issues under debate, which have also been major themes of the Arab enlightenment debates and headlines of the Arab uprisings, included atheism, authority, censorship, education, enlightened rule, enlightenment, emotions, faith, freedom of the press, instincts, law and order, a legal constitution, liberty, morality, reason, religious reform, revolution, state employment, state loyalty, tradition, and violence.

The relative freedom to discuss these issues was reduced with the death of Frederick the Great in 1786 and his succession by his conservative (some would say obscurantist) nephew, Frederick William II, who it is said was drawn to Christian mysticism. His advisor, Johann Christoph Wöllner, played an important role in reversing the relatively liberal trend initiated by the late monarch. In 1788 he issued a religion edict to reestablish religious orthodoxy, followed by a censorship edict to silence criticism against the first edict. The idea behind the two edicts was that orthodoxy and traditional Christian faith were essential for the Prussian state. These edicts were followed by concrete measures: pastors were called upon to abide by the old orthodoxy that was not "distorted" by the Enlightenment, and the liberal head of the Prussian Ecclesiastical Department, K. A. Zedlitz, was replaced by Wöllner himself.

Theology was indeed at the heart of the German Aufklärung debate. In the 1770s and 1780s some Berlin theologians had developed a rationalist current of theology known as "neology," which advocated an understanding of Christian faith that could correspond to enlightened reason, devoid of superstition, fanaticism, and prejudice. The emphasis was on moral rectitude and social responsibility. Revelation was maintained but made accessible to natural human reason. The scriptures were interpreted historically and critically. The question was, To what extent could this understanding of Christianity remain consistent with teachings that upheld an essential otherworldly dimension that transcended natural human reason? This new rationalist theology was criticized by thinkers like Friedrich Heinrich Jacobi, who believed that the rational approach to religion could lead to atheism and fatalism, taking Baruch Spinoza's philosophy as an example.[83] The Prussian religion edict further animated discussions about the importance of customary religious beliefs in maintaining the coherence and peace of civil society. The question was, Which was a more secure foundation for political stability, orthodoxy or enlightenment? The edict's aim was to prevent Enlightenment thinkers from developing and disseminating free and innovative interpretations of Christianity. After the publication of Kant's *Religion Within the Limits of Reason Alone*, Frederick William II threatened him with unpleasant measures should he go on disparaging the teachings of Christianity.

With the outbreak of the French revolution in 1789, and as echoes of the dramatic events in neighboring France reverberated across Germany, state repression targeted not only the religious discussions but also the political ones. In fact, the revolution in its successive phases provoked all sorts of feelings in German intellectuals, ranging from enthusiasm and admiration to disapproval, condemnation, and fear, especially fear of chaos, violence, and civil war. In the beginning some thought the revolution did not threaten the Prussian monarchy, which was "benevolent" and "enlightened," unlike the French one; others believed that as long as the revolutionaries tried to limit the monarch's abuses of power by imposing a constitution, they deserved sympathy. Fears for the Prussian state grew with the execution of Louis XVI in 1793. The escalating violence and chaos transformed much of the early enthusiasm into disillusionment and anxiety. It became increasingly important to sort out the linkages between Enlightenment values and the gruesome course of the revolution: between enlightenment and civil and political order, revolution, and political reforms, and between reactions to the French revolution and moral progress. Was it possible or justifiable for proponents of the Enlightenment to defend the revolution? If yes, then on what grounds and how? If not, then was enlightenment to accommodate despotism?

Conservatives considered themselves vindicated by the horrific developments in France, while proponents of revolutionary change found it difficult to defend their position. Moreover, those developments reinforced the arguments of those who believed in gradual reform. In brief, the French revolution affected the German Aufklärung debates in at least two ways: by challenging core tenets of enlightenment, such as liberty, reason, autonomous thinking, the right to revolt, and the importance of challenging authority; and by exposing them to greater censorship, as the monarchical state grew weary of the potential destabilizing effect of the revolution next door. This double impact can be traced in some of the inconsistencies and ambiguities in Kant's work:[84]

1. After being against the revolution, Kant started affirming it in the late 1780s then again rejected it in the late 1790s. Indeed, as Kant himself writes, by the mid-1760s his reading of Jean-Jacques Rousseau led him to realize the importance of social and political equality, to reject elitism, to espouse republicanism as the best form of government, and to regard the right to rebel against arbitrary and unjust rule as legitimate. However, it is believed that under the pressure of strict censorship, especially after the French revolution, Kant did not want to provoke the authorities and risk what little freedom of expression remained. So he started qualifying his statements by saying that while he defended the right of revolution, he disagreed with its method, or that he was for the rights of man but not those of revolution.

2. Kant seems to have been a loyal civil servant, as a university professor, and an admiring subject of the king, Frederick the Great. As a man of his time and place, Kant did not believe in organized political action and expected reform to come from the monarch, who had promised to introduce a constitution. Apparently, Kant could not imagine rebelling against a king who encouraged ideas of reason and liberty and allowed intellectual exchanges to take place in public. Kant hoped reform would come from the king's responses to these ideas and debates, but his hopes were dashed by Frederick's death and the succession of his son, who was uninterested in enlightenment ideas. This is the Kant who, on the other hand, advocated the autonomous use of reason without tutelage and rejected paternalism, even for the sake of happiness. Apparently, practicing autonomous reasoning and expecting conditions for that practice to come from a ruling authority did not seem inconsistent to him.

3. Despite Kant's affirmation of the rational and autonomous individual as the maker of enlightenment, he firmly believed in the progressive orientation of history and in the power of providence in bringing about enlightenment, with the help of enlightened kings and individuals if possible.

These contradictions and ambiguities in one of the most critical and rational systematic works of philosophy show the possible tensions between, on the one hand, an emphatic call for the universal, autonomous use of reason in view of enlightenment and, on the other hand, entrusting charismatic state leaders with the task of achieving reform and enlightenment. Trust in the sincere dedication of a leader to enlightenment goals cannot be seen as the most rational mechanism for achieving those goals, and yet Kant, as one of the prime Enlightenment philosophers, seems to have strongly betted on it.

It seems inevitable that once the German Aufklärung challenged political, religious, or social authorities, questions about elitism, journalism, freedom of the press, religion, and education would arise. They were the concerns of most of the participants in the Enlightenment debates in Europe, including the French philosophes, many of whom looked at the people with fear and contempt and regarded them as unworthy or incapable of enlightenment, though in need of an education geared toward an enlightened social order. The enlightened state was to carry out this educational training, inspired by the enlightened ideas of the philosophes.[85] Indeed, the role of the state in shaping an enlightened and free society, through education, discipline, and rationalization, has been part and parcel of Western society since the age of the Enlightenment. The paradoxes, ambiguities, and dialectics of this role and its Enlightenment goals have been at the core of the subsequent Western debates. They have also been an integral part of the Arab tanwir discussions, which have had inflections of their own, as is seen in the Egyptian and Syrian debates.

PART II

Damascus

THREE

Tanwir Debates in Syria in the 1990s

The Sisyphean Moment

THE SAME 1990s that witnessed the heated tanwir debates in Cairo saw the publication of tanwir essays, books, and journals in Damascus. However, although the main tenor of the general ideas was the same in the two debates, the circumstances, objectives, foci, scale, and nature of the Syrian debate were quite different from those in Egypt. The common plea in the two debates was for reason and freedom against oppression and fanaticism, but the addressee and the setting were different. A few broad comparative remarks can be useful both to introduce the Syrian debate and to situate it with respect to the Egyptian one. First, the primary opponent that Syrian tanwiri discourses addressed was not political Islam, as it was for the Egyptian ones, but the state's despotism, corruption, and brutality. Islamists had been persecuted, arrested, and assassinated a decade earlier in Syria; political Islam was declared criminal and to a great extent disappeared from Syrian soil. Second, the public realm of the Syrian debate was much more restricted than that of the Egyptian one, as a result of more systematic repression of opposition figures and movements across the political spectrum. Third, the Syrian government at the time, unlike the Egyptian one, had no interest in the tanwir discourse. Finally, given the heavy censorship in Syria, those who dared to speak spoke in general terms, referring to "Arab society," "the Arab state," "Arab regimes," and so on. Things were not given specific names until the death of Hafiz al-Assad and his son's succession in June 2000. In his inaugural speech Bashar al-Assad promised an opening to pluralism and modernization. This encouraged many dissident voices, including those who were skeptical about his promise, to become more precise in their critiques, giving rise to what came to be known as the Damascus Spring, which did not last long.

On the other hand, the nahda and its evaluation as a source of inspiration or a cause of disorientation and failure remained as central to the Syrian tanwir debate as it was to the Egyptian one. Moreover, certain Egyptian nahda figures became important references for Syrian tanwiris, Taha Husayn foremost among them. The question of the nahda was for these Syrians, as it was for the Egyptians, a ground for discussing identity, tradition, change, modernization, westernization, secularization, elitism, and conciliatory thinking (al-tawfiqiyya).

In the years that followed independence from the French mandate in 1945 and 1946, Syrian political life was parliamentary, though highly unstable. The union with Egypt between 1958 and 1961, which gave rise to the United Arab Republic, brought an end to parliamentary politics. Under Gamal Abdel Nasser's leadership, political parties were abolished and all aspects of democracy eradicated, similar to what was imposed in Egypt. For Syrian thinkers like Tayyeb Tizini and Michel Kilo, as we shall see, this elimination of political life was the founding moment for the despotic Syrian regimes that followed. The union was terminated in 1961 by a Syrian coup d'état led by Syrian army officers, who resented the Egyptian centralized diktat that turned out to be disadvantageous to Syrian public life and the economy. At first, those officers allowed the traditional Syrian elites to come back to power; however, their rule remained unstable. Eventually, the officers took power in 1963. They declared a state of emergency and imposed martial law, which remained in effect until 2012, when it was replaced by a version of martial law allegedly aimed at fighting terrorism. The war with Israel was increasingly used to justify decades of martial law, while lifting it remained a constant demand of the opposition.[1]

The officers were members of the growing Baath Party.[2] They claimed to rule in its name and for the sake of its goals: Arab unity, socialism, and freedom. Since the party's inception in 1947, there had been different ways of interpreting and plans for implementing those goals, leading to division and conflict. However, despite those differences, the ambition was for an independent, united, and revived Arab nation, strong in its inherent cultural and moral forces. Socialism was liberation from oppression, especially for peasants and workers, and it called for state economy. Freedom was primarily freedom from colonial control but also meant democracy within what became the ruling party, which would lead state and society, at least through a transitional period. Contesting this one-party rule, prescribed by paragraph 8 of the Syrian constitution, was another recurring opposition activity. Under the pressure of the uprising, the constitution was changed to affirm political pluralism and democratic rule.[3]

Tensions and conflicts continued to plague the Baathists. Just a year after they came to power, discontent spread across the country because of the mishandling of liberties, disrespect for civil rights, and abuses of power. Demonstrations were fought, and force was used to muzzle various protest actions.[4] Moreover, a whole set of economic policies that were supposed to advance socialism, including nationalization measures in agriculture and industry, disrupted major sectors of production and alienated big industrialists, landowners, and businessmen, causing capital flight. It was in this turmoil that Hafiz al-Assad grabbed power in 1970 in what he called a "corrective movement" in the Baath trajectory, beginning a rule that lasted until his death in 2000.[5] Assad tried to regain the trust of entrepreneurs and opted for a less rigorous socialist economy. The result was centralized state capitalism, in which nonruling economic collaborators were co-opted in a tightly controlled system of enticement and threat, leading to a growing web of corruption. The "corrective" measures benefited some sectors; however, they did not prevent major economic crises from breaking out in the mid-1970s, as large sectors of the population suffering from those measures, including professional unions, students, and political parties, took to the streets to protest. In the mid-1980s the economy again faced a set of severe crises, which were dealt with by new liberalization policies. These policies increased socioeconomic disparities and led to the further growth of the mercantile sector close to the circles of power. By then, corruption had become an endemic part of the Syrian economy.[6]

On the political level, in 1972 Assad put together the National Progressive Front (Al-jabha al-wataniyya al-taqaddumiyya), composed primarily of the Baath Party in addition to a number of minor leftist, mainly socialist and communist, parties, which accepted Baath leadership and rule. The Front parties were then reduced to an instrument of the governing power, and their ideals became shallow state slogans. The National Progressive Front was the only political body in the country allowed to participate in public life, serving as the pluralistic and inclusive facade of the autocratic regime.[7] In 1980 a decree was issued canceling all standing professional unions, in a further step of Gleichschaltung. The lawyers' union had been particularly vocal in protesting against Assad's abuses of human rights.[8] Full and lasting control became Assad's main goal, with repression as the main response to dissent. For this purpose, organizations for indoctrinating and mobilizing were established across Syrian society, including schools, universities, professional unions, religious institutions, the arts, and the media. In addition, secret police, intelligence services (the famous Mukhabarat), and paramilitary organizations were set up and manipulated by the central power. Assad's cult of personality was installed, with omnipresent pictures and monuments representing him as the perpetual leader of the country, now called "Suria al-Asad" (Assad's Syria). Pupils, students, state employees, and union and tolerated political party members would be forced into "spontaneous" demonstrations whenever an extra show of allegiance was deemed necessary. Criticism of minor issues targeting lower-level employees would be permitted, but higher levels of the power hierarchy and certainly the leader, his closer family, and collaborating circles would stay outside the remit of any public critique. Such criticism would be mercilessly punished. At the same time, the regime knew how to "champion" culture and manipulate it for its own purposes, sometimes blurring the line between the forbidden and the permitted, making it even more difficult for artists and writers to negotiate its red lines. It would for instance support the production of socially critical films and the publication of dissident books but forbid their distribution, thus making them inaccessible to the public.[9] This elaborate form of censorship not only stifled cultural production but also silenced public opposition and killed politics, leading to the atomization of society, whereby people could not trust each other and express opinions without risking denunciation and its consequences.[10]

The first wave of repression took place in the late seventies against protestors across the country, but mostly against the militant, armed Muslim Brotherhood, which had launched a campaign of violence against the regime, including assassinations and bombings.[11] Their conflict with the regime was not primarily political or economic; rather it was religious and sectarian. They saw the regime as an un-Islamic, sectarian Alawi power that oppressed the Sunni majority. The response, as is well known, was a merciless clampdown on the movement and its adherents, with the infamous Hama massacre of 1982 and the destruction of large areas of the city, an operation led by the president's brother, Rifaat al-Assad. There were tens of thousands of victims, with thousands more jailed, tortured, and executed. The result was the dismantling of the organization in Syria and the criminalization of its membership. But the repression was not limited to the Islamists. It included communists and Iraqi rival Baathists as well. During the 1980s large numbers of Syrians were incarcerated for their political opinions, often for over a decade and for arbitrary reasons, under brutal conditions, with the help of martial law and a politicized judiciary.[12] It is in the wake of this long and ruthless repression that the few tanwir discourses emerged in the 1990s, as the iron grip of power loosened up slightly, after having established an effective reign of terror and silence.[13]

If the Syrian interior looked stable and sounded pacified, without really achieving economic and developmental breakthroughs, the Assad regime became a major player in regional geopolitics, manipulating the Lebanese and Palestinian scenes brutally and masterfully. Syria was acknowledged by world powers to be an efficient regional force and a patient and clever negotiator in the Arab-Israeli conflict. Its interior did not interest outsiders, or at least it was not in their interest to raise questions about it.

In the first section of my analysis of the Syrian tanwir discourses, we will explore the notions, metaphors, and realities of darkness and light in the discourses of Ahmad Barqawi, Michel Kilo, Mamdouh Adwan, Burhan Ghalioun, Abdulrazzaq Eid, Sadeq Jalal al-Azm, and Tayyeb Tizini. We will also look at the light shed on the nature and effects of the Syrian regime in the early 1980s by French sociologist Michel Seurat. In the second and third sections, we will look at two Sisyphean figures of Syrian tanwir, Saadallah Wannous and Faysal Darraj. We will also discuss the journal *Qadaya wa-shahadat* as an important forum for Syria's Sisyphean tanwir.

Darkness and Light in Syria's 1990s: Barqawi, Seurat, Kilo, Adwan, Ghalioun, Eid, al-Azm, and Tizini

A good entry point to the Syrian landscape of light and darkness is Ahmad Barqawi's essay "Ma al-tanwir?" (What is enlightenment?), published in 1996 in the Lebanese leftist journal *al-Tariq*.[14] Barqawi, of Palestinian origin, was professor of philosophy at the University of Damascus at the time. He starts

his essay by noting the recurrence of the question of tanwir in the twentieth century fin-de-siècle Arab world and proposes to grasp this notion of
tanwir by investigating the darkness from which the question is raised. The
answer to the question regarding the nature of tanwir, he writes, cannot
come from Immanuel Kant or Jean-Jacques Rousseau or even from Farah
Antun (1874–1922)—a main nahda figure who championed secularism, rationalism, and liberty. It has to be dug out of the darkness experienced here
and now. Going West and turning to early local traditions for answers have
failed. So, he concludes, "Let us search in our darkness to formulate our
enlightenment" ("Idhan, fal-nabhath fi dhalamina min ajl siyaghat tanwi-
rina").[15] As illustration of this darkness, Barqawi mentions the unraveling
of nation-building in Iraq and elsewhere in the Arab world, whereby societies are regressing from national political bodies to primary communities
such as tribes and religious groups. He mentions the rise of despots and religious fundamentalism and writes about Algeria, Egypt, Palestine, and
Sudan without ever naming Syria. The regressive process of fragmentation
(al-tadhardhur) is an important indication for him of the state's failure to live
up to society's potential. In this context, he writes, tanwir consists, on the
one hand, in unveiling and explaining those realities and, on the other, in
offering alternative visions in which the state is no longer an impediment
to the fulfillment of society's potential. Tanwir is then an ongoing critique
of the present, understood in its historical context; that is, in a desacralized
form. The state, he adds, is an important aspect of this present. Tanwir is to
contribute to the development of the conscious agency (fa'iliyya wa'iya) of
people and societies. The idea is not to reject the state in a utopian or anar-
chical sense, but to call for a state that corresponds to that agency. This
agency can only be realized when people get together freely, beyond their
primordial allegiances, to form a civil society (mujtama' madani) composed
of political parties, professional unions, clubs, and associations and to work
toward a rational state that they can check and control. This is why tanwir
is fought by the existing state as well as by an opposition, whose narrow horizons do not correspond to tanwir.

Tanwir thus confronts the idol of the state (sanamiyyat al-dawla) but also
the idol of Islamic theology (sanamiyyat al-lahut al-islami). It goes against the
idea of divine rule (hakimiyya), which is a denial of the social contract and a
tool to repress freedom of worship. Reform theology (al-lahut al-islahi) tries
to adapt religion to society and works for religious laws that respect change.

In this critical function, it comes close to tanwir, but contrary to tanwir, which is by nature worldly, it remains tied to religious doctrines. Tanwir is to help us understand the role of religious awareness in social and political behavior. Ultimately, tanwir has to remain critical of its own ideas in order to avoid their determinism and despotism. It should be a constant critique of reality as well as a critique of our representations of reality, de-idolizing history, state, theology, and even ideas themselves.

Barqawi's answer to the question "What is tanwir?" focuses on three concepts that constitute the keywords of Syrian tanwir: state, civil society, and to a lesser extent, Islamic fundamentalism. Syrian tanwir centers on the antagonism between state and society, lamenting the destructive effect of the former on the latter under the prevailing regime. It is a call for the creation of a civil society, against all odds, to counter that effect. State and civil society were also the keywords of the Damascus Spring, when the odds became slightly favorable for a brief moment. A decade later all three keywords would characterize the dramatic Syrian uprising.

But in what way did the state antagonize society? In those years, Barqawi could not detail the problems of the state more specifically, and certainly not those of the Syrian state. However, French sociologist Michel Seurat (1947–1986) had done so a decade earlier and probably paid for it with his life.

In 1983 and 1984 Seurat published two articles in the French journal *Esprit* under the pseudonym Gérard Michaud, analyzing the nature of the Assad regime after the repression of the late seventies and early eighties. They were "L'état de barbarie: Syrie, 1979–1982" (The state of barbarism: Syria, 1979–1982) and "Terrorisme d'état, terrorisme contre l'état: Le cas syrien" (State terrorism, terrorism against the state: The Syrian case).[16] As the titles indicate, the main characteristic of the Syrian state, according to Seurat, was barbarism—the unbridled use of brutal force to maintain power for Hafiz al-Assad, who had appropriated the state for himself.

In these articles Seurat argued that attempts to describe the Assad regime in terms of simple opposites, such as Left versus Right, rural areas versus cities, or minority versus majority, or oppositions between sectarian communities or social classes, fail to render the real mode of functioning of this regime. According to him, the regime functioned through the cynical manipulation and exploitation of these factors to keep all confessions, classes, regions, and religions under control, to the advantage of the ruler. These groups would be threatened, divided, and lured into collaborating with the regime. Syrian thinker Tayyeb Tizini summarized this mode of functioning as corrupting whoever has not yet been corrupted, in such a way as to contaminate and condemn everyone when need be (*yajib an yufsad man lam yufsad ba'd bihayth yasbah al-jami' mulawwathan wa mudanan tahta al-talab*). Combining corruption with violence, observed Seurat, the Syrian regime became the negation of the state, sealing the abortion of the whole project of the modern state. The ruler, together with his compliant servants, functioned like a gang (*jama'a*), taking everything and leaving nothing. Over three decades later, political scientist and keen observer of Syrian social politics Thomas Pierret agrees with Seurat's description of the Syrian state, which, he opines, is technically neither a military dictatorship, a police state, nor a regime under one-party rule, in so far as it is not run by the military, the security forces, or the party as institutions. It is instead run by a circle of people held together by common interests, headed by the president.[17] This gang logic knew no ideological commitment; it operated by means of violence, not only inside the country, but also in the region, using what Seurat called the "diplomacy of terror." He thought that the West condoned this diplomacy in view of the services it rendered to the regional power balance. The West also overlooked the internal violence, including the horrors of Hama, in the name of the secular nature of the regime (not very different from international positions regarding the situation after the 2011 uprising). A secular regime was deemed preferable to the religious clerics who had just taken power in Iran. In a nutshell, the three principles guiding the Assad regime were divide and rule, corrupt and rule, and terrorize and rule, and its goal was to appropriate everything and control everyone.

Seurat was kidnapped in 1985 in Beirut by the Jihad islamique, as part of a wave of kidnappings of foreigners by Islamists in Lebanon at the time, when the country was under Syrian control. His kidnappers declared him dead in March 1986, but he had actually died months earlier from lack of medical attention.[18]

The Syrian opposition, wrote Seurat, realized that what was urgently needed was the restoration of politics and the establishment of democracy. Until the late seventies one could hear quite daring criticisms of the regime, its policies, and style of governance. In the wake of the severe economic crisis of the midseventies and the protest movements that had swept the country by the end of the decade, the government reached out to the various sectors of society, supposedly to engage them in a dialogue on solutions. The National Progressive Front invited unions for meetings, including the Union of Arab Writers in Syria.[19] From that meeting we have short recordings of statements made by two prominent Syrian intellectuals, Michel Kilo and Mamdouh Adwan.[20] These statements are remarkably bold, and this is probably why such meetings were never repeated.

In the meeting Kilo (born 1940), a leftist activist, opinion writer, and major Syrian oppositional figure, stated bluntly that the Front was constituted to repress independent political forces and emasculate interest groups, and it was not perceived by people as a representative body in which their interests were voiced. The central question, in his opinion, was of responsibility for the regime's policies and measures, taken with the Front's approval, that had led to the country's disasters. What needed to be clarified, he added, was the real relation of the Front to the regime.

Moreover, the assumption behind the recent debates, he said, was that mistakes were made and shortcomings and technical problems occasionally emerged, but that the broad political orientation of the country's leadership was sound. External conspiracies had also been invoked. Indeed, Kilo admitted, there had been conspiracies against the Syrian people. Israel was surely responsible for one of them, but that was not the only conspiracy. The loss of liberties and political life resulting from the establishment of the union with Egypt was another crucial one. The political disenfranchisement of the people had been one of the worse consequences of those losses. Syria, while facing severe crises, missed the engagement and political participation of its people. The problem lay not in technical errors and sporadic mistakes but in the country's flawed power structure. This flaw, he believed, had been intentionally put in place over the past decades. Its devastating consequences were perceptible in education, health care, and the various economic sectors. The same dismal failures could be seen in the broad Baath causes that the regime claimed to serve, such as pan-Arab unity and socialism. Perceiving all these failures, people could not help but antagonize such a structure. So long as those outside the regime and the Front were not permitted to participate in the decision-making process, dialogue had no importance. At the end, he asserted that he also made these criticisms for the record, to disclaim any responsibility, and hence complicity, that might one day be imputed to the people regarding the orientation of the country's leadership. Kilo was arrested in the early 1980s and held for a year and a half, after which he left for France. He later returned to Syria and published oppositional writing in the Arab press outside Syria.[21] A decade later he participated in the Damascus Spring, as we shall see. He signed the 2005 Damascus Declaration (I'lan Dimashq), demanding radical governmental reforms, then the Beirut-Damascus Declaration in 2006 (I'lan Beirut-Dimashq), which called for the normalization of relations between Lebanon and Syria, which would entail Syria recognizing the sovereignty and independence of Lebanon, and for diplomatic relations between the countries to be established. Soon after that he was arrested and condemned to jail for three years, along with other signatories. With the outbreak of the Syrian uprising he left the country, becoming an important spokesman for the Syrian revolution and a member of the Syrian National Coalition in 2013 for a short period.[22]

Mamdouh Adwan (1941–2004) was a prominent Syrian poet, novelist, and playwright and an audacious oppositional figure. In the same 1979 Damascus meeting of the Union of Arab Writers and the National Progressive Front, Adwan began by stating that the Front, and behind it the regime, had called for the meeting because there was a gap between it and the people and a credibility crisis due to the regime's mendacity. Not only were reports about war untrustworthy, he said; even weather reports were doctored. The media as the voice of the regime were full of lies, and the regime lied because it feared the people and that they might discover its truth.

On the other hand, the regime also disregarded the people. For instance, it did not explain why at one point it regarded the Iraqi regime as an enemy and then suddenly not an enemy. Moreover, when the regime admitted, through the Front or the Baath Party, that some of its policies had led to bad results, it did not apologize to the people. Stories of corruption had become common without the regime or the political parties taking responsibility for them. Officials did not explain why corruption was happening at such a scale, or why it had been impossible to stop. Instead, people who criticized those faults were accused of treason. Furthermore, nothing was said about the misdeeds of the paramilitary troops and the intelligence services (Mukhabarat). As an example, Adwan called out the Saraya al-difa', set up for the regime's defense and led by the president's brother, Rifaat. It was heavily involved in the Hama repression. In 1984 it was merged with the army to become the infamous Fourth Troop and the Presidential Guard, after Rifaat was forced to leave the country after a conflict with his ruling brother. The Fourth Troop and the Presidential Guard were now headed by another of Hafiz al-Assad's sons, Maher al-Assad, known as one of the most ruthless in the clan. Maher took an active role in the violent suppression of the 2011 uprisings.

Naming the Saraya al-difa' and the Mukhabarat was quite a bold move on the part of any public speaker, even then, before the great repression of the eighties. Moreover, Adwan deplored the regime's silence on its own sectarian nature or behavior. It was true, he said, that people had a tendency to be sectarian, but seeing the regime exacerbate this was disquieting. Finally, he expressed outrage at the regime's silence on the system of privileges that ran across the army and security services. These were all issues that would lead to the explosion of the country three decades later, after Bashar came to power in 2000 and when all peaceful attempts at reform were aborted.

Adwan continued to touch on these matters in his poetry, fiction, and television dramas, as well as in his nonfiction. In *Haywanat al-insan* (The animalization of the human), published in 2003,[23] he addressed the phenomena of brutalization (*tawahhush*), repression (*qam'*), habituation to violence (*ta'awwud*), and torture (*ta'dhib*). The first half of the book is drawn from world literature and some social scientific studies of these matters. The second half speaks about violence and corruption in terms that suggest he is talking about Syria without saying so clearly. He analyzes the Shabbiha, gangs of outlaws who worked for prominent regime figures and were allowed to steal, smuggle, and brutalize people. These gangs were above the law, demonstrating that the application of the law was at the whim of the powerful. He describes the workings of a despotic and corrupt regime and their effects on society and individuals. In the preface he refers to a passage he wrote in his 1985 *Difa'an 'an al-junun: Muqaddimat* (In defense of madness: Preliminaries), published a few years after the writers' union meeting.[24] It was composed of several essays meant as introductions to different works, all celebrating dissent, madness, and revolt against a world that was too conformist or oppressive. His praise goes to artistic and creative madness, as in the essay on Syrian painter Louay Kayyali (1934–1978), who suffered depression and mental unrest. The passage from the book he refers to in *Haywanat al-insan* is the following:

The human[s] had a beautiful dream about themselves. They aspired to their human condition. But the flow of circumstances opened a wound in that dream.

And the dream started to bleed and wither away. And as it shrank, it started to take forms and names.

And every now and then, the human[s] realize their terrible loss, and they become aware that they are exhausting themselves to prevent themselves from falling from their human level to that of the animal. And when they resist, their resistance takes the form of a madness.[25]

The outcry of those Syrians who rebelled against the Assad regime in 2011, expressed in the iconic statement "I am a human, not an animal, and all these are like me" ("Ana insan, mani haywan, wu hadul killun mitli"), could be seen as the ultimate "mad" response to the decades-long dehumanization process. That process consisted, as we saw, in the suspension of social and political norms, telling people that no normative or ethical principle would regulate their treatment but that the unbridled force of the rulers determined their fate. The cry "I am a human, not an animal" came from Syrian citizen Muhammad Ahmad Abdel Wahhab on television in the early months of the Syrian uprising, as soldiers rounded up him and his fellow villagers, forced them to lie facedown in the village square with their hands tied behind their backs, and started jumping on them, beating them, kicking their heads, and forcing them to kiss and lick the boots of their torturers. The television clip went viral on social media and was shown on Arab satellite TV channels. It was one of the first recordings to come out of the repression of the Syrian uprising. Abdel Wahhab's outcry became an icon of the Syrian revolution and captured that mad affirmation of basic humanity in the face of brutality.[26]

Nowhere was this brutality clearer than in the extensive Syrian penitentiary world, where the suspension of political, social, and human norms was carried to its extreme. The growing Syrian prison literature that started to appear in the late 1990s sheds light on the "state of barbarism" Seurat observed in the early 1980s. This radical anomie, orchestrated by the regime for decades, ultimately destroyed much of the country's societal, moral, cultural, economic, and political fabric. Inevitably, the damage affected the latent opposition as much as the society at large. For many survivors of the Syrian penitentiary world, the regime's unrestrained violence against the rebels after the 2011 uprising is in continuity with the violence practiced in Syrian prisons. Whether before or after the uprising, the idea of dissent, let alone rebellion, was unacceptable for the Assad state. Rebellion against brutalization and subjugation was dealt with by using more brutalization. In this sense, the prison memoirs contain insightful reflections on the nature and logic of the Assad regime.[27]

Among the survivors of the Syrian penitentiary system is Yassin Haj Saleh (born 1961). He was a twenty-year-old third-year medical student in Aleppo when he was arrested in 1980 for sympathizing with the Communist Party faction that refused to accept the dictate of the regime. He spent sixteen years in Syrian prisons, the last one in Tadmur (Palmyra). He completed his medical degree in 2000 after being released in 1996. Today he is one of Syria's foremost thinkers and writers. Reflecting on the 1979 meeting between the Front and the writers' union, shortly after Michel Kilo's second incarceration, he mentions that a recording of the meeting circulated as a secret document that challenged the "official truth," and that the tape was called the "tape of the Front" (*sharit al-jabha*).[28] More importantly, he thinks that this meeting was the birthplace of the Syrian intellectual (*muthaqqaf*), defined as a person who possesses symbolic capital and puts this capital at the service of a public role, speaking truth to power, which is what he believes Michel Kilo did in that meeting and continued to do until his second arrest.

Analyzing the circumstances of that 1979 meeting, Haj Saleh thinks that the regime saw a confrontation with the Islamists coming and wanted to win over the secularists or non-Islamist intellectuals, expecting them to attack and blame the Islamists for the country's crisis. Yet those intellectuals, most of whom, like Kilo and Adwan, had no sympathy for the Islamists, instead attacked the regime and denounced its vices. What was urgent for them was to refute the suspicion of agreement with the regime on the basis of a supposedly shared secularist value system. Only truly independent thinkers, such as Kilo and Adwan, could offer up-front criticism of the regime. Few Syrian intellectuals had that autonomy, a sine qua non for dissidence.[29] Given the antagonism between the regime and the Islamists, it was tempting for many non-Islamist intellectuals to give in to this ambiguous agreement with the regime. This ambiguity, Haj Saleh reckons, has been one of the hindrances to the formation of a dissidence tradition in Syria. Clearly, conditions were not favorable for the development of such a tradition. But dissidence, he adds, has never been a convenient and safe option.

In 2013 Kilo himself underlined the importance of individual autonomy for the effectiveness of the intellectual's work. In an article entitled "Muthaqqaf al-taghyir" (The intellectual of change), he spoke of two phenomena that had developed in recent years for many Arab intellectuals: first, their gradual move away from partisan affiliations, and so from politics in the narrow sense, and their coming closer to their own personal experiences; and second, their greater involvement in civil society, understood as the community of free citizens. Both developments, Kilo believed, gave intellectuals greater freedom and more effectiveness in their public role in an oppressed society seeking freedom.[30] As a result, they have started to become intellectuals of change.

A year after the 1979 meeting, writes Haj Saleh, the intellectuals dispersed. Kilo was sentenced to prison for a year and a half, and a wave of persecution, censorship, and arrests inaugurated what came to be known as the "kingdom of silence" (*mamlakat al-samt*).[31] Some intellectuals were jailed, some were forced into exile, some stopped speaking up, and some chose to combine an abstract critique of despotism with adherence to general causes like pan-Arab nationalism or that of Palestine. Abstract critique was a safe choice but hid resignation, helplessness, or passive acquiescence, and often the symbolic capital of "intellectuals" who chose this critique was trivial, and the role they claimed for themselves clearly inflated.

What also prevented real dissidence, according to Haj Saleh, was ideological commitment, whether progressive, communist, nationalist, or Islamist. Such commitments deprived intellectuals of the necessary intellectual and political independence for true dissidence. Kilo was among the rare intellectuals who preserved this independence. After the uprisings, Haj Saleh insisted on his independence by refusing political posts with the opposition. Syrian Marxist thinker Yasin Hafiz (1930–1978), Haj Saleh adds, was the first and most prominent theoretician and critic of ideologies, including the socialist and Baathist ones. But he had to flee Syria to Beirut after an incarceration period of one year in 1968, and he died prematurely in Beirut in 1978.[32] His work influenced a number of Arab and Syrian intellectuals, including Kilo.

Another Syrian critic of ideology was Burhan Ghalioun (born 1945). He left the country in 1969 to study at the Sorbonne and then became professor of sociology there. In 1983 he was one of the founders of the Arab Organization for Human Rights. He was elected president of the Syrian National Council for 2011–2012. In his French exile Ghalioun became a prolific writer of essays in Arabic, which were widely circulated and discussed in Syria and the Arab world. Among his main themes was the critique of ideology and the antagonism between state and society. He was among the first Syrian thinkers to demand democracy, albeit from Paris, and until the 1990s in general "Arab" terms, without explicitly naming Syrian realities.[33] In 1978 he published a manifesto for democracy, *Bayan min ajl al-dimurratiyya*, in which he argued that the main flaw of the national question (*al-mas'ala al-qawmiyya*) was its being centered on the state instead of the people.[34] Modern Arab history, he believed, was presented as a history of national liberation, while in reality it had been a history of people's disenfranchisement, exclusion, and enslavement by an elite that took power and ended up serving its own narrow interests. This modern history showed that no religious, social, political, and economic development was possible without a popular democracy in which people could represent and control their interests. The "people" here, he explained, was the set of social and political relations—organized around professional unions, local councils, and political parties—that could produce a free press, an independent judiciary, and rule of law. Hence, no revolution could be successful if it was not led by the people and in the spirit of freedom. No vanguard could teach people freedom, which was a basic survival drive. A freedom taught would be no freedom.

What happened in modern Arab history, Ghalioun added, was the foundation of states by elites dependent on, and subservient to, procapitalist, pro-Western interests and values and disconnected from the majority of people in their countries. This gave rise to a "class-state" (*al-dawla–al-tabaqa*), whose interests did not lie with those of the majority. Education systems, economic structures, and cultural choices were established that were unresponsive to people's needs, interests, and orientations. A gap emerged between the elite and the majority and kept growing until today's polarized situation.[35] The elite sought a vision that reconciled tradition with modernity, religious thought with modern methods, but that vision, according to Ghalioun, was bound to fail intellectually, socially, and politically. It could only appear to work if one of the sides of the conciliation equation was distorted. In a sense, the efforts of the nahda were mistakenly based on the success promised by this conciliatory strategy. In *Ightiyal al-'aql: Mihnat al-thaqafa al-arabiyya bayn al-salafiyya wa al-taba'iyya* (Assassination of reason: The crisis of Arab culture between Salafism and dependency), first published in 1985, he called upon his fellow Arabs to liberate their minds and culture from the despotism of ideology and to abandon the illusion of finding solutions in conciliatory, unified ideologies.[36] For him, the double rejection of fundamentalism (*usuliyya*) and modernism (*tahdithiyya*) did not consist in some conciliatory merger of the two, but in freedom of thought. The civilizational delay could not be solved verbally, by developing some new doctrine, but instead by developing a proper democracy and a truly national economy.

An elite-serving education system left people without education, and a procapitalist economy left them without socioeconomic justice. The elite complained about an ignorant population that hindered the spread of secularism and scientific thinking and stood in the way of progress in general. The Left criticized the elite for not serving the interests of the people and for lacking the "scientific ideology" that would have otherwise led it to change its policies. Ghalioun thought that it was not a matter of a missing ideology, but of the nature of that elite class-state, which dictated policies that were detrimental to the majority. This elite practiced intellectual consumerism, borrowing from and dialoguing primarily with the West, and took the nahda as its ideology. Given this power and interest structure, he affirmed, no religious or intellectual reform could succeed. Secularism became a form of factionalism confronting a resisting majority.[37] The solution, he concluded, was not a return to Islam or to traditional forms of power, but the critique of all power (*naqd kull sulta*) and the establishment of a democratic power representing the people.

In the preface to the 1986 edition of his manifesto for democracy, Ghalioun deplored the violent reaction of Arab governments to peoples' revolts against exclusion and injustice. He was probably referring, among other things, to the bread riots, which broke out in several Arab countries: in 1977 in Egypt, in 1981 and 1984 in Morocco, and in 1983–1984 in Tunisia. People, he added, had been deprived of their dignity, self-respect, sense of self, and hope for a better future. The reaction included military confrontations and massacres. Two decades later, in the preface to the 2006 edition of the book, Ghalioun mentioned the new chances and the new challenges he saw for democracy in the Arab world. On the one hand, he saw the bankruptcy of the Arab regimes and the reemergence of social movements despite all the repression; he saw the encouraging democratic changes in Eastern Europe and the end of the cold war, which favored support to many a dictator in the region. But on the other hand, he deplored the extensive damage done by those bankrupt regimes, the general ruin (*al-kharab al-shamil*) that they had produced, and the destruction they had done to the structures of the modern state. So the emerging pluralist, democratic aspirations had to face this bitter harvest. In Ghalioun's opinion, the impending confrontation did not offer much optimism for the democratic forces. In a premonitory passage, which reads like a Cassandra call for what would materialize a few years later with the outbreak of the 2011 revolution, he formulated his fears about the upcoming day of reckoning:

> It is also not sure that the disappearance of the old security control and the fall of the wall of fear which will come with [the emergence of plural systems] will lead to the development of the social and political dynamic forces that those systems need for their life, working and consolidation. It is much more probable that the transitional period and the fall of the dreadful security regimes will show the extent of the helplessness and collapse that civil society suffers from and show the shortcomings and deep flaws produced by a whole era of systematic destruction and killing of the sense of individual and collective responsibility as well as carelessness about the common good. Perhaps it will, on the contrary, be an occasion for the explosion of numerous mines that the previous regime planted in all domains of action, life and social relations. . . . And with the prevailing vast economic disparities in the distribution of wealth and the profound feeling of injustice and absence of social solidarity, we cannot be reassured that resorting to force and breaking the law won't be the strongest temptation of those communities and sectors that were deprived of their humanity and that harbored feelings and values of despair; and we cannot be reassured that it won't be the strongest temptation of those who have been benefiting from the situation and who won't hesitate to use any means to keep their exceptional positions and privileges to empty pluralism of its content and disrupt the democratic transformation in any way possible.[38]

In a January 2016 interview Ghalioun asserted that his manifesto retained its pertinence, that more than ever the problem was the disempowerment of the people, and that the question was still the question of power (*sulta*), of its organization and management. He recognized the rise of the counterrevolution but affirmed that no stability could be established without recognizing people's rights; that is, without democracy. Cultural, economic, civil, and political elites had to draw lessons from their past mistakes and engage the people in their democratic yearnings. They should strive to overcome their estrangement from the people. With the outbreak of the revolutions, many in the elite, he added, seemed more scared of the people's victory than the regime's. The revolutions showed the lack of deep interaction between the elite and the people, as well as the lack of trust in the people's humanist aspirations. This has been disruptive for their collaboration. Paradoxically, the elite speaks about democracy and behaves otherwise, while the people, who might not have a democratic education, make sacrifices for the sake of democracy. In some sense the elite, which acts like a secularists' sect (ta'ifat al-'ilmaniyyin), believes that the regime, with which it supposedly shares a secularist-modernist ideology, protects it from the people—whom they both despise. In return, the people make a counterideology of their religious faith, feeding the polarization. At the end of the interview, Ghalioun laments the loss of secularism's emancipatory and egalitarian potential, on the one hand, and the loss of the solidarity values of religion on the other.[39]

Fellow Syrian leftist opposition writer Abdulrazzaq Eid (born 1950) disagrees with Ghalioun's characterization of the nahda. He does not believe that the nahdawis, the major figures of the nahda, advocated secularism to empower despots, when so many of them criticized and struggled against despotism. They were fought by the elite, not the people. He mentions the cases of Abd al-Rahman al-Kawakibi (1855–1902) and Ali Abdel Raziq (1888–1966). The former wrote strongly against despotism, and the latter argued that Islam did not advocate a specific form of government and that the caliphate was wrongly believed to be an Islamic dogma.[40] Since the nahda, Eid adds, secularists have been confronted by the ruling elite's autocratic sword as well as by the religious establishment's theocratic sword. And these two forces have a lot in common: both are conservative, imitators, and traditionalists. The opposition between them has never been an intellectual conflict, but rather a struggle over power and religious legitimacy. Secularists find themselves besieged by both. Gamal Abdel Nasser fought the Salafists politically but empowered them culturally. To say that the nahda, including its secularist and tanwiri ideas, has been an oppressive ideology is a dangerous claim that reinforces the position of those two camps; namely, those of the ruling elite and the religious establishment. The blaming and criminalizing of the nahda (ta'thim wa tajrim 'asr al-nahda), and the call to go back to "authentic" tradition, is one of the main manifestations of the "tanwir crisis" (azamat al-tanwir), according to Eid. Ghalioun, by attacking the elite and associating it with the nahda, distorts the reality of the nahda and gives credit to the elite that it has not earned. Ghalioun's defense of people's traditional cultural specificity becomes an apology for civilizational retardation. Eid writes that he agrees here with his fellow Syrian scholar and translator Georges Tarabichi (1939–2016), who thought that Ghalioun's call could be justified if people had boarded a drifting boat that needed to be reanchored. But in the Arab case, Tarabichi added, it looked more like a boat that was incapable of setting out in the first place. This is Eid's main argument in his 1997 book *Azamat al-tanwir: Shar'anat al-fawat al-hadari* (The crisis of tanwir: The legitimation of civilizational delay). It is not true, he wrote, that the nahda was anti-Islamic and alien to its environment.[41] On the contrary, it was firmly rooted in the realities of its epoch. But after the defeat of 1967, the nahda was increasingly blamed for much of the Arabs' miseries. There is, Eid added, a consensus that the post-1967 period witnessed the setback of many nahda ideals, including reason, modernization, popular nationalism, and socialism. The nation-state endeavor has failed, and there has been a regression to tribal or sectarian allegiances. Regimes have become increasingly totalitarian and distant from their populations. The obsession with identity and tradition indicates the failure to deal effectively with the challenges facing society. The crisis of tanwir is, for Eid, the use of reason to develop apologies for this failure, in the name of a cultural specificity from which rationality, modernity, and secularism are excluded. According to Eid, Muhammad Abed al-Jabiri's (1936–2010) theory about the constitution of Arab reason belongs to this apologetic orientation.[42] Finally, he adds, tradition (*turath*) was one of the elements of the nahda's conciliatory strategy (*al-tawfiqiyya*), and the other element was modernity. After 1967, modernity disappeared from the equation, and tradition became the dominant one.

Syrian leftist philosopher Sadeq Jalal al-Azm (1934–2016) agreed that there had been a mounting attack on the nahda since 1967. In a dialogue with Palestinian writer Saqr Abu Fakhr on enlightenment, secularism, and Salafism, he said that in the 1960s he and his fellow leftists had criticized the nahda for its insufficient efforts to implement its ideals, which were in any case not radical enough.[43] The assumption that nahda ideas could be taken for granted and improved upon was shown to be false by the 1967 defeat. That defeat revealed the fragility of those ideas. In the face of the growing demonization of the nahda, leftists were now defending it and its tanwir. Interestingly, al-Azm, like so many other Arab thinkers, equated nahda with tanwir. He admitted that in the past the leftists had neglected the importance of democracy, liberty, civil society, and human rights. He too recognized Yasin Hafiz's pioneering work of self-critique, produced by drawing attention to those values. Moreover, he thought the Marxists had been too shy in upholding secularism, instead humoring the religious inclination of the masses at a time when insisting on the necessity of secularism was important. Al-Azm, for one, was never ambiguous about it.[44] According to him, Abdel Nasser had missed an opportunity by not declaring secularism a state principle at the height of his popularity, during the nationalization of the Suez Canal. Finally, al-Azm too believed that the nahda was not purely an intellectual movement but also a socioeconomic and political phenomenon that affected the wider region, starting in the Ottoman Tanzimat period (1939–1876).[45]

In 2005, a year before the fifth edition of Ghalioun's manifesto appeared, Syrian Marxist philosopher Tayyeb Tizini (born 1934), then professor at the University of Damascus, published a manifesto on the Arab nahda and tanwir, *Bayan fi al-nahda wa al-tanwir al-arabi*.[46] It was a plea for democratic reform as the only way to rise up from the Arab wreckage (*al-hutam al-arabi*) caused by corruption, emergency laws, and consumerism and by the absence of pluralism and tolerance. It was a call for societal political participation, for a pluralistic media, for accountability, and for an active civil society—all deemed necessary for nahda (renaissance) and tanwir. Tizini insisted on the deep connection between the Arab project of the new tanwiri nahda and the involvement of civil society in controlling political action.[47] Finally, it was an appeal for the defense of freedom and reason that bring about a culture of tolerance, solidarity, equality, and conviviality.

Nahda and tanwir had not been on Tizini's intellectual agenda for most of his career up until the mid-2000s. His initial project was a Marxist reading of tradition that would provide the elements of an Arab cultural, and eventually political, revolution. He formulated that reading in his 1976 *Min al-turath ila al-thawra* (From tradition to revolution), part of a trend in which Marxist thinkers read Marxist ideas into the Arab-Islamic traditions.[48] In a 2008 interview Tizini explained the change in his outlook from revolution to nahda and tanwir in the following way. He said that in light of the latest developments, including the collapse of the Soviet Union, the new world order, and the invasion of Iraq, ideas needed to be reconsidered and adapted to these developments. What the new circumstances demanded was tanwir and nahda, not revolutions carried by only certain classes, like the working classes. Moreover, one could no longer exclude social movements such as Islamism. Change was imperative but needed to be inclusive and plural. It required a large and open societal dialogue, unrestricted by ideological constraints. The cancellation of political parties at the time of the union with Egypt, he added, was a mistake that had profoundly damaged Syrian political life.[49] There was an urgent need to correct this mistake, reform the state, reconsider previous intellectual and political projects, and construct a new thought that responded to the wreckage (*hutam*) produced by decades of abuse.

Already in 2003, Michel Kilo had directed a scathing attack on Tizini's claim about a "new thought."[50] Revisions of Marxist theory from a humanist, enlightenment perspective that emphasizes individual and collective liberty had already been undertaken by Marxist Syrian thinkers such as Yasin Hafiz and Elias Murqus (1929–1991).[51] Kilo thought that Tizini had been late both in reading reality and in adopting a tanwiri and nahdawi orientation. He also believed that Tizini remained an old sympathizer of the Baath ideology, and that his bet for reform had been for too long on the state rather than on civil society. Finally, his intellectual shortcomings coupled with his political inexperience made his presumptuous claims to philosophical innovation unacceptable.

In 2001 Tizini published a critique of the 2000–2001 Damascus Spring, *Min thulathiyyat al-fasad ila qadaya al-mujtama' al-madani* (From the trilogy of corruption to the issues of civil society).[52] One of his criticisms was that supporters of civil society had exaggerated expectations for it, while he believed that the starting point of reform should be the reform of the state.[53] Despite his conflicts with those involved in the Damascus Spring, Tizini signed the two major declarations of the Syrian opposition: the 2005 Damascus Declaration and the 2006 Beirut-Damascus Declaration, which we will address in chapter 4. A few days after the beginning of the Syrian uprising, in March 2011, he was among the several hundred demonstrators who demanded the release of political prisoners in front of the Ministry of Interior in Damascus. He was beaten and held for a brief time by the state security forces. On October 7, 2011, he participated in the national conference convened by the regime in Damascus to discuss the crisis. Kilo was also among the two hundred participants. In his speech Tizini listed the demands that should be met before any national dialogue began; namely, no firing at fellow Syrians, the release of political prisoners, the application of the rule of law, the abandoning of security state principles, and the reconstruction of the media to make room for a real national debate. The executive committee of the conference that would follow satisfaction of these demands should be the product of a dialogue between the regime and the opposition, not convened by the regime on its own.[54] Similarly, Michel Kilo asked for the immediate cessation of the security approach to the situation, and for constitutional amendments that would allow opposition forces to form legal political organizations. Like Tizini, he demanded the release of political prisoners and the end of state violence against demonstrators as preliminary conditions for the pursuit of dialogue.

These Syrian debates clearly show the need for a tanwir, one made from the lived darkness—a darkness experienced in the repression put in place by those who grabbed power in the 1960s and 1970s. Like the tanwir advocated by Egyptian deconstructionists, the tanwir demanded by Syrian critics is anchored in the lived experiences of the people and made by their coming together as a free civil society. Unlike the 1970s dialogue between the regime and the unions, the tanwir called for by the critics demands the restoration of real political life. Moreover, according to these critics, the contribution of intellectuals to this tanwir necessitates independence not only from the state but also from rigid ideology. Finally, the nahda occupies a central place in the Syrian debate, as it did in the Egyptian one: the nature, identity, and significance of the nahda legacy for genuine tanwir are subjects of heated discussion. Whether the nahda had been an ideology used by the powerful against the people or a promising project aborted by the regime was one of the main questions of that discussion.

Saadallah Wannous and the Journal *Qadaya wa-shahadat*

Toward the end of the dark 1980s, in the midst of the general ruin (*kharab shamil*) and heavy silence, three prominent Syrian thinkers launched a journal that would shine a light in the darkness: writer and playwright Saadallah Wannous (1941–1997); philosopher and literary critic of Palestinian origin Faysal Darraj (born 1942); and Saudi, Iraqi, Jordanian, and Syrian novelist Abdel Rahman Munif (1933–2004). They invited Egyptian literary critic Gaber Asfour (born 1944) to join them to give the journal a wider Arab dimension, but he did not play much of a role in its production. Entitled

Qadaya wa-shahadat (Issues and testimonies), the journal appeared between 1990 and 1992, in six volumes.[55] Wannous fell ill, which was one of the major causes of the journal's being phased out. A seventh and final volume appeared in 2000 in homage to him. The other causes given by Darraj are the absence of a supporting readership, direct or indirect censorship by a number of Arab countries, and the ongoing post-1967 defeat situation.[56]

The major themes of the journal were rationalism, democracy, modernity, modernization, the nahda, national culture, dependency, tradition, and history.[57] Each volume had an introduction that articulated the relevance of and approach to the issues it addressed. Wannous wrote the introductions to the first four volumes, Darraj introduced the fifth volume, and Munif the sixth. These editors belonged to a disappointed postindependence generation disillusioned by political militancy and the "aftermaths of sovereignty," to use David Scott's phrase.[58] However, having known the gloom of depression, they also saw the necessity of sustaining hope, reconstructing the human, and reestablishing faith in the critical and creative faculties, despite and against the prevailing brutality.

Together with the editorial statement that appeared on the front page of every volume, their introductions served as the journal's program. The editorial statement read as follows:

> Here is a periodical that aims at a collective cultural work, starting from the questions of everyday reality that concern the intellectual and his role as well as the ordinary person searching for bread, freedom and national dignity. The journal aims to connect the present Arab democratic culture with its cultural past, a culture that had struggled for rationality and human dignity as well as to build a civil society in the service of the common good, based on speech, action and a sense of endeavor. The review does not seek new answers to existing questions as much as it attempts to reformulate them.[59]

The statement's keywords—democracy, cultural past, daily reality, intellectual, ordinary person, collective work, bread, freedom, national and human dignity, rationality, history, civil society, public good, old questions, and new formulations—set the program of the journal. To reconnect their readers with the Arab cultural past that had articulated the impulses toward democracy, rationality, and freedom, each volume contained documents (*watha'iq*), selections (*mukhtarat*), and testimonies (*shahadat*) from modern

Arab thinkers like Mikhail Nu'aimy, Taha Husayn, Zaki Naguib Mahmud, Hasan Muruwweh, Yasin Hafiz, Abdallah Laroui, Mahdi Amil, Salim Khayy-ata, Ghassan Kanafani and Sadeq Jalal al-Azm, Gamal Ghitani, Sonallah Ibrahim, and Haydar Haydar. Some of the volumes also contained transla-tions from foreign texts, including some from Jean Baudrillard, Walter Ben-jamin, Marshall Berman, Frantz Fanon, Fredric Jameson, and Edward Said. Of course, with its advocacy for democracy and freedom, the journal did not get coverage by the Syrian official media and could not be part of a public debate. However, the quality of its texts and the prominence of its contributors make it one of the most important publications of this period in Syria and the Arab world. The contributors and editors were well aware of the impossibility of effecting any immediate change to Syrian and Arab realities, but at the same time they seem to have felt the urgency of witness-ing and presenting alternative, imagined possibilities; hence, the Sisyphean character of their work.[60] No one articulated this aspect of the journal's character and mission better than Wannous.[61]

Saadallah Wannous studied journalism in Cairo, but his main interest and creative work was in drama. He wrote some two dozen plays in his relatively short career, many of which are considered among the major works of mod-ern Arab drama, such as *Haflat samar min ajl khamsa huzairan* (Entertainment evening for June 5, 1968), *Al-Fil ya malik al-zaman* (The elephant, oh king of time, 1969), *Al-Malik huwa al-malik* (The king is the king, 1977), *Al-Ightisab* (The rape, 1990), *Munamnamat tarikhiyya* (Historical miniatures, 1994), *Tuqus al-isharat wa al-tahawwulat* (Rituals of signals and transformations, 1994), and *Al-Ayyam al-makhmura* (The drunken days, 1997). Some of his plays were translated into foreign languages, including English, French, Ger-man, Italian, Polish, Russian, and Spanish. He pursued his interest in drama in France, Germany, and Russia. Upon his return to Damascus, he worked for the Syrian Ministry of Culture and wrote for the cultural supplement of the Syrian daily *al-Baath* and the Lebanese daily *As-Safir*. For many years he was editor of the Syrian theater magazine *Hayat al-masrah* and taught at the High Institute for Theatre Arts in Damascus. He also wrote theoretical essays on his understanding of the nature of political theater and its role in raising critical awareness. Most of his plays and other writings denounced demagogy, mendacity, oppression, empty lyricism, hypocrisy, and most of all the abuses of political and social power. Their goal was to nurture pub-lic discussion about matters of common interest and to liberate people from imposed and self-imposed constraints. Sometimes his plays were banned (e.g., *Haflat samar min ajl khamsa huzairan*), sometimes they were severely criticized (e.g., *Al-Ightisab*), but in general they did reach a considerable public across the Arab world.[62]

In the 1960s Wannous was enthusiastic about the socialist modernizing projects undertaken in Syria, only to be disappointed by their mismanagement and the increasing limitations on freedom of expression. But as for most Arabs, the shock came with the 1967 defeat. It led to anguished soul-searching regarding the causes of the debacle and who was responsible. Many Arab thinkers sought answers in the cultural domain, leading to a cultural malaise and culturalism in its analysis. Wannous was among the few Arab thinkers who early on identified the causes of the disastrous defeat as being in the political domain, and more precisely in the disenfranchisement and disappearing of the people from the public sphere (*taghyib al-sha'b*). *Haflat samar min ajl khamsa huzairan*, written in 1967 and 1968, presented this analysis unambiguously and hence was banned from Syrian stages. The disappearance of the people and the confiscation of political life (*musadarat al-hayat al-siyasiyya*) were to become leitmotifs in his writings.[63]

But a more severe shock was to hit Wannous in the late seventies with the Camp David Accords of 1978 and 1979 between Egypt and Israel. The accords were for him the ultimate betrayal of the Arab and Palestinian causes, and the collapse of the dreams of Arab unity, liberation, and justice. His despair was so total that he contemplated suicide, as he related in a long interview conducted on a hospital bed while he received treatment for cancer, shortly before his death in 1997.[64] He only recuperated from his depression and resumed writing in the second half of the 1980s. The early eighties, as we know, had also witnessed the Syrian repression and the Israeli invasion of Lebanon, including the occupation of Beirut. In a 1986 interview Wannous said that those gloomy years made him deepen his self-examination and led him to eventually resume his work and his struggle for freedom and truthfulness, albeit with more humility and determinacy.[65] A year before his death, in 1996, UNESCO commissioned him to deliver the message for World Theatre Day. His message was entitled "Al-Ju' ila al-hiwar" (The hunger for dialogue).[66] In it he pleaded for dialogue and democracy and cautioned against the internalized tendency toward authoritarian monologuing nurtured by years of despotism. He ended his speech on a Sisyphean note, saying, "We are condemned to hope" (*Innana mahkumun bi al-amal*).

Qadaya wa-shahadat belongs to this postdespair phase in Wannous's career and is part of his work toward the reconstruction of the Arab tanwir project. The introductions to the first four volumes deal with the nahda and its central figures, including Taha Husayn, Rifa'a al-Tahtawi, Kheireddin Tunisi, Malik Bennabi, and Sayyed Qutb, and reflect on modernity, modernization, culture, and politics. His introduction to the first volume, "In Lieu of an Introduction," reads like a tanwir manifesto. In it he states that the journal takes a stand and bears witness (*mawqif wa shahada*):[67] it stands for reason, historical thinking, independence, and progress; for the dream of a civil society; and above all for the revival of attempts at Arab tanwir, in view of connecting these attempts into a coherent and effective whole (*ihya' muhawalat al-tanwir al-arabi, wa rabtiha fi siyaq mutalahim wa fa'al*).[68] In this endeavor, he thinks that one must start with the work of Taha Husayn (1889–1973), who produced the most radical tanwir project (*mashrou' tanwiri jadhri*) in modern Arab intellectual history.[69] Unfortunately, he adds, we have been severed from Husayn's project, which, instead of being transmitted and advanced, has been fought and spoiled by politicians, intellectuals, and people at large. It is time to try and reclaim (*istirdad*) Husayn as a light in the darkness, he writes, and it is for this purpose that the first volume of the journal is devoted to his work.[70]

According to Wannous, five main features of this work constitute the tanwiri orientation that needs to be reclaimed. First, Husayn examined Islamic history, including some of its canonical texts and founding events, as historical phenomena, shifting away from a sacralized, theological approach. By so doing, he introduced the relative and the human into this history and opened a margin of freedom and self-confidence in Arab culture that is no longer available. He looked at history as a human becoming (*sayrura insaniyya*) and no longer as a sanctified entity.[71] In other words, he took the liberty of submitting the authority of tradition to his rational examination. Second, Husayn openly and unambiguously criticized the teaching methods and curricula of the Azhar, the central religious institution in his country (and the Sunni Muslim world)—no one would dare to make his critique nowadays, adds Wannous. Husayn demanded that all religious teaching be subjected to the republican rules of a secular state. Third, Husayn avoided the pitfalls of cultural specificity and cultural superiority/inferiority, even when he affirmed Egyptian identity, by underlining the equality of cultures and the universality of the human mind. Fourth, Husayn was always eager to connect his ideas with reality, writes Wannous. Contrary to his detractors, the changes he advocated were meant not for a select elite but for the largest possible number of people. The education he pleaded for was for everyone, not for a few. Moreover, and again contrary to the claims of many critics, he remained consistent in his approach, even when he turned to Islamic topics. Some saw in this turn a renunciation of his critical approach and a submission to popular taste. In reality, it was his further critical appropriation of the religious historical field. He did not want to leave a field so significant to the masses to the uncritical religious authorities. Finally, Husayn never lost sight of the importance of anchoring ideas and tanwiri projects in the lived realities of people and in the policies of the state. These five features of Husayn's tanwiri project also characterize, for Wannous, the whole of the nahda as a tanwiri movement, notwithstanding its variety of tendencies and figures. And it is these features that got lost under the political and intellectual coups of the 1950s onward. As a result, the Arab tanwiri project was not brought to fruition and a whole enlightenment legacy was severed from our awareness, instead of being accumulated (murakama) and owned for further development. The journal is an effort to recuperate this legacy, but a few intellectuals cannot achieve this recuperation on their own. It needs the efforts of all social and political forces, Wannous writes, insisting that the project cannot be a purely intellectual-cultural one.

One of the most important blows against Husayn's Arab tanwiri project is located in politics, according to Wannous, and more precisely in Abdel Nasser's 1952 military coup, also known as the Free Officers revolution or the July revolution. By canceling political parties—ironically, with popular support—and thus annulling political life, Abdel Nasser instituted an authoritarian regime that eliminated critical reason and freedom from public life. Even at the height of the popular enthusiasm for Abdel Nasser's policies, Husayn raised his voice against the general orientation and stated that no revolution that denied reason and freedom could be acceptable.[72] Eventually he was marginalized, and his project was left to crumble. Abdel Nasser was not even capable of using Husayn's ideas in his fight against Sayyid Qutb and his Salafi followers. Abdel Nasser's pragmatism, narrow horizons, and conciliatory thought (fikr tawfiqi),[73] which tried to conciliate conservative, religious thinking with socialist, revolutionary thinking, could not tolerate Husayn's liberal and tanwiri thought. Despite some achievements, Nasserism eventually led to the major failures Arabs have since witnessed, because of the disenfranchising of people, the confiscation of political work, and the conciliatory mode of thinking.[74] Moreover, in the intellectual sphere even progressive thinkers such as Mahmud Amin Alim and Abdel Adhim Anis turned against Husayn, accusing his work of representing intellectual feudalism.[75] Wannous believes the Arab tanwir project, which started in the nahda and was advanced by Husayn, unraveled because of these political and intellectual developments, leaving following generations disconnected from it.

In his introduction to the second volume of the journal, "Bayn al-hadatha wa al-tahdith" (Between modernity and modernization),[76] Wannous discusses the ideas of two major nahdawi figures, Tahtawi and Tunisi. Again, what he finds significant in their work is not so much the answers they offered as the questions they raised, particularly the confidence, freedom, and optimism with which they raised them. Many of their questions are still being raised today, deplores Wannous, but with less resolve and less courage. What remains inspiring from their epoch is an intellectual vitality connected to sociopolitical realities, geared toward change and modernization, and supported to some extent by the political rulers in charge. Tahtawi undertook his writing and founded the translation and language school in Cairo thanks to the support of Muhammad Ali Pasha (ruled 1805–1848). Similarly, whatever political reforms Tunisi was able to implement in Tunis or even Istanbul was thanks to favorable political support. Their respective rulers were able to keep conservative forces in check, as they saw benefits for their own power in the modernization process. In addition, European colonialism had not yet come to the region and complicated the perception of European modernity.

For those nahdawis, Europe represented an advanced civilization, based on principles of political justice, economic success, and cognitive progress—principles that they believed they could adopt and indigenize without much conflict or concern for identity. They saw the close connection between those principles and their products. They warned against accepting the latter without grasping the former—a mistake later generations made in the name of preserving identity. By limiting their borrowing from the West to consumable products in order to protect indigenous values, later generations ended up deepening their dependency on the European other. With the advent of European colonialism, Europe showed its aggression, greed, and racism, making the discernment of its values and the call for their adoption a more complex matter. Modernity became a more intricate phenomenon to grasp, and modernization a more skewed process to manage. Since then, adds Wannous, Arab history has been a series of successive attempts at rising and discouraging falls, damaging the course of modernization and aborting the tanwir project. This failure in modernization and tanwir cannot be explained exclusively in cultural and intellectual terms, as has generally been done, writes Wannous; it has to be accounted for politically (*fal-tafsir la yakmun fi al-thaqafa bal fi al-siyasa*).[77] The failure of Arabs to enter the present age (*al-'asr*) has arrested them in an ever-recurring problematic of "us and them" and lost modernization. By searching for the causes of failure in culture, that failure is made to seem more abstract and less painful. In fact, what is constantly and conveniently silenced, he writes, is the political root of the failure, and more precisely the role of the postindependent state and political regime. By silencing this role, the discussions remain innocent, safe, and elitist. In reality, the national or postindependence state promised modernization and a unified nation that would regain its dignity and enter the present age with ease, by burning stages if necessary. But here we are, in the nineties, he observes, and we are still backward countries, in which human beings are worthless, threatened by hunger, and inhibited by fear and despotism. Instead of working toward thorough modernization in all sectors of society, supported by education and civil rights, the social fabric was torn apart, and modernization was limited to appearances, to buildings, cars, televisions, and so on, and it led to a dependent economy. Not only was the modernization dreamt of by the likes of Tahtawi lost, but the skewed partial modernization became an instrument of despotism and an extension of it[78]—an assessment reminiscent of Burhan Ghalioun's.

Wannous pursues his critique of this culturalist approach to the Arab predicament with modernity in his introduction to the journal's fourth volume, "Al-thaqafa al-wataniyya wa al-wa'I al-tarikhi" (National culture and historical awareness).[79] He responds to the approach adopted by most participants of "Al-turath wa tahaddiyyat al-'asr fi al-watan al-arabi" (Tradition and the challenges of the present age in the Arab homeland), a 1984 Cairo conference organized by the Centre for Arab Unity Studies.[80] The theme of the conference in itself, he writes, implies a whole set of problematic assumptions that are taken for granted; namely, that we know "tradition" and the "present age" as well-defined and well-studied entities, that we have the freedom to pick and choose from them whatever suits our interests, that the destiny of the nation depends on those choices we can make, and that history has room for our contemplations and hesitations.[81] None of these assumptions are warranted, according to Wannous. *Turath* (tradition) is used like an incantation to evade reality, confine Arab debates to issues of identity, and conveniently avoid subjects that disturb regimes, such as the unjust distribution of wealth within and between countries and the abuse of power. What is also eluded is history—more precisely, the historicity of tradition and contemporaneity. Finally, what is bracketed is reality. Real Arab history includes the brutality of despotism (*sharasat al-istibdad*), the abuse of the independence and wealth of nations, the manipulation of sectarian divisions, the suspension of laws and constitutions, the absence of civil society, backwardness, and dependency: all of these bitter realities are conveniently avoided by focusing on issues of cultural specificity, tradition, and identity.[82] Wannous criticizes the same lack of historical thinking in the cultural theories of Algerian thinker Malek Bennabi (1905–1973) and Egyptian Islamist ideologue Sayyid Qutb (1906–1966).[83]

In this tendency to avoid historical thinking, Wannous sees a defeat of the awareness that Arab intellectuals, like all third world intellectuals, have to confront, at a time when they are weakened by local and external factors: by the absence of democracy, poverty, illiteracy, a dominating and futile media, and ramping capitalism. Nevertheless, he adds, the intellectual

> like Sisyphus has to carry the rock and climb the mountain. He is condemned to carry the rock, and condemned not to expect—especially in these gloomy days—any compensation. He has to accept his marginality, and to continue his work, to be a witness and a leaven. To be a screaming voice in the wilderness and to be an impulse [*irhas*]. And it is important that he does not entertain any illusions about his role, and let inadvertently the defeat creep into his awareness and defeat it.
>
> So, let us carry the rock . . . and continue.[84]

His introduction to the journal's third volume is a conversation with Syrian philosopher and thinker Antoun Maqdisi (1914–2005) on issues of modernity and modernization.[85] The two men agree that the notion of modernity—in the comprehensive sense still operational in the sixties, including personal, social, and political emancipation and development—has been lost in the haze of consumerism and opportunism, the pressures of repression, the wave of Salafi violence, and the general Arab collapse.[86] Maqdisi accuses intellectuals of having participated in this collapse by supporting coups, sometimes believing that these could accelerate the course of progress, and often out of opportunism and greed for power.[87] They also agree on the need to build a modest civil nucleus, in which people can think and exchange their thoughts freely, in view of developing a new public opinion, especially among the youth, and of coming out of the dismal Arab fall. Equally important for them is the building of a historical awareness for the generations that have been cut off from the modernization efforts that came before the era of military coups. What is absolutely needed, they believe, is the reconstruction of the human being (*bina' al-insan*). The question is where to start and how to undertake such a reconstruction under conditions of repression, with an education system that has been ruined and teachers who have been robbed of their spirit. On a Sisyphean note, Maqdisi admits that he is aware of the discouraging gloominess of the picture (*ana a'lam an al-sura qatima wa muhbita*) and has moments of despair, which he overcomes by telling himself that he will go on trying until he dies.[88]

Maqdisi studied philosophy and literature in France and taught philosophy in high school upon his return to Syria. Together with Akram Hourani (1911–1996), he was among the founders of the Syrian Socialist Union Party (Hizb al-ittihad al-ishtiraki). He wrote its program and inner regulations. He later participated in writing the merger document when the party merged with the Arab Baath Party to become the Arab Baath Socialist Party, which in 1963 became the ruling party. However, as soon as the party took power, he left it and retired from political work. He then devoted himself to writing and translating. He participated in founding the Arab writers' union in 1969 and in establishing the philosophy faculty at the University of Damascus. In 1965 he was appointed head of publications and translation at the Syrian Ministry of Culture. He was highly respected for his moral integrity and professional dedication and stood out for his modesty in an epoch of endemic corruption, opportunism, and servitude. A decade after his conversation with Wannous, he wrote the first open and critical letter to the newly "elected" President Bashar al-Assad. He was then sacked by the ministry, after thirty-five years of dedicated service. A few months later, in September 2000, he opened the series of talks and discussions at the Atassi forum that marked the beginning of the Damascus Spring. His talk was on civil society. Maqdisi walked the walk after talking the talk, crossing from the Sisyphean tanwir years of the 1990s to the Promethean ones of the Damascus Spring. Wannous, unfortunately, did not get to that bridge. He died of cancer a few years before the Spring.

Samar Yazbek (born 1970), a Syrian feminist novelist, screenwriter, and engaged activist in the revolution, wrote a moving homage to Maqdisi a few months after his passing, while she was working on a documentary film on him.[89] In her homage she lamented the fact that only in the last few years had she gotten to hear about "a man who lived for almost a century." How could she have heard of him, while growing up with the only three local official newspapers in the country, she wondered. As a woman in her thirties, she saw herself as belonging to a generation that was from early on indoctrinated in the one-party organizations, with one color, one thought, and one language, that of always obeying orders. She admired this man who came from another generation, a generation that knew multiple colors, pluralism, dialogue, and freedom; a man who kept his integrity in the midst of ubiquitous corruption, only to be humiliated at the end of his life by being dismissed from his position after years of loyal service, dedicated to the world of ideas and values. The stubborn optimism of this man and his faith in the coming human being (tafa'uluhu bi al-insan al-qadim) inspired her generation, which had nothing to expect but ruination (jili la yantadhiruhu siwa al-kharab); it inspired her with hope. This was a man, she added, who said that we were citizens, not subjects. He was a respectable intellectual, unlike so many of today's intellectuals, who fight one another and struggle to earn a livelihood, in times that respect neither intellectuals nor culture. Her testimony speaks for a new generation searching for references of respectability and culture and trying to weave for itself a moral and intellectual genealogy disrupted by decades of dictatorship.

There was certainly a Promethean element in those Sisyphean moves of the 1990s, bold intellectual attempts at emancipation from despair, servitude, and dehumanization. The Promethean moment a decade later would have its own Sisyphean moment, this time tragic, as the Damascus Spring was repressed; and its tragic character would be aggravated another decade later when the Syrian revolution was crushed and mired in a bloody conflagration.[90] Faysal Darraj, a colleague of Wannous and Maqdisi, witnessed the struggle and the tragedy.

Faysal Darraj: Thought and the Context of Thought: The Nahda and the Present Age

Born in Palestine in 1942, Darraj moved with his family to Damascus in 1948, after the Nakba, the first defeat of the Arabs by Israel and first major wave of Palestinian dispossession. He studied philosophy in Damascus and Toulouse and wrote a dissertation on alienation in Marx's philosophy. Back from France, he worked for various Palestinian and Arab research centers and publishing houses, living in Damascus, Beirut, and Amman. He became a prolific literary critic, with a profound knowledge of modern Arab literature and thought and sharp insight into Arab sociopolitical realities.[91] Throughout his intellectual career he remained a secular, leftist critic of those realities and a staunch, if critical, defender of the nahda and tanwir, especially when the latter came under attack in the 1990s.

Like Wannous, Darraj underlined the necessity of addressing the question of the postindependence state and the captive human (al-insan al-mu'taqal) it produced.[92] Similarly to Wannous, he found the issues of authenticity and identity to be fake ones, nurtured by the dominating powers and the false consciousness they created; like Wannous, he found the champions of authenticity to be the most effective servants of dependency, contrary to what they claimed.[93] Like Wannous, he perceived the nahda in its sociohistorical context and emphasized the ethos it could bequeath the present generation, if they could reconnect with it: an ethos of intellectual daring, freedom of debate, and social embeddedness. Husayn represented the Arab tanwiri par excellence, for Darraj as for Wannous. Darraj wrote about Husayn in the first volume of Qadaya wa-shahadat in 1990 and expanded on the topic years later with a comparative study of Husayn and the poet Adonis.[94] In his introduction to the fifth volume of Qadaya wa-shahadat, Darraj compared and contrasted the nahda thought with the present one.[95] Furthermore, he pursued his examination of tanwir beyond the journal in the following decade, discussing the substance, merits, and shortcomings of the nahda for today.[96] In what follows, we will examine Darraj's understanding of Husayn's tanwir, then his comparison between the nahda period and the present time, and finally his grasp and critical defense of tanwir.

Darraj's contribution to the first issue of Qadaya wa-shahadat, devoted to Husayn, is a seminal essay aimed at teasing out Husayn's conception of modern knowledge, its characteristics and differences from the traditional knowledge practiced and taught in Egypt during his lifetime. Darraj's presentation "Al-sheikh al-taqlidi wa al-muthaqqaf al-hadith" (The traditional sheikh and the modern intellectual) is based on his reading of Husayn's memoirs,[97] published in three volumes in Cairo in 1929 (volumes 1 and 2) and 1973 (volume 3). These memoirs, entitled *Al-Ayyam* (The days), covered Husayn's childhood in rural Upper Egypt, then his years of study at the Azhar in Cairo, and finally his years in France.[98] In them, Husayn depicted the rural setting he grew up in, city life in Cairo, and the European modernity he discovered in France. One theme that ran through the three volumes was the type of education and knowledge each setting offered him. His primary education was in the traditional religious school of the village, the *kuttab*. In 1902 he entered the Azhar in Cairo to study religion and Arabic. But his years there seem to have been frustrating for him. He complained about the boring teaching methods, the uninteresting curricula, the rote-learning requirement, and the overall poor training and culture of the teachers. In 1908 he joined the newly founded Cairo University. He became its first graduate in 1914, with a thesis on the rationalist freethinker, poet, and philosopher Abu al-'Ala' al-Ma'arri (died 1057). In France he studied at Montpellier and the Sorbonne and graduated with a thesis on Ibn Khaldun (1332–1406) in 1917, becoming the first Egyptian to obtain a doctorate degree in France. Back in Cairo in 1919, he was appointed professor of history at Cairo University. In 1950 he became minister of education, advocating free and universal education for all. His thoughts on knowledge and education articulated in his memoirs constitute the focus of Darraj's essay.

Indeed, in these memoirs Husayn contrasts his different educational experiences in his village *kuttab*, at the Azhar, then at the French universities and describes the nature of modern knowledge he discovered in the process. Darraj draws from Husayn's observations a typology of the traditional sheikh and the modern intellectual in Egypt in the twentieth century, regarding their views of history, the authority they speak with, the sources they refer to, the social group they rely on, and how they relate to that group. The traditional sheikh, notes Darraj, relies on an obedient public, defined as the community of believers, that bestows legitimacy and authority on him, based on the social and institutional role he represents, not on his actual cognitive merits. In this role the sheikh unifies in an authoritarian way the religious and cultural functions in his person. His sources consist of religious texts, and his ultimate reference for a virtuous city (*madina fadila*) is a golden past, in which history had come to total perfection, independently of human will. The modern intellectual, on the other hand, needs to bring a supportive public into existence, by advocating and disseminating literacy—not in the technical sense of reading and writing, but in the wider sense of opening up to knowledge and thought. Society will be civil and democratic, composed of heterogeneous groups—certainly not an elite minority, contrary to what critics of Husayn have often claimed:[99] hence the critical significance of the school reform and of the political will to carry out this reform. For Husayn, the formation of a truly literate public, the school reform necessary for this, and the political will to realize it were all interconnected matters and an integral part of his intellectual and sociopolitical tanwir project.[100] Moreover, the authority of the modern intellectual comes from the quality and validity of knowledge she dispenses, and her understanding of her function is strictly cultural, not religious. Her sources are reality (*al-waqi'*), and history for her is an open possibility; the virtuous city is an objective to be reached by human effort, by a search for the rational human (*al-insan al-'aqil*). The modern intellectual defends the free human (*insan taliq*), who is able to move from a reality that cancels the human to one that submits to human wishes and reason.[101]

For Darraj, Husayn's project stems from the confrontation between these two types of cultural workers, and he clearly sides with the modern one. The confrontation, however, remarks Darraj, is not between science and religion. Husayn's challenging of the religious establishment of his time is based on his discovery of the nature and virtues of modern knowledge. The question for him is not between atheism and faith, but between knowledge and ignorance, between rationality and irrationality. Husayn's negative depiction of the traditional sheikh is not an attack on religion, but an attack on the historical circumstances that produced him: ignorance and backwardness.[102] The emergence of the modern intellectual, adds Darraj, took place at a transitional juncture, Egypt in the first half of the twentieth century, when a secularization process was in the making. Darraj emphasizes the relevance of historical circumstances to the rise of certain types of knowledge and intellectuals. These types were embodied for Husayn in the mosque (*al-jami'*) and the university (*al-jami'a*), as he got to know them: the mosque required sanctification, submission, and passive rote learning; tied language to religion; practiced indoctrination; and transmitted a completed knowledge. The university encouraged discovery, freedom of thought, and the open-endedness of human knowledge. Contrary to the mosque, the university applied a methodology of historical and causal thinking, made room for contradiction and difference, invited questions about origins, acknowledged the universality of human knowledge, encouraged the understanding of the other, and linked knowledge to life and lived realities.[103]

The secularizing context in which Ali Abdel Raziq advocated the separation of religion from politics is also the one in which Husayn advocated the separation of religion from knowledge. But the secularism of that epoch in general was an ambiguous one (*multabis*), writes Darraj, except for some cases, like that of Husayn and Ahmad Lutfi al-Sayyid (1872–1963). Its ambiguity lay in its attempt to reconcile two different logics, that of reason and that of myth, that of science and that of religion. Its conciliatory strategy (*al-tawfiqiyya*) was plagued by an inner contradiction. Science could not be an inner moment of religious awareness, and religion could not be an inner moment of scientific awareness. The ambiguity of that secularism reduced it to a mere encouragement to adopt science and modern technology. Attempts at religious reform, on the other hand, wrongly assumed that revolutionizing religion would lead to a revolutionizing of society. In fact, the impulse for religious reform came, according to Darraj, from the general drive of that epoch for change. In this religious reform of the nahda, the human being and reality took precedence over the religious text and its absolute independence. The text was to be read in light of the changing times; and so the matter was not an abstract opposition between science and faith, as it is viewed nowadays, adds Darraj, in times of defeat and deterioration.[104]

With the socioeconomic and political defeats of the postindependence state, starting with Abdel Nasser's, Husayn's project no longer had societal support, nor could it strive to create that support. In fact, writes Darraj, the postindependence state compensated for its defeats and ensuing loss of legitimacy with traditionalist ideologies and the destruction of rational and democratic forces. This gave rise to the neotraditional sheikh (*al-sheikh al-taqlidi al-jadid*), who had neither the consistency of the old traditional sheikh nor the commitment to modernity of the modern intellectual. The trick of this new sheikh was to overcome the defeat of society with a made-up thought (*fikr talfiqi*), based on a wishful blend of modern ideologies, such as Marxism, and traditional religious beliefs.

As examples of this neotraditional sheikh, Darraj names Egyptian thinkers Hasan Hanafi (born 1935), who tried to merge Marxism with Islam under the label of the "Islamic Left," 'Adel Husayn (1932–2001), who moved from Marxist nationalism to Islamism and advocated the Islamization of knowledge, and Anwar Abdel Malek (1924–2012), who moved toward mixing Arab nationalism with Buddhist theology.[105] In all these cases, writes Darraj, the references have been an amalgam of textual sources disconnected from lived realities.[106] Husayn, on the other hand, emphasized the importance of a thought anchored in life and of an objective knowledge of reality, believing them necessary elements in the production of a civil society. The persistence of the old traditional sheikh and the emergence of the neotraditional sheikh are not to be explained by the lingering cultural legacy (*al-mawruth thaqafi*) or the psychological reservoir of the masses (*al-makhzun al-nafsi li al-jamahir*),[107] but by the nature of the ruling bourgeoisie and its failures.[108] As for Husayn and the modern intellectual he both advocated and embodied, they became, with the deteriorating sociopolitical circumstances, an intellectual type with no model (*muthaqqaf la nasaq lahu*), a stranger with no support.[109]

Egyptian historian Ghali Shukri also criticizes the perpetuation of the conciliatory mode of thinking: the difference between its use during the early nahda and the present time is that while it might have been helpful then, it can no longer be the task of present thought to "conciliate Islam with the present age"; a more revolutionary task is needed. Moreover, studying the sociohistorical aspects of the Islamic tradition might be a commendable endeavor, and underlining the progressive elements of this tradition might be interesting. But this is one thing, and democracy and socialism are another. A progressive interpretation of religion cannot move popular religious ideology to side with progress, but a national progressive program might attract believers to support it.[110] Progressive achievements in the various sectors of society (i.e., a true nahda) are, according to Shukri, the indispensable requirements for tanwir. The latter cannot come from the ruins of the former. And the Arab world has been on a ruinous course for decades.[111]

Darraj concludes his essay by addressing the question of the judiciousness of reclaiming a thought like Husayn's, which has been defeated. He answers by asserting that Husayn's thought was defeated not because of the untenability of its content but by the historical circumstances that did not allow it to develop and take root. In reality, he writes, this thought was more progressive than the "progressive" Nasser regime that eventually destroyed it—a regime that remained traditionalist and believed only the state represented the people and its truth. Only a popular, democratic movement could sustain a project like Husayn's, he adds.[112] Any appropriation of his legacy in the absence of such a movement would be an abstract endeavor estranged from history and reality. To move beyond Husayn's thought, he concludes, one first needs to get acquainted with and accept it.[113]

In his introduction to the fifth issue of *Qadaya wa-shahadat*, Darraj insists on the contextuality of thought:

> The question of thought is the question of the relation of thought to its context [*siaq*]. And if the dominating Arab thought at present is closely related to the domination of the defeated reality [*al-waqi' al-mahzoum*], the domination of the nahda thought in the past was in close relation with an Arab reality that looked for a new horizon, and perhaps what makes the difference between the former and the latter is the attitude toward reality. The first dominating thought affirms the defeated reality and matches [*yatawa'am*] with the givens of the defeat, whereas the nahda thought rejected reality and searched for a sociocultural project that offers a new horizon.[114]

Is Darraj reducing thought, particularly tanwir thought, to sociocultural and political circumstances? Moreover, is he reducing tanwir to political mobilization? His argument is that to understand the gist of nahda/tanwir thought, or of any thought, one needs to set it in its context. Otherwise, one is left with unclear abstract concepts: unclear not because abstract but because unsituated, and hence truncated and imprecise. Such concepts would lead to futile discussions about absolute opposites such as religion versus science, or Islam versus democracy, which Arabs have often put themselves in. Once the concepts are contextually grasped, then one can elaborate on them for more conceptual precision. It is with this contextual approach that Darraj went on defending nahda and tanwir in the late 1990s.

In "Difa'an 'an al-fikr al-'arabi: Fikr al-tanwir bayna al-naqd wa al-tazwir" (In defense of Arab tanwir thought: Tanwir between criticism and vilification), published in 1997, Darraj affirms that Arab tanwir thought (meaning nahda thought) was never a thought for the sake of thought, walled in closed circles, but was from the beginning engaged with concrete realities, confronting oppressors and the powers that be (al-sulta). The present-day thought, he adds, avoids such confrontations, not only because it lacks a genuinely critical edge, but also because it mistakes those powers that fight Islamist obscurantism for tanwir powers. It misses the fact that the obscurantism is produced and sustained by those powers, that the two are of the same nature, and that their opposition is one over power, not thought. People, on the other hand, resort to religion to make their miserable lives under Arab regimes bearable, in an atmosphere of ignorance, hunger, defeat, and injustice caused by the regimes and then exploited by religious obscurantism.[115]

The nahda had its own myths, Darraj admits, but they were noble ones. Its ideas and actions were premised on humanistic assumptions about the equality of humans and the capacity to carry out a sociocultural and political project that ensures the humanity of all. It looked at social reality as something that can be changed, and it perceived intellectuals as important contributors to this change, not in the sense of a class distinction, but rather in the sense of having a particular responsibility. Liberating minds and establishing democratic rule were an integral part of this project. In this sense, he writes, the nationalism or patriotism of this tanwir thought lay precisely in its enlightening project (wa bi hadha al-ma'na, fa inna wataniyyat al-fikr al-tanwiri taqum fi istinaratihi).[116] The nahda tanwir connected with the actual issues of the homeland, the society, and the human, not with the alleged eternal "Arab mind" (al-'aql al-arabi), the empty rhetoric of a national soul (ruh al-umma), or some scholastic bases of knowledge removed from reality (qawa'id al-ma'rifa), as most Arab thought does today.[117] Arab nationalism and socialism relinquished those tanwir components, primarily humanism and historicity, and by doing so defeated themselves. In other words, those ideologies defeated tanwir, and the defeat of tanwir defeated them in turn. There can be no defense of nationalism and socialism without a defense of tanwir.[118]

According to Darraj, the failure to appreciate the content, value, and importance of tanwir is a sign of the troubled present age. Burhan Ghalioun, by imputing the present misery to the nahda modernity adopted by the regimes, misses the fact that modernity was never thoroughly adopted, and that partial attempts to do so, including Abdel Nasser's attempt, were foiled by the West. More importantly, the priority of modern Arab thought was never grabbing power, in the sense of monopolistic state power, but rather the moral rise of state and society toward the "excellent human," to use Husayn's term (*al-insan al-mumtaz*). Along the same lines, when Jamal Barut sees the present gap between a secular-modern elite and a Muslim nation, he forgets that Arab nahda tanwir was never secular in a European sense, that it never ignored or rejected Islam, and that it rather called for its reform—a reform that would allow Islam to speak to people's present lives. Muhammad Imarah, on the other hand, after seeing likeable Marxist and then nationalist features in the nahda, turned against it in the name of Islamism and equated thought with religious identity.[119] All these skewed and failed readings of the nahda tanwir indicate for Darraj the poverty and misery of the present thought. The point, however, is not to bring back the nahda as it was. Times have changed, he writes. Nor is it possible to idealize the nahda, for it was, according to him, far from flawless. In fact, Darraj directs three main criticisms at the tanwiri intellectuals: a certain teleological view of history (*mafhum gha'i li al-tarikh*), meaning an overly optimistic view of progress; too great a faith in the power of knowledge (*quwwat al-ma'rifa*), meaning too much focus on the dissemination of ideas and not enough attention to the social conditions necessary for spreading tanwir; and confusion about the difference between a point of view and a theory (*al-khalt bayn wujhat al-nadhar wa al-nadhariyya*), or a sense of certainty about possessing the truth. The last phenomenon is particularly manifest in nationalism and Marxism, and their belief in the inexorable victory of "the nation" or "the working class."[120] But Darraj distinguishes a legitimate and necessary critique (*naqd*) of tanwir from derision (*hija'*). Going back to the nahda is impossible, but for him it represents a moral and cognitive moment (*lahdha akhlaqiyya wa ma'rifiyya ma'an*), and as such a valuable and inspiring moment in Arab history.[121]

Apart from this moral and cognitive moment, writes Darraj, it is not possible to speak of the nahda as a firmly shaped epoch defined in terms of deep societal transformations. One can speak of impulses toward such transformations, but these impulses did not have the time to develop into full-fledged historical changes.[122] When contemporary thinkers assess the nahda, they do not take this fact into consideration, and read the ideas of the nahdawis independently of their historical circumstances. The complaint about the failure of the nahda to make an epistemological break (*qat' ma'rifi*) assumes a bookish, intellectualist conception of such a break, without due attention to its societal requirements.[123] There was a time, he adds, when innovators such as Husayn and Abdallah al-Nadim (1843–1896) could find popular support when attacked by conservative forces. This support waned quickly under the growing authoritarian pressure of the postindependent state.[124] The intellectualist view of the nahda and the tanwir is a fallacy that even thinkers such as Gaber Asfour fell for, though he otherwise grasped tanwir quite well, in Darraj's opinion.[125] It is also the fallacy of Adonis, who essentializes the "Arab mind" and looks at the nahda as yet another manifestation of that mind's incapacity to be creative and rebel. Moreover, Adonis sees the present state of Arab culture as a result of the realization of the nahda, while Husayn lamented its failure.[126] Darraj sees in this opposition the difference between a thought (Husayn's) that developed in the nahda's ascendant moment and one (Adonis's) that grew in its moment of defeat.[127] Yet they both called for a rebellion against certainties and championed freethinking.[128] Nasr Hamid Abu Zayd agrees with Darraj that the sociopolitical context should be central in evaluating the nahda and the tanwir endeavors. Like him, Abu Zayd thinks that the 1967 defeat significantly impacted the nature and effectiveness of those endeavors. It left the tanwir intellectual isolated, with no sociopolitical support, caught between the West and the Arab-Islamic past, and threatened by growing conservative public opinion. People were looking for an identity that could provide them with a sense of psychological security in the midst of the general collapse. That identity was religious tradition. This atmosphere accentuated the taboo nature of that tradition and made it even more difficult for the intellectual to analyze it in a critical, historicizing manner. But without such an analysis, no tanwir is possible, according to Abu Zayd.[129]

In 2004 Darraj participated in "Hasilat al-'Aqlaniyya wa al-tanwir fi al-fikr al-arabi al-mu'asir" (The harvest of rationalism and enlightenment in contemporary Arab thought), a pan-Arab conference organized in Beirut by the Center for Arab Unity Studies. In his paper, "Fi ma'na al-tanwir" (The meaning of tanwir), Darraj reiterated his main views on the nahda tanwir. The participants came from Egypt, Iraq, Jordan, Kuwait, Lebanon, Morocco, Palestine, the Sudan, Syria, and Tunisia. The papers, comments, and discussions were published in a 2005 volume.[130] Suffice it to say, the main discussant of Darraj's paper was Muhammad Salim al-'Awa (born 1942), a prominent Egyptian Islamist and at the time secretary-general of the world union of Muslim ulamas. 'Awa disagreed with Darraj's designation of the nahda as "tanwir," saying that he would rather call it *"nahda"* ("rise" or "renaissance") or *"islah"* (reform), because according to him, the main gist of the nahda movement was to revive the Arab-Islamic nation and reconnect it with its religious origins. 'Awa deplored the fact that Darraj had omitted the main revival movements from his account of the period: the Salafi-Wahhabi movement, founded by Muhammad bin Abdul Wahhab (1703–1792); the Sanousi movement in Libya, founded by Muhammad bin Ali al-Sanousi (1787–1859); and the Mahdi movement in the Sudan, founded by Muhammad Ahmad bin Abdullah al-Haj, known as the Mahdi (1843–1885). As for the work of Jamal el-Din al-Afghani, Khayr al-Din al-Tunisi, Muhammad Abduh, and al-Kawakibi, presented in the customary tanwir discourse as among the main figures of the nahda, he thought they were in reality figures of an Islamic renewal project (*mashru' tajdidi*). Finally, he rejected Darraj's pessimistic view of the harvest of the nahda movement.[131] Clearly, 'Awa's comments are reminiscent of those of his fellow Islamist Muhammad Imarah on the Egyptian tanwir discourse: they connect the discussion of tanwir to that of the identity of the nahda, as well as to identity in general, defending the Islamic nature of both.

At the end of this review of Wannous's and Darraj's thoughts on tanwir, what characteristics of the Sisyphean moment in the Syrian tanwir debate can be identified? Three main topics seem to dominate the debate: first, the wide-ranging destruction (*al-kharab al-shamil*) and the urgent need for the reconstruction of the human (*bina' al-insan*); second, the prominence of the idea of civil society as an indispensable agent of reconstruction; and third, the importance of reengaging in politics. Indeed, after the regime's systematic brutalization (*tawahhush*), a Syrian finds herself in a society torn apart and a country devastated. Understandably, the emphasis of tanwir here is less on the disenchantment of the world than on its rehumanization. Moreover, rebuilding and reactivating civil society is seen as the way to engage in a public debate about the country's economy, politics, education, health care, civic life, and sectarian tensions. Finally, individual and collective involvement in the res publica is called upon after the disappearing of the people (*taghyib al-sha'b*) and the confiscation of political life (*musadarat al-hayat al-siyasiyya*) by the autocratic ruling circle. During the 1990s, it was clear to all participants of the debate that no margin of action was available and that any move to act on any of these concerns was doomed. But as soon as an opportunity for action arose with the founding dictator's death, people convened to organize debates around issues of public concern, including the need for economic and political reform; they formed associations, issued public declarations, and mobilized themselves for public matters. By doing so, they expressed their need to reclaim their humanity and citizenship. Many of the participants in the Sisyphean debate became active participants in the Promethean moment, starting with the elderly Antoun Maqdisi, who in August 2000 wrote an open letter to the new president and inaugurated one of the main discussion fora that opened that summer, with a speech on the necessity of civil society. Other participants from the Sisyphean moment, such as Sadeq Jalal al-Azm, Abdulrazzaq Eid, Burhan Ghalioun, Michel Kilo, Mamdouh Adwan, Tayyeb Tizini, and Faysal Darraj, translated the ideas of the 1990s into concrete steps by formulating public statements and manifestos; by joining meetings to discuss, formulate, and sign declarations; by giving talks at the various fora; by writing for the media about their activities; and by getting involved in exchanges with the opposition or even the regime.

That window of opportunity did not last long before it was shut down with the old repressive methods, indicating that the regime's nature persisted, despite the new president's promises of change. This short "spring" led up toward the end of the 2000s to the outbreak of the Syrian revolution in March 2011. The thematic continuity between the debates of the 1990s and those of the early 2000s makes them part of the same tanwir endeavor, even if the term *tanwir* appeared less frequently in the 2000s debates. This is probably due to the fact that in this second moment, the primary concern was no longer theoretical and the priority was no longer the reconstitution of a dismembered intellectual, moral, and political memory. The urgent drive was to seize the long-awaited opportunity to act on matters that had crystallized in the Sisyphean moment. However, the ideas and ideals of the 1990s tanwir, as we shall see, continued to serve as the ground for actions proposed and analyses offered. Those ideas would also be present in the demands of the 2011 rebels for freedom and humanity. While the tanwir discourses of the 2000s in Egypt denounced those of the 1990s, the discourses in Syria moved on a continuous line from the theoretical to the more practical. In both cases, the two decades led to an outbreak of unprecedented mass protests demanding human dignity, freedom, and political participation—three demands that were at the heart of tanwir in both countries.

FOUR

Tanwir and the Damascus Spring at the Turn of the Millennium

The Promethean Moment

The First Decade of Bashar al-Assad's Presidency, 2000–2010

THE PROMETHEAN MOMENT was prompted by the passing of Hafiz al-Assad after thirty years of personalized rule. Hafiz had carefully prepared for his son's succession and made sure that the system he had built would persist after him. Yet his death inevitably heralded the end of an era, and it was obvious that a transition phase had started. No matter how well the succession had been planned, people felt that things were somehow bound to change, without being able to predict the nature and extent of the change. The personality that Hafiz al-Assad projected would not be easy to replace, and the regime he had established was to a great extent his own creation.

But changes had already started to take place in the last decade of Hafiz al-Assad's rule. Indeed, he had begun to evoke the need for change himself in the early 1990s. After the collapse of the Soviet Union and the transformations in Eastern Europe and Latin America, he felt the need to affirm the stability of his rule, which he claimed was based on the democratic nature of his regime, adding that Syria had its own style of democracy in line with its own history, culture, and circumstances. However, he also called for more inclusiveness in representation, encouraging and allowing some independent candidates to participate in the 1990 elections. He repeatedly demanded that authorities curb corruption and improve legal services. He released large numbers of prisoners, while keeping freedom of speech in check. However, the more pressing need for change came from the ailing economy. The public sector had failed to generate capital, and too many public funds went into financing the many intelligence and security agencies. Funds were also used to provide state benefits in terms of jobs, patronage, and subsidies. Private capital had fled the country and was discouraged from returning by the scale of corruption and the absence of legal guarantees for making investments. Aid from the Arabian Gulf countries and the Soviet Union had secured some rents to the state independently from society. But in the late 1980s the economic crisis became aggravated, and the state had to cut social benefits and shrink the public sector, leaving large sectors of society in dire need. Strict import limitations were imposed, causing a huge smuggling business to develop, primarily in the hands of the army and security agents.

Some measure of economic liberalization from overwhelming state control had become necessary. Hafiz al-Assad wanted to make sure this liberalization did not entail a political liberalization leading to a democratization process. He went for a "calculated decompression as a substitute for democratization," in the words of political scientist Raymond Hinnebusch.[1] This calculated decompression consisted in granting some room for private capital, including diaspora money, to operate, while controlling the bourgeois civil society it would bring about. But Assad's maneuver, according to Hinnebusch, was bound by the very structures he had put in place: a Bonapartist state led in an authoritarian way, with military support and anti-elitist, conservative rhetoric co-opting the demands of the popular classes. The Baath Party, for instance—which catered to a vast constituency, including peasants, students, public employees, and workers, who depended on statist policies and investments—could not be turned into a party of businessmen without causing mass discontent. The new bourgeoisie, composed of the military (mainly Alawi high officers) and urban merchants (mainly Sunnis), depended on the regime's support and network for its earnings. Moreover, some tensions seemed to have developed in this collaboration: the sons of those in power (*awlad al-sulta*) felt at some point empowered to take the lion's share of the business, to the detriment of the merchants; the middle merchants, on the other hand, had managed to keep some form of autonomy from the state.[2] The intelligentsia was incorporated into state-controlled unions and hence did not form an independent political force. The traditional civil society of the souk preserved its autonomy to some extent, but its political inclinations went toward political Islam, which was not tolerated. In this socioeconomic and political landscape, little room was left for private economic initiatives, and little chance for sociopolitical autonomy outside state control. The challenge for Assad was to keep this state of affairs while encouraging the much-needed private economic revival. The result was some softening of authoritarianism while keeping the repressive apparatus ready against any transgression.

What the new president, Bashar al-Assad, did during the first half of his presidential term, according to Volker Perthes, was modernize authoritarianism, and not modernize tout court, as some of Assad's early statements might have suggested. Modernizing authoritarianism amounted to rejuvenating the administrative and political elite, giving more importance to technological skills, and lending authoritarianism a more institutionalized form, with appearances of rational and due process. Assad cautiously encouraged pluralism, in the media and in political formations, but made clear that this pluralism was strongly controlled. He prioritized economic modernization, however, with the least amount of risk for his political power.[3] In 2005 he advocated a form of "socialist market economy" that looked more like the Chinese model: an economy governed by neoliberal policies, with no concern for social safety nets and no fair redistribution, with ongoing political authoritarianism, and with little, if any, prospect for democratization.[4]

In a seminal essay, "Upgrading Authoritarianism in the Arab World," political scientist Steven Heydemann showed that a number of Arab regimes, including those of Algeria, Egypt, Jordan, Morocco, Syria, and Tunisia, had managed to absorb their peoples' growing demands for political representation, economic opportunities, rights, and liberties by "upgrading" their authoritarianism through a process of "authoritarian learning."[5] In this way, they had managed to resist those demands and preserve and even consolidate their own power. The key features of this authoritarian upgrading were appropriating and containing civil societies, managing political contestation, capturing the benefits of selective economic reforms, controlling new communication technologies, and diversifying international linkages. Together with fellow political scientist Reinoud Leenders, Heydemann showed how this learning had proved effective in helping regimes react to the uprisings and counter the learning process of the people, who had learned to mobilize and voice their demands despite despotic conditions.

Regime learning was obviously strengthened by states' willingness to use violence against their own populations.[6] On the basis of this analysis, Heydemann predicted in 2013 that the Syrian regime would emerge even more authoritarian from the conflict, contrary to analyses that expected civil war to annihilate authoritarian state structures.[7]

In "Syria: From 'Authoritarian Upgrading' to Revolution?" Hinnebusch argued that an unbalanced authoritarian upgrading might have led to the outbreak of the revolution. He showed that Bashar al-Assad, by wanting to rejuvenate the elite, especially in the Baath Party, had let go of those who for years had established the clientelist system of patronage and instead bonded large sectors of society, particularly in the rural areas, to the regime. By carrying out neoliberal policies without paying attention to equitable distribution, and by privatizing the public sector instead of reforming it, he had jettisoned the social base of the regime. Through the change of guard, he had also narrowed the base of the ruling clan to his family circle. On the other hand, he had not allowed a political formation to emerge in support of the neoliberal transformations.[8] Carsten Wieland wrote of a "decade of lost chances" in describing the first ten years of Bashar al-Assad's rule, particularly regarding the chances he missed to react positively to the civil society opposition movement. Wieland deplored the three waves of repression Assad used against that movement, at the beginning, in the middle, and toward the end of the decade. Assad's unwillingness to meet at least some of the movement's demands led, in his opinion, to the 2011 explosion.[9]

In addition to the need to adjust to economic pressures and secular political demands, the Assad regime had to address its relation to Sunni religious organizations, and for two reasons: first to uplift its religious legitimacy among the Sunni majority, especially after the brutal repression of the Muslim Brotherhood in the 1980s; and second, to deal with growing poverty, caused by economic liberalization and the reduction in public social benefits, by relying on the charity work of religious organizations. Since the beginning of Assad rule in 1970, the regime had shown no interest in training a state clergy; instead, it had co-opted regime-friendly clerics and fought the others. It had increasingly tolerated nonpoliticized, pietistic religious organizations, such as Qubaysiyyat, popular among upper-class Sunni women, and Zayd, popular among the urban merchants. Both organizations affirmed Sunni identity against the ruling Alawi one, but without stepping into political action, at least not then and not directly. The

Assad regime had found it expedient since the 1990s to tolerate and collaborate with such organizations, without, however, being able to co-opt them, given their substantial autonomy.[10] It has had to rely on their charity assistance, especially the Zayd movement's, which tapped into the resources of the merchant class in big cities, especially Damascus, and offered relief and education services through a vast grassroots network. For Thomas Pierret and Kjetil Selvik, the autonomy of these organizations limited the Syrian state's "authoritarian upgrading."[11]

The "modern" image projected by the new president and his wife was welcomed by Syria's Christian minority. This image affirmed in their eyes the secular character of the regime, which despite its many shortcomings considered them citizens, not Christians tolerated and "protected" by a Muslim majority, as was the case in most of the region. On the other hand, the Assad regime, particularly under Bashar, prided itself on this inclusiveness and saw in the Christian minority's loyalty a confirmation of its secular and modern image. Comparing their own situation to that of other Christians in the Arab world, Syrian Christians had real reasons to believe they were safer under the regime. In Egypt, Copts were discriminated against and often exposed to various forms of aggression; Lebanese and Iraqi Christians were victims of civil war conflict, often targeted as Christians, and threatened by waves of dispossession, deportation, and killings.[12] While such waves also affected other religious communities in Lebanon and Iraq, they endangered the existence of the relatively small numbers of Christians.[13] Syrian Christians felt most menaced by Islamist forces, and so they felt that Assad's regime ensured their existence, physical as well as religious and cultural. Given this set of priorities, they were ready to forgo political rights and put up with authoritarianism. In this sense, argues anthropologist Andreas Bandak, their allegiance to the regime was not "as if," as Lisa Wedeen argued was the case for the largely Sunni majority, but instead "as is."[14]

But the Christian minority was not the only group ready to forgo political rights for other things. Wedeen argues that a certain sector of urban society felt attracted to a model of the good life, an affluent and modern life, inspired to some extent by the image of the presidential couple, and promised by the neoliberal prospects of social mobility. For these people, social liberties and economic opportunities were more important than political liberties. They were not ready to shake up the system for democracy. But then they had to reconcile their aspirations with the system's coercive control.[15] The tensions that such choices entailed were also seen in the cultural sector under the new president and with the new, limited liberalization policies.

The first cultural censorship organ, Al-irshad al-qawmi (National Guidance), was established in Syria in 1959. In the 1960s and 1970s, culture and art were to be socially useful to the nation and follow social realist guidelines. Censorship became harsher starting in the 1980s, with the wave of repression, until the relative loosening of control in the late 1990s. Culture, like the economy, was opened up for privatization; and as in the economy, the new entrepreneurs were people from, or close to, the regime. Still, some small enclaves of independent culture emerged, though the general red lines of the regime remained in force.[16] One of the booming sectors in Syrian culture at the turn of the millennium was television drama. Syrian private producers as well as rich Arabian Gulf investors poured money into the television industry. Many Syrian television series became successful and even more popular than well-established Egyptian ones. This implied a double influence on the style and content of drama: an influence from the Gulf, with its more conservative and religious social values, and an influence from the regime, through its private producers and its own direct and indirect guidance. The regime red lines became more blurred, and it became more difficult to grasp the rules of the game, except for the more obvious ones regarding the well-known taboos on religion, sex, and high politics. Gulf influence was easier to fathom, but not always easy to reconcile with the interests of the Syrian public. However, artists still had room to maneuver around those lines.

The regime wished to use television drama to represent its reform guidelines, and in this sense to enlighten the masses, by addressing sensitive issues such as religious fanaticism, gender, the intelligence services, and corruption, including the complicity of the people, and by showing them how to think about these matters. Some of the best drama directors were interested in a more incisive cultural and political critique. They sometimes got away with incisive critique, as in the famous series *Buq'at daw'*, directed by Layth Hajju. This required great subtlety and caution,[17] but it showed that even with the political agendas of the regime and private producers, artists could struggle for goals of their own. Sometimes those agendas and goals intersected, as in social critique and tanwir, often in the elitist sense of "enlightening the masses" about the way forward.[18]

While these transformations were taking place on the domestic level, Syria witnessed three external events that were to impact it in many ways. First, the September 11 attacks in the United States deflected attention from Syrian events in the international media and thus deprived the Syrian opposition of support; on the other hand, they gave Syria a new role in the fight against terrorism on the world scene. Second, the 2003 invasion of Iraq by the United States and its allies destroyed Iraq's infrastructure, destabilized its society, and exacerbated its religious tensions. The invasion created chaos, with violent repercussions across the region. For Syria, it meant the fear of invasion and the imperative of closing ranks against divisions that could weaken it in the face of such a menace. In times of national peril such as this one, the regime could equate dissidence with treason. The opposition, on the other hand, could argue even more strongly for the urgency of democratic reforms that would bring about unity between the people and the government in the event of such an attack. Third, the 2005 assassination of Lebanese prime minister Rafik Hariri in a Beirut car bombing, when Lebanon was still under tight Syrian control, provoked worldwide outrage. An international tribunal was established, with the Syrian regime as its prime suspect. Syria had to withdraw its troops from Lebanon after thirty years of hegemony in the country. The withdrawal had political, military, and economic consequences for the Syrian regime, not least political isolation on the international scene. Yet the regime managed to weather these crises and pull itself out of isolation again.[19] It continued to consolidate its internal power and ignore opposition demands until the outbreak of the Syrian revolution, which changed the destiny of the regime, the opposition, and the Syrian people.

This is in brief the decade during which Syrian militants struggled for civil society, democracy, and political reform. Our focus next will be on the first two years of that decade, during which the short Damascus Spring unfolded.

The Promethean Damascus Spring and Its Demise: Civil Society and Tanwir, 2000–2001

The Damascus Spring time frame runs from Bashar al-Assad's inauguration speech on July 17, 2000, to the arrest of prominent activists in

September 2001. Their trials followed in summer 2002.[20] The three main collections that document the activities of the period are Ridwan Ziadeh, ed., *Hiwarat "Muntada al-Hiwar al-watani"* (The dialogues of the "National Dialogue Forum"), which contains the eleven talks delivered at the National Dialogue Forum, established by prominent oppositional figure Riad Seif, and the discussions that followed them, in addition to some of the main declarations; Abdulrazzaq Eid, ed., *Yas'alunak 'an al-mujtama' al-madani: "Rabi' dimashq al-maw'ud* (They ask you about civil society: The buried Damascus Spring), which comprises many of the polemical newspaper pieces written around Eid's positions in the movement; and finally, Muhammad Jamal Barut and Shamsuddin al-Kilani, eds., *Suria bayn 'ahdayn: Qadaya al-marhala al-intiqaliyya* (Syria between two epochs: Issues of the transition phase) from 2003, the most comprehensive of the three sources, with pieces from the opposition and the regime.[21] Each collection includes an informative introduction about the activities and their context. The standard English references about the movement are Alan George's *Syria: Neither Bread nor Freedom* (containing some of the declarations translated into English) and Carsten Wieland's *A Decade of Lost Chances: Repression and Revolution from Damascus Spring to Arab Spring*.[22] The two main fora of this period's debates were the National Dialogue Forum and the Jamal al-Atassi Forum (Muntada Jamal al-Atassi), the second of which was run by Suhair al-Atassi (whose father, Jamal al-Atassi [1922–2000], was a prominent Syrian Arab Nationalist politician and one of the earliest leading members of the Baath Party). The principal leading figures of the movement were Michel Kilo, Riad Seif, and Riad al-Turk. In examining some of the speeches and writings of the Damascus Spring, our purpose is to capture the main ideas of the debates and compare them with those of the 1990s debates.

The public outing of the opposition in this transitional phase of the Assad regime entailed a confrontation in which both sides had to make careful calculations. Moves had to take into consideration uncertainties about the other side, at a time when strategies were tentative, parties were testing each other, and stand offs were to be avoided, especially by the weaker party, the opposition. Moreover, in each camp there were disagreements on judicious tactics, the degree of potentially fruitful provocation, and the measure of risk to be taken. The result was contradictory signals of rigidity and openness, escalation and appeasement. The opposition wanted to reassure the regime that its demand was for gradual reform that would not imperil the country, while at the same time stressing the urgency of reform and political participation. The regime, on the other hand, wanted to preserve a facade of reform and modernization for as long as it could without putting its own power in peril. But it was no longer clear how many decision makers there were in the regime, and who among them had the upper hand. Between Bashar al-Assad's election on July 10, 2000, his July 17 inaugural speech, and the wave of arrests in August and September 2001, events began to accelerate.[23] In October 2000 the new president released some six hundred political prisoners. In January 2001 he permitted the publication of independent newspapers, among them *Al-Doumari*, published by the famous Syrian caricaturist Ali Farzat. The permit was revoked in 2003.[24] The government approved a law for the establishment of private banks, and the information minister announced that martial law was suspended. In February 2001 the regime started to curb the activities of the opposition by imposing forbidding conditions for the organization of talks in the newly opened fora. Debate fora were not limited to Damascus but were also opened in Homs, Hasakeh, Qamishli, Aleppo, and Tartous.[25] In the same month Vice President Abdul Halim Khaddam addressed the faculty of Damascus University, warning against the opposition's course, which would in his opinion lead Syria to the fate of Algeria or Yugoslavia.[26]

The opposition undertook bold moves soon after the presidential election. In mid-August Antoun Maqdisi sent an open letter to the president, and Riad al-Turk published critical articles in *al-Hayat* and the cultural supplement of *an-Nahar*, with more to follow in the coming months, along with a few satellite television talk show appearances. In mid-September Seif announced the opening of the National Dialogue Forum in his home, and later in the month *Bayan al-99* (Manifesto of the 99) was published by Friends of Civil Society; it was followed by *Bayan al-1000* (Manifesto of the 1000) in January 2001, which elaborated on its themes, and *Tawafuqat wataniyya 'amma* (General national common-ground declaration) in April 2001.[27] The main demands of these declarations were for the cessation of the emergency laws, the release of all political prisoners, and the establishment of the rule of law, liberties, and political pluralism. In January 2001 Syrian lawyers addressed an open letter to the president asking for the rule of law and a revision of the constitution.[28] In mid-January the opening of the Jamal al-Atassi Forum, for debates independent from political parties, was announced. At the end of January Seif announced his intention to found a political movement called the Social Peace Movement (Harak al-silm al-ijtima'i) and presented its program for discussion in his forum.[29] In March 2001 the Muslim Brotherhood published a basic national honor agreement (*mithaq sharaf watani*) from London, seeking peaceful cooperation with the opposition and the regime under political pluralism.[30] In July 2001 activists held a meeting in Damascus at which they announced the formation of a human rights organization and elected Haytham el-Mallah as its president.[31] In May 2001 Seif openly criticized the regime's corrupt cell phone deal and in August published a detailed study of it. The regime received all of these moves with increasing suspicion and ultimately outright hostility, leading up to the arrests of the principal opposition figures in summer 2001. The arrested included Anwar al-Bunni, Walid al-Bunni, Kamal al-Labwani, Riad al-Turk, Aref Dalila, Ma'mun el-Homsi, Habib Issa, Hasan Sa'dun, Habib Saleh, and Fawwaz Tello. The last arrests were on September 11, 2001. The September 11 attacks robbed the opposition of international attention at a critical juncture in its confrontation with the regime. In what follows, we will focus on some of the most important documents that shaped the opposition's moves.

Ridwan Ziadeh, a Syrian human rights activist and scholar, prefaces the National Dialogue Forum's collected essays (*Muntada al-hiwar al-watani*) with a brief history of the forum and its initiator, Riad Seif, entitled "Muntada al-hiwar al-watani: Al-takwin al-ijtima'i wa al-hirak al-siyasi" (The National Dialogue Forum: Social formation and political action).[32] It begins with Seif's parliamentary election campaign toward the end of 1998, during which he organized open gatherings to discuss sociopolitical, legal, economic, and environmental matters. This was made possible by the previous president's encouragement of change.[33] With the appointment of a new prime minister in March 2000 and the condemnation of the previous one for corruption and mismanagement, people felt emboldened to talk about politics, according to Ziadeh. A group of intellectuals had started to meet to discuss the pressing need for change. The first meeting was in the home of Syrian filmmaker Nabil el-Maleh in Damascus in late May 2000.[34] Seif joined the meetings, and in September 2000 he approached Vice President Khaddam for a license to transform the gathering into an official association. The vice president declined and asked him to wait for the upcoming law of associations and political parties. In mid-September Seif launched his dialogue forum and sent out invitations quoting the new president's call for inclusiveness in the development of society from his inaugural speech. The talks given in the forum addressed three major themes: civil society, the economy, and legal rights. Antoun Maqdisi gave the first talk, on the necessity of civil society ("Darurat al-mujtama' al-madani"), followed by a talk by Ahmad Barqawi on civil society in the context of the development of state and society ("Al-mujtama' al-madani fi itar tatawur al-dawla wa al-mujtama' "), then one by Muhammad Said al-Halabi on the role of social organizations in development ("Dawr al-jam'iyyat al-ahliyya fi al-tanmiya"), and finally, one by Muhammad Jamal Barut on the problems of Arab social organization in the context of globalization ("Mushkilat al-jam'iyyat al-ahliyya al-arabiyya fi itar al-'awlama"). Three papers were presented about the economy: Muhammad Riad al-Abrash's "Muhawalat al-islah al-iqtisadi fi suria: Al-haqiqa al-da'i'a ma bayn al-hilm wa al-haqiqa" (Attempts at economic reform in Syria: The lost truth between the dream and the illusion), Aref Dalila's "Mutatallibat al-islah allati yatrahuha waqi' wa mushkilat qita' al-tijara al-kharijiyya" (The reform requirements raised by the reality and problems of the external trade sector), and Seif's "Kayfa nabni iqtisadan wataniyya?" (How do we build a national economy?). They were followed by three papers on legal rights: Shibli al-Shami's "Haq al-qawl" (The right to speak), Youssef Salameh's "Al-islah al-siyasi: Ma'nah wa hududuhu" (Political reform: Its meaning and limits), and Ziadeh's "Al-ma'zaq al-siyasi wa ishkaliyyat al-ta'aththur al-dimuqrati fi suria" (The political deadlock and the problematic of democratic blockage in Syria).

According to Ziadeh, the talks were well attended, even by the younger generation. They soon started to get local and international press coverage. The attendees included Baath Party members, who were given the floor to express their views. This was meant to demonstrate a will for inclusive national dialogue. Encouraged by the momentum, in late January 2001 Seif announced his new Social Peace Movement. He presented its program in the forum, where it was discussed over two days. All this raised the suspicion of the regime and led it to promulgate a new regulation, demanding that permission for each talk be applied for, including the title of the talk, the name of the speaker, the list of invitees, and so on, which made fora activities practically impossible. Seif was then summoned to appear before a judge to explain his movement. Seif stepped back and applied instead for a permit for his forum from the Ministry of Social Affairs, which was not acknowledged. In July 2001 Seif announced the resumption of forum activities, and in early September Burhan Ghalioun flew from Paris to give a talk, "*Mustaqbal al-islah wa al-taghyir fi suria: Nahu ʿaqd watani jadid*" (The future of reform and change in Syria: Toward a new national contract). Ziadeh recalls that over five hundred people attended the event. The talk was firm but at the same time moderate in its formulation, avoiding unnecessary provocations toward the regime. The discussion that followed was apparently very animated, with attendees from the regime and the opposition hugging at the end. Yet the next day, instead of being rewarded for facilitating such an encounter, Seif was arrested. It is important to note here that a few months earlier, in May 2001, Seif had denounced the cell phone deal. In response to Seif's arrest, fourteen dialogue fora convened in his house and issued a protest statement.[35]

Riad Seif (born 1946), a self-made industrialist, joined the Syrian parliament in 1994 and quickly became an outspoken critic of corruption and the mismanagement of the economy. Retaliation came in the form of a smear campaign and an accusation of tax evasion, which led to his bankruptcy but not yet to his political demise. He won a parliamentary seat again in 1998 and denounced a cell-phone deal arranged for the president's family that was detrimental to the state. The deal passed, and he was arrested and sentenced to five years in jail. His fellow independent parliamentarians, economics professor Aref Dalila (born 1942) and Ma'mun al-Homsi, a lawyer, also ended up in jail, for publicly critiquing the regime and demanding reform and constitutional law. But the formal accusations never mentioned their denunciations of the regime's corruption or their demand for genuine rule of law and democracy. Most arrested activists were accused of wanting to change the constitution in illegal ways, of spreading lies that weakened the resolve of the nation in a time of war, and of preventing state institutions from implementing their tasks. After the 2011 uprising Seif fled the country to Berlin, and in 2016 he was elected head of the National Coalition for Syrian Revolutionary and Opposition Forces (Al-I'tilaf al-watani li qiwa al-thawra wa al-mu'arada al-suriyya).

Antoun Maqdisi gave the first National Dialogue Forum talk on September 13, 2000. A month earlier, on August 14, Maqdisi had issued one of the first public addresses to the newly elected president, in the form of an open letter published in London in the Saudi-owned pan-Arab daily *al-Hayat*. It deserves to be quoted in full:

To Mr. President Doctor Bashar al-Asad,
President of the Arab Syrian Republic,

I allow myself to congratulate you for the first presidency, and also for the truly promising words that came in your announcement (respect for other opinions, priority to the state point of view instead of that of the leadership . . .), and for the measures that you took and implemented: cancellation of publicity, forbidding of marches, closing down of reception gatherings [in honor of the elected president]. . . . It is the beginning of a long path, which if we take, could take us gradually from bedouinism and tribal rule to the rule of law and the entry in the twenty-first century. We have had enough oh Sir of pompous words: gains of the people, achievements of the people, will of the people. *The people have been absent, oh Sir, for a long time,* their paralyzed will aims at two tasks today: on the private level, *working day and night to insure bread for their children,* and on the public level, *saying what they are asked to say, and behaving the way they are asked to behave (marches, slogans . . .).* What holds this people back from destruction is the fact that they live with this bad situation as with *a chronic disease.* Perhaps this people started to sense their existence in the mid-forties, after a long struggle against the foreigners, but soon after that the military putsches followed one another, and all that was left to them was to return to their cocoon, *waiting for orders. . . . The general situation, briefly, oh Sir: general collapse, political and economic and also cultural and human.* Maybe in the seventies, after the disaster of 1967, and after the collapse of the tribal structures, Syria needed a strong rule that would bring people together, but today, as you said Sir, we are in the twenty-first century. What the people need first and foremost is to regain confidence in themselves and in their government—and the two are one—and this is not an easy thing. It might need years of taking the other's opinion into consideration, as you said, and then it could gradually move from a state of subjection to the state of citizenship. I wish you, Sir, success on a path full of dangers of all kinds.

Please accept my utmost respect,
Antoun Maqdisi.[36]

We find again the themes that Maqdisi elaborated in his conversation with Wannous a decade earlier: the disappearance and oppression of the people and the political, economic, cultural, and human destruction of the Syrians. These themes were no longer being shared with a fellow intellectual but openly addressed to the president of the republic and formulated as a political demand: quite a Promethean leap!

A month later, in his forum address, Maqdisi spoke about the necessity of civil society. He recalled that back in 1983, UNESCO had organized a conference on the hundredth anniversary of Karl Marx's death. Participants were asked to state what they imagined Marx would say to their cities or nations, were he alive. Maqdisi said he had thought Marx would ask the great powers to lift their hands off his country and the countries of the third world, whose populations were capable of progressing with their own capabilities. But, he said, there was another thought that had come to his mind, which he had silenced. He could state it now: that despots of the third world should lift their hands off their own people, so that these people could form civil societies and progress. As long as people were deprived of freedom and sovereignty, he added, rulers were going to indoctrinate them with self-serving rational, intellectual, and moral ideas that justified their own rule; people deprived of sovereignty meant the end of everything. Everything should be done, he concluded, to liberate the people and allow them to form a civil society.

In the discussion that followed, Dalila added that after ideological indoctrination came a worse phase of despotism, in which rulers focused on their power and economic privileges and their readiness to sacrifice and even kill their people for the sake of preserving those privileges. Others expressed alarm at the scope of the predicament, to which Maqdisi, as always, responded by stressing the importance of not giving in to despair, of speaking up, and of trying to open a dialogue with the regime.

Barqawi spoke about the gap between state and society across the Arab world, which had engendered deep societal discontent, sometimes expressed in violent form—as in the case of religious fundamentalism—and which often brewed in festering silence. Only an active and peaceful civil society could bridge this gap. Neither violent movements nor outside forces could be the right response. Barut pointed to the problems of civil society organizations in a globalized world, in which networking and funding could serve neoliberal foreign interests rather than local ones. He recalled that in the Arab world, the notion of civil society had not always been used in a neoliberal sense, as it seemed to be at present. Interestingly, he mentioned its use in *Qadaya wa-shahadat*. Having been a steady contributor to that journal, Barut said, he could attest that the notion was used there to counter fundamentalism and to reform the Left. Moreover, civil society should serve politics in the broader sense, not the narrow one of dealing with party and power politics. Several discussants disliked Barut's cautionary attitude toward civil society: Was this caution meant to keep down civil society under the pretext of not harming the prevailing state? Was internal funding necessarily less suspicious than external funding? Did it make sense to expect a state that benefits from the absence of civil society to create one? Wasn't civil society in the Arab world associated with the struggle against all forms of hegemony rather than just neoliberal projects?

Most of the talks on economy and legal rights combined historical overviews of modern Syria with assessments of the present situation. Like Maqdisi, Seif deplored the destruction of the human in a system that spoiled the entire value structure of Syrian society. The prevailing system had made it impossible to work and produce according to constructive norms. Fundamental reform had become critical. Haytham al-Mallah responded by adding that from his forty-five years of practice as a lawyer, he knew that no technical improvement, like a raise in salaries, could reform the judicial system, which had been ruined and emptied of its purpose.

Ghalioun's talk turned out to be the last one in the forum, as Seif was arrested the following morning, and came after an interruption of several months in forum activities. Ghalioun had traveled from Paris for the occasion. His talk was solemn but moderate in tone. It was divided into five parts: a description of the current situation, an analysis of the nature of the Syrian crisis, a call for social reconciliation and work toward a new national contract, the conditions for national reform and its goals, and finally, the role of the opposition and of democratic forces. It addressed the main opposition themes that had recurred in the other talks and dwelled on the violent rift in Syrian society since the 1960s; namely, the coming to power of a rural and tribal leadership and the sudden and total exclusion of the traditional urban elite. The abrupt change and the violence and lawlessness required to maintain it created, said Ghalioun, a state of severe civil tension among Syrians. No reform and no progress could be made without first addressing this social fracture and engaging in a process of civil reconciliation. He expressed his wish that the new president would commit himself to such a process and let the state lead the way by organizing free elections and securing civil and political liberties. This, according to him, was the historical challenge of the new presidential era. Only if this challenge was met could a new process of healing, moral recovery, and confidence building begin, upon which a new social contract could be elaborated among free individuals. Only then could feelings of despair, pain, misery, insecurity, and resignation be overcome and faith in a better future be nurtured. This would be the prerequisite for much-needed reform in the various sectors of public life. Democracy should be seen as the means to reach such a new social contract. Such a process would necessitate a genuine social debate, an honest self-examination, and the realization that the choice is between change and total bankruptcy.

The reaction from Baath members was strong: one discussant thought that Ghalioun's talk was full of "poisons"; that he spoke as if the country were in a state of civil war, when in reality everything was fine; that one had to show respect to others and acknowledge them; and that great conspiracies were being woven against Syria and needed to be defeated. Dalila wondered why they had to convene in a private home and were not given the right to meet in public places to discuss public matters, and why they were deprived of a newspaper where they could express their ideas and concerns. Would such rights empower Israel? He worried that the country was in a deep crisis that could lead to a civil war, which would be fed with the money robbed from people's pockets, as had happened in Lebanon. Urgent measures in the form of new policies should be taken to avoid that bleak scenario, he added. Some raised concerns over the arrests of Riad al-Turk and Ma'mun al-Homsi and feared that the same could happen to Ghalioun. Others confirmed Ghalioun's concern about the climate of fear in which the country was kept, including the mutual fear between the regime and the opposition.

In the talk he gave at the Jamal al-Atassi forum, "Thaqafat al-khawf" (The culture of fear), Abdulrazzaq Eid described and criticized the culture of fear that the absence of democracy had created. Oppression and the regime's arbitrary rule, he deplored, had killed moral and legal norms for the individual.[37] In the introduction to his book *Yas'alunak 'an al-mujtama' al-madani*

(They ask you about civil society), entitled "In lieu of a preface: Civil society in Syria, from the Society of Friends to the Revival Councils,"[38] Eid explains the two manifestos, that of the ninety-nine (*Bayan al-99*) and of the one thousand intellectuals (*Bayan al-1000*). In introducing *Bayan al-99*, he recalls the contributions of Riad al-Turk and Saadallah Wannous, which led, despite their absence (al-Turk having spent seventeen years in prison and Wannous having passed away), to a declaration that brings back to Syrian culture its vanguard and tanwiri roles.[39] Both documents, Eid says, were the labor of about twenty intellectuals, who came together to formulate societal demands for reform. The main point of the declarations was the urgency of political reform as a prerequisite for economic and social reforms. The texts were the expression of a society that had at the beginning of Baath rule willingly accepted its own cancellation to facilitate faster progress through revolutionary putsches. With time this had led to society's decay and collapse. Syrian society had lately tried to take back some of its vigor and come out of its predicament. For Eid, the notion of "reviving civil society" came from the wish to grasp and underline this important societal trend. It is not true, he adds, that the use of the term *civil society* is only a fashion or imported concept. If one were to reject imported terms, then one would also have to discard communism and nationalism, in the name of which the notion of civil society was being criticized—in the case of communism, to warn against the collapse civil society had led to in the Soviet Union; and in the case of nationalism, to warn against fragmentation and division. In reality, says Eid, it is in the historical experience of Syria and the region that the cancellation of civil society had proved disastrous. By reviving the role of civil society, intellectuals were reconnecting with Syrian and Arab societal struggles against Ottoman, and later Western, imperialism in the quest for freedom, modernity, rationalism, and tanwir. Briefly put, Eid says, civil society is the subjection of public affairs to public opinion through political parties and a free press. Who would fear such control apart from thieves and corrupt people?

In a conciliatory note, he adds that the calm and rational reaction of the regime to *Bayan al-99* had been encouraging. In light of this encouraging response, the manifesto authors had elaborated on its text, adding theoretical foundations and political analyses to clarify their position, thus producing *Bayan al-1000*. The main intention, he affirms, was to stress the peaceful, nonviolent mode of exchange regarding these social and political matters. Interestingly, he states that the manifestos and the whole idea of the "civil society revival" are the political equivalent of the Arab nahda revival, with its slogans of tanwir, rationalism, progress, and modernity—the revival being based on the belief that nahda thought had real historical continuity with contemporary national culture, not some neotraditionalism that sought continuity with Ibn Rushd, Ibn Hazm, or Ibn Khaldun.

In the first piece in *Yas'alunak 'an al-mujtama' al-madani* (They ask you about civil society), called "Yas'alunak 'an al-mujtama' al-madani" (They ask you about civil society),[40] Eid writes that those who fear the term *civil society* might invite fragmentation or dissociation between state and society do not realize that it is totalitarian regimes that produce such results by jettisoning democracy. The Baath Party had done this by not heeding the warning of its own theoreticians, like Yassin Hafiz, who called time and again to combine Baath ideals and actions with democracy.

Indeed, while the notion of civil society was the central theme of the opposition, its definition and judiciousness were also the subject of much discussion and even disagreement among members of the opposition.[41] The regime, on the other hand, moved between co-opting the notion and vilifying it. Much of the fray around this notion was documented in Barut and al-Kilani's *Suria bayn 'ahdayn* (Syria between two epochs). The volume comprises four parts: on the main declarations and statements issued by the various opposition and regime parties; on interviews and opinion pieces published during the Damascus Spring by its main protagonists, mainly in the Lebanese dailies *an-Nahar* and *as-Safir*, in the pan-Arab daily *al-Hayat*, and in the Syrian state dailies *Tishreen*, *al-Baath*, and *al-Thawra* (in the early days of the Spring *al-Thawra* had opened its pages to oppositional voices, albeit for a short while); on articles devoted to economic reform; and finally, on some of the debate fora talks. Most of the gathered pieces date from late fall 2000 to spring 2001, and the editors' introduction put this eventful period in the longer historical perspective of Syria since the 1960s.

Whether through official spokesmen—such as Vice President Khaddam and state newspaper editors, including Turki Saqr, editor in chief of *al-Baath*, and Mahmud Salameh, editor in chief of *al-Thawra*—Baath Party declarations, or anonymous statements, the regime made it clear that the movement around civil society was an attempt to destabilize and divide Syria.[42] Civil society was a foreign concept, introduced through the channels of globalization, or even through conspiratorial organizations such as the Freemasons, to sow chaos and weaken the state in the name of political participation. According to the regime, the Baath Party and its allies in power had from the beginning ensured the active participation of different sectors of society in the country's political life through numerous school, youth, university, workers, peasants, and professional organizations. For Barut these organizations, created by the revolutionary power that established itself as the state in 1963 and consolidated itself in 1970, never really expressed the will of the sectors they were supposed to represent; rather, they expressed the will of the state imposed on society.[43] The real civil society, he adds, was marginalized and disempowered.[44]

On the other hand, proponents of the civil society movement, such as Michel Kilo, Riad Seif, Riad al-Turk, and their collaborators, viewed the revival of civil society's agency as the necessary condition for reforming the country.[45] The country, they said, had reached an ominous impasse, and only the reinstatement of the freedom for citizens to debate, gather, and participate in public life could usher them out of the predicament. The organized participation of the free citizenry was not to be seen as a movement against the state: regime and society needed to collaborate together peacefully to solve the problems that had resulted from decades of absolute power. No modern, democratic state could come into being without an active civil society. Moreover, the reempowered citizenry in a democratic setting, guaranteed by a solid constitution, would construct genuine national unity across regions, religions, and primordial affiliations. The empowerment of civil society required the reestablishment of human, civil, and political rights and an end to the emergency laws that had covered the arbitrary rule of the regime for so long.

Tayyeb Tizini, in one of his articles in *al-Thawra*, argued that the transitional period in Syria, as in the rest of the Arab world, required the establishment of a truly strong state—something that in his opinion Arabs had failed to accomplish. Only such a state, governed by the rule of law, could empower civil society. Calls to empower society first, before the establishment of such a state, would lead to the further weakening of the state, he believed.[46] He was severely criticized by Michel Kilo a few months later. Kilo thought that the whole discussion as to which should come first, state or civil society, was a useless one. A strong and democratic state could not emerge from the void. Instead, efforts should be made to mobilize the existing vital forces in state and in society. Idolizing or demonizing civil society rendered no service toward this urgent task. Finally, he added, proponents of a strong civil society needed no lessons in rejecting dependency and servitude to globalization.[47] Around the same time, Antun Maqdisi expressed similar concerns about the fixation, and confusing elaborations, on the notion of civil society. Similarly, he found the opposing proposals to prioritize state or society unhelpful.[48] Moreover, he thought that these disputations remained enclosed in intellectual circles and did not speak to the people. For him, it was obvious that no proper state could emerge without a free and enabled civil society, free to organize and control its public affairs. He reiterated his call for the regime to lift the siege on the people (*fakk al-hisar 'an al-sha'b*) and to focus on the free human being, as an individual and a collectivity.[49] Faysal Darraj and Syrian historian Aziz al-Azmeh also believed that raising political awareness in society was more important than conducting elitist discussions on civil society.[50] Finally, with the onset of repression by the regime in February 2001, Burhan Ghalioun admitted that the notion of civil society could lend itself to confusion and manipulation by both the opposition and the regime. Still, he thought that its core idea of a politically active society was a crucial one for putting the country on a salutary path. He insisted on the importance of dialogue between those in power and those who were left out of it.[51] Once again, in a Cassandra call, Ghalioun warned the regime against avoiding that dialogue. Failing to constructively engage the emerging democratic movements, manifested in the discussion fora and the public debates, would leave the floor to extremist currents that would easily fill the void. The equation, as he saw it, between the security agencies and the extremist currents could only be broken by allowing a democratic current to come into being. Otherwise, the country would head toward a violent confrontation between those two forces. In the absence of a democratic outlet, oppositional fundamentalist radicalization would easily grow. Deprived of political frames of opposition, people would be led to express their discontent under the banner of some fundamentalist religious legitimacy or participate in chaotic outbursts of violence.[52] Sadly, we know today that this is exactly what happened: the state refused to acknowledge and engage the democratic opposition, civil society was crushed, and the Islamists were allowed to fill the oppositional void, often encouraged by the state in order to demonize all opposition and justify unbridled violence against it. The regime followed through on slogans like *"Al-Asad aw nurhriqu al-balad"* (Assad or else we burn the country), found on the walls of Syrian cities, and brought the logic of the barbaric state described by Seurat in the early 1980s to its bitter end. And as in the 1980s, the regime seems on its way to being rehabilitated by the international community, with the justification that it is the only alternative to the Islamists.

One of the most prominent victims of this state logic of barbarity has been Riad al-Turk (born 1930), a Syrian lawyer and veteran opposition figure and political prisoner. Early on in his life he adhered to the Syrian Communist Party but disagreed with its lack of commitment to the pan-Arab cause and its submission to the Soviet Union. When the leader of the party, Khaled Begdash (1912–1995), decided to give his allegiance to Hafiz al-Assad, al-Turk declared his dissent and the formation of a separate body called the Syrian Communist Party—Political Bureau. He was arrested in October 1980 for his political opposition and kept in prison for eighteen years under inhumane conditions. During most of those years, he was kept in solitary confinement and often subjected to torture. He was released in 1998 without having renounced his political principles. Soon after the amendment of the constitution that allowed for the election of Assad's son in June 2000, he expressed his objection to the lack of respect for the constitution in an interview with *Le Monde*.[53] His dissenting voice was the only one to go public in Syria at the time. A few days after Bashar al-Assad's inaugural speech, al-Turk published a soon famous article in the cultural supplement of *an-Nahar*, "Min ghayr al-mumkin an tadhall suriya mamlakat al-samt" (It is not possible that Syria remains the kingdom of silence);[54] this was three weeks before Maqdisi's open letter to Assad. The main theme of his article was the fear that had come to dominate life in the country: people fearing the absolute and corrupt power of the regime, and people fearing each other for lack of trust, created by the security agencies through decades of voluntary and involuntary denunciations. Al-Turk called on Syrians to remember their history did not begin with Assad rule and that it would not end with it. He exhorted them to recall the more democratic past, in which even the Baath Party had expressed the genuine will of a certain constituency, unlike the mass party that became a puppet of Assad's power. He gave the example of the Soviet Communist Party, which eventually collapsed, despite its official massive following. The problem, he wrote, was not Bashar al-Assad the person, but the power mechanisms that made him president, transforming the republic into a hereditary system of family rule. The republic, he recalled, had been built by Syrians struggling against colonialism and foreign interference. It needed to be preserved, not least because it was the only system that could tackle the country's problems. The first step to reinstating republican democracy was lifting the weight of fear and silence through the peaceful mobilization of all sectors of society. Al-Turk concluded by saying that now that Bashar al-Assad was president, he would be expected to rule with justice.

Al-Turk developed the same themes of fear and the urgency of a democratic transition in his August 2001 talk at the al-Atassi Forum.[55] He warned against violent change and called instead for the mutual recognition of all parties involved, inside and outside the regime. The regime needed to admit its past mistakes and injustices and present reparations (*radd al-madhalim li ahliha*). He closed his talk by stating that the Syrian people had suffered too much and that it yearned for freedom, dignity, and security. He was arrested a month later, condemned a year and a half later to a two-and-a-half-year prison sentence, and released after fifteen months. Upon his release in December 2002, he reiterated his belief in the primary goal of taking Syria from dictatorship to democracy and expressed optimism at people's open support for his release and for the cause of freedom.[56] At the outbreak of the Syrian uprising he went underground, actively supporting the revolutionaries and their demand for freedom, dignity, and security.

Were the moves of the Syrian intelligentsia involved in the Damascus Spring naive, politically unsavvy, and doomed from the outset? Were they isolated acts of an estranged elite, disconnected from people at large? Were the risks taken by speaking up and acting on ideas of civil mobilization worth their while, given the predictable price? Whatever the answers to these questions, events, including the outbreak of massive demonstrations in March 2011, showed that the ideas, moves, and people involved in the Damascus Spring were not disconnected from the general mood of the country. They seem to have been in tune with the pervasive alarm at the deterioration of things politically, economically, and socially, with the urgent need to address that deterioration rationally and publicly, and with the despair and humiliation that kept on growing in large sectors of society. Those ideas, minus the moves, were also there in the 1990s writings of the Sisypheans. To the question "Where are the intellectuals?" so often heard at the outset of protest movements across the Arab world, particularly in Egypt and Syria, one should answer by pointing out all those writings (and sometimes moves) produced by Arab critical thinkers during the long years that preceded those movements. I am not arguing that the writings and ideas led to the movements in some causal way. Rather, I am noting the similarity of concerns, yearnings, and endeavors expressed by the writings of the Sisypheans, the moves of the Prometheans, and the demands of the Syrian protesters. That similarity could also be observed between the Egyptian deconstructionist thinkers described in chapter 2 and the Egyptian protesters. They all articulated in their own ways the darkness of their prerevolutionary predicament and the brighter possibilities they envisioned for the future.[57] The complex Arab revolutions and their transformations will no doubt be the subject of numerous investigations to come. But the tanwir debates can already be identified, delineated, and analyzed. I shall argue in the conclusion that what they advocated was a form of political humanism.

Conclusion

Tanwir as Political Humanism

THE EGYPTIAN AND Syrian fin-de-siècle writings on tanwir are quite explicit: their subject is the darkness of their times spread by the ominous developments of the postindependence regimes. The darkness they address is concrete: their authors' future and the future of their fellow citizens doomed by corrupt and violent states. It is the darkness of present times overwhelmed by endemic socioeconomic and political problems and the systematic prevention of people from participating in dealing with them publicly and rationally. It is also the darkness of a past that one could refer to in order to position oneself intellectually and politically in search of alternative futures, a past that is now blurred by an overwhelming state ideology. It is the fear and mistrust imposed by repression and violence, the darkness of state prisons and torture cells, and the darkness of state mendacity, cynicism, and opportunism. It is feelings of impotence, humiliation, insecurity, and despair. It is deprivation of basic health care, education, liberties, civil rights, and even human rights.

The Cairene and Damascene tanwir discourses I analyze in this book are intellectual attempts to come to terms with this darkness, to grapple, diagnose, and propose remedies for it, even when it has been clear to their authors that implementing those remedies was not possible, as in the case of the Syrian Sisypheans. Making lucid sense of the late twentieth-century Egyptian and Syrian predicaments, and searching for and debating about the right explanations and conceptual tools to face it, are the central objectives of those discourses. Shedding light on the nature and causes of the present situation and igniting a glimmer of hope in a better future are essential aspects of the tanwir work undertaken by the debaters. Denouncing the hypocritical and abusive state discourse on tanwir, as we saw in the Egyptian case, and naming and resisting the manifold state abuses of power in both Egypt and Syria are the most salient endeavors of the critical writings on tanwir. Religious fundamentalism and Islamist violence are also targeted, but these are perceived to a great extent as epiphenomena of a more fundamental problem; namely, the regimes that have confiscated their states and prevented the development of democratic processes and policies. Contrary to the claims of the Egyptian and Syrian regimes that they are fighting the dangers of religious extremists, they have consistently manipulated the Islamists to legitimize and reinforce their own power, while presenting themselves as enlighteners or modernizers. They have also nurtured various forms of confessionalism and sectarianism under the guise of secularism and moderation.

For the critical tanwiris, the predicament is primarily political, and its remedy lies in reclaiming the right to political participation. Only through participation, they believe, can the abuse of power be fought and the damage produced by it stopped. The damage is seen in all sectors of life—as indicated by the recurring term *"al-kharab al-shamil"* (the general ruin)—but most importantly in the destruction of the human being. Tanwir, in the sense of the practice of reason and freedom, is to contribute to the reconstruction of the human (*"bina' al-insan"*), to serve her emancipation, and to restore her dignity and well-being. Hence, I argue that this tanwir amounts to a political humanism, a view that has at its center and as its goal the human being, through the restoration of political life and democracy.

Why did the postindependent era reach this level of darkness? What went wrong with nation-state building, development, liberation, and modernization? Why did life in these countries become so brutish, unsafe, and desperate? These questions had already started to be raised by Arab intellectuals and Arabs in general a few decades after the wave of independence in the Arab world. The Arab defeat of 1967 and the establishment of military regimes since the mid-twentieth century aggravated these anguished interrogations. But the ensuing years of autocratic rule (in various forms) pushed many Arab societies to ever-worsening socioeconomic and political conditions, reaching ominous levels in the 1990s and 2000s. This exacerbated those interrogations further, and the tanwir debates came to serve as an expression of the urgent need to name, address, and react to those menacing ills.

What share of responsibility did ideas, ideologies, and culture have in causing this disaster? Culturalistic readings of the "aftermath of sovereignty" abounded in the 1960s, 1970s, and 1980s, blaming tradition, national character, religion, westernization, mentalities, modes of thinking, worldviews, and damaged identities for the unfortunate course of the postindependence era. Minority reports, however, as I argued extensively in my previous book, pointed quite early on to political disenfranchisement and the confiscation of political life. It is this political reading of the aftermath that comes to the fore in a most pointed way in the critical tanwir debates of the 1990s and 2000s.

Interestingly, this political reading involved a rereading of the history of ideas that had accompanied these countries during Ottoman rule, through the French and British mandates, and to independence—in other words, a reading of the nahda. The nonculturalist approach did not mean discarding the significance of ideas, for ideas were important in understanding the course of events, discerning their causes and effects, and indicating the way out of the predicament. Rather, it meant a nonreductionist understanding of ideas that perceives them in their historical contexts and sees them in interaction with lived realities, as expressions of those realities and as tools to deal with them.

The centrality of the nahda in both the Egyptian and the Syrian debates was unmistakable. In fact, as I also showed in my previous book, the significance of the nahda for the postindependence era had already been the topic of much discussion since the 1960s: What was the nahda about? What did it amount to? Did it succeed or fail, and for what reason? Was it an aberration caused by an unhealthy infatuation with the West, leading to an estrangement from the self? Was it a form of religious renewal? Was it a trend in secularization? Was it an ideology of modernization imposed on people to overpower them? Did its ideas connect to actual policies? Did people in general relate to them in any way? What were its strengths and weaknesses? What impact did it have in its time and what effects, if any, are to be found in the present time? These questions were raised for decades before the tanwir debates, but they gained additional significance in the debates. That significance came with the growing realization of the failures of independence. Did these failures reflect the failure of the nahda; that is, the failure of the ideas of reform, progress, modernization, development, and liberation? The prevailing assumption among most Arab discussants in the second half of the twentieth century was that the nahda, at least in its basic impulses, was indeed oriented toward those projects, whether they were eventually misled or not. Hence the question about the fate of those projects was also a question about the nature and fate of the nahda.

According to some Egyptian thinkers, the regime used this earlier intellectual history, called the nahda, to misrepresent itself as the bearer of nahda values and ideas, and as a way of distinguishing itself from the obscurantist Islamist fanatics. Egyptians, like many others in Arab countries, were presented with these two options for leadership: the "enlightened and tolerant" regime or the Islamist extremists. Egyptian critics denounced this misappropriation and misrepresentation and called for the actual practice of those values and ideas, basically those of reason and freedom. Such a practice would produce an enlightening understanding of the socioeconomic, cultural, and political phenomena of the present and uphold those values concretely and consistently. Egyptian critics also criticized how these values and ideas were practiced during the nahda; namely, with authoritarianism and elitism. For Syrian critics, on the other hand, the problem was that Syria had been severed from the nahda legacy through the political system put in place in the 1970s. They found their fellow Syrians and Arabs in general estranged from that legacy, and that when mentioned, it was misunderstood and blamed for the present predicament.

The challenge for Syrian critics was to remind people that there was a time before the Assad regime, and to encourage them to believe that there could and should be a time after it too. It was important for them to show that there had been a time when plural ideas were given a margin of free expression and when free debates were conducted. For the autocratic regimes had confiscated not only political life but intellectual life as well, particularly in Syria. This had led to an intellectual and cultural desertification in addition to the political one. It was crucial to reconnect with an intellectual and political history that existed beyond the Assad era, a history that offered a vision different from that of the Assad reality. "Al-Asad ila al-abad" (Assad forever) was to be challenged by bringing in history, ideas, and a cultural legacy that could inspire and empower. The nahda was for these critics a promising democratic Arab culture that could or should be an enabling narrative for change. In the case of Saadallah Wannous and Faysal Darraj, this remembering was not resigned nostalgia for an idealized epoch or a wishful "back to nahda" movement. Rather, it retrieved an alternative politico-intellectual narrative to the one imposed by the Assads. It was also, more broadly, an alternative option to the choice presented by many an Arab regime: "Either us or the Islamists!"

Why was this alternative politico-intellectual narrative affiliated with the nahda characterized as tanwir? Indeed, a great number of Arab thinkers used nahda and tanwir interchangeably, without justifying or explicitly explaining this characterization. Students of Arab thought have made this implicit characterization as well.[1] French political scientist Jean-Noël Ferrié tried to draw clear distinctions between the two terms. In "Réformisme, renaissance et contingence: La justification de la justice chez Nubar Pacha et Khayr al-Din," Ferrié argued that not every nahda reform or reform proposal could be defined as an enlightenment reform: it depended on how it was justified.[2] If the reform was defended on the basis of a transcendental reference, such as a religious one, then it could not qualify as an enlightenment reform. What was specific to the enlightenment mode of thinking, he wrote, was its appeal to contingent norms that were discursively established by a public, with no extrahuman validation. Reason, taken as the new principle replacing God as validation, was understood in discursive terms, knowable by all. It was how the rejection of despotism and the demand for a just, nonarbitrary state were justified that was not specific to enlightenment. An enlightenment reform was one that proposed a new order without the sanction and legitimation of a preexisting, extrahuman order. With this distinguishing characteristic of enlightenment, Ferrié contrasted the reform endeavors of two figures of late nineteenth-century Tunisia and Egypt, Khayr al-Din al-Tunisi (1820–1890) and Nubar Pacha (1825–1899), respectively. Both struggled to modernize and improve their states and wrote about their experiences. Al-Tunisi wrote a treatise in Arabic;[3] Pacha wrote his memoirs in French.[4] What interested Ferrié was how they accounted for their ideas and actions in their writings. He rightly noted that while al-Tunisi was considered a reform thinker and politician in the established nahda narrative, Pacha was not given a comparable place in the narrative. Yet Pacha, according to Ferrié, deserved the designation of an enlightenment reformer; although he did not justify his reforms with a systematic theory, he related them to his own experiences, which could be articulated, shared, and recognized by fellow humans. Ferrié mentioned, as an example, Pacha's reporting on his reform of forced labor, in which he related specific biographical incidents that moved him to undertake that reform. Al-Tunisi, on the other hand, wrote Ferrié, pleaded and struggled for a modern, just state ruled by law by appealing to the divine order revealed by the Prophet. His arguments for reform and justice were based on the authorized opinions of the religious tradition and shown to be in conformity with Islamic law. Such a reform thought, according to Ferrié, could not be equated with enlightenment, and so nahda should not be conflated with enlightenment.[5]

If we were to follow this distinction, the question would still remain as to whether the recourse to religious justifications was more strategic than dogmatic. In other words, were religious references used to facilitate the acceptance of proposed reforms? And if so, would such expediency jeopardize the consistency of the reforms in question? Israeli historian Israel Gershoni addressed this question in "The Theory of Crisis and the Crisis in a Theory: Intellectual History in Twentieth-Century Middle Eastern Studies." He reviewed the crisis narratives of modern Arab and particularly Egyptian intellectual history produced by prominent Western historians, including Hamilton A. R. Gibb, Gustave E. von Grunebaum, Nadav Safran, and Wilfred Cantwell Smith. These historians saw in the intellectual careers of modernist Egyptian thinkers such as Muhammad Husayn Haykal and Taha Husayn a retreat from their modernist views of the 1920s and a move toward more traditionalist, religious positions in the 1930s and onward. They deplored this retreat as a crisis in Egyptian and Arab modernist thought. Gershoni also examined the deconstruction of this crisis narrative by later historians such as Pierre Cachia, Marcel Colombe, Albert Hourani, and Charles D. Smith, who saw not a retreat but a concern to connect with a wider public, still with a view toward modernism and change.[6] Alain Roussillon subsumed the different and sometimes seemingly contradictory orientations of those early Egyptian modernists under the complex phenomenon of reform.[7]

Be that as it may, the nahda seems to have been characterized as tanwir by participants of the 1990s and 2000s tanwir debates because of its vibrant intellectual production and the involvement of ideas with the concrete development projects of the time. Tanwir in these debates was much more about the reconstruction of the human, the rehumanization of the world, than its disenchantment. Tanwir at that historical juncture was not so much about how to cognitively grasp the world. Nor was it about the metaphysical grounds on which to justify reform. Rather, it was about how to make dignified life possible again and how to acknowledge and affirm the humanity of people and their dignity, rights, and liberties. It was not about being for or against a certain metaphysical or religious worldview or mode of life. These questions were perhaps bound to be raised at some point, but first the space of free expression and exchange of ideas had to be reopened. The 1990s and 2000s tanwir debates in Cairo and Damascus were about the search for a moral and intellectual compass to lead Arabs out of their doom. It meant the actual practice of free and public reason, not in the Kantian sense but in the more straightforward sense of public expression and rational debate on affairs touching the humanity of people, their dignity, their livelihoods, their safety, and their integrity. The yearning for life-affirming views and actions and the quest for a humanist democracy were already leitmotifs of post-1967 Arab thought, as I showed in my previous book. The 1990s and 2000s tanwir debates are a pronounced and urgent expression of that yearning and that quest.[8]

Few took the trouble to articulate what they meant by "tanwir" when referring to the nahda and when characterizing their own projects in relation to the nahda. Wannous articulated that meaning when explaining how he saw Taha Husayn's work as an inspiring tanwir project. He emphasized five points, as we saw in chapter 3: historical thinking, the rejection of bigotry, the assertion of universal humanism against narrow forms of particularism, the anchoring of ideas in sociopolitical realities and projects, and the commitment to democracy and the refusal of elitism. These are the principles and impulses that Wannous saw in the nahda and advocated with his fellow tanwiris for their own times.

This tanwir was primarily political, formulated in plain language to express basic demands in reaction to real experiences. It was neither utopian nor cynical. The debates were not "academic," despite the fact that many of their participants, whether Egyptian deconstructionists or Syrian Sisypheans and Prometheans, were academics. Their discourses were not learned elaborations on an academic subject but reactions to lived experiences of the time.

Furthermore, they were not meant to serve didactic purposes—to "enlighten" the masses. Obviously, the authors of the discourses did not speak with the authority of a better-knowing vanguard. Rather, they understood themselves primarily as victims like everybody else. Their addressees were those in power, mainly the rulers of their respective countries. Their allies were their fellow countrymen and women, whose involvement they regarded as crucial for bringing forward their demands. I do not think it was clear to the debaters in the 2000s to what extent they were in tune with the rest of their respective societies, but the uprisings a decade later showed that they were indeed in tune. In 2011 the demands voiced on the streets of Egypt and Syria were the same as those of the prerevolutionary tanwir debates: human dignity, freedom, social justice, accountability, and political participation.

The tanwir debates and the revolutionary demands showed that a political demand for participation and emancipation had already started to form in the minds of people, intellectuals or not, many years before the outbreak of the uprisings. Observing the early phases of the revolutions, Palestinian-American sociologist Mohammed A. Bamyeh wrote: "In overcoming not one's own but state-imposed immaturity, one demonstrates that the overcoming of a self-imposed immaturity has already taken place, inaudibly, and long before any revolution."[9] The decades-long yearning for freedom burst into the streets of Cairo and Damascus, and in many other cities of the Arab world, in astounding mass demonstrations. These were crushed by the respective regimes. Repression turned Egypt into another *"mamlakat samt"* (kingdom of silence), and unrestrained violence transformed Syria into killing fields, mass graves, and ruins. Can one still repeat today what Wannous affirmed in 1996: "We are condemned to hope, and what is happening today cannot be the end of history"?[10] The leap of faith he called for then has become much harder to make today, and the glimmer of hope he struggled to preserve has become even more tenuous. The struggle for tanwir has now become, more than ever, a steep uphill one.

Notes

Introduction

1. See Kassab, *Contemporary Arab Thought*.

2. See, in particular, Kassab, introduction and conclusion to *Contemporary Arab Thought*. For more on the regional and international geopolitical context of the late twentieth-century Arab world and its intellectual history, see Hanssen and Weiss, "Introduction: Arab Intellectual History Between the Postwar and the Postcolonial," in *Arabic Thought Against the Authoritarian Age*, 1–35.

3. Demands for political participation through civil society and freedom of expression, and for revolt against despotism, were also voiced by Saudi intellectuals around the turn of the millennium and especially after the 2011 Arab uprisings. However, these demands were articulated from within Islamic thinking and as a critique against both the dominating Salafi clergy and the ruling family. Its spokespeople aimed to formulate a third path that would advocate change toward freedom, reason, and political participation and at the same time preserve the Islamic worldview, though a modernized version of it. They were labeled "modernists," "rationalists," and sometimes "tanwiris." They were attacked and repressed by the clerical and political establishment. Their ideas and debates were documented and analyzed by Saudi-British scholar Madawi al-Rasheed in *Muted Modernists*.

4. Hourani, *Arabic Thought in the Liberal Age*.

5. Here are some of the latest publications in the field: The two volumes edited by Jens Hanssen and Max Weiss, *Arabic Thought Beyond the Liberal Age* and *Arabic Thought Against the Authoritarian Age*, both published on the occasion of the fiftieth anniversary of Hourani's *Arabic Thought in the Liberal Age*. For a recent bilingual nahda anthology, see el-Ariss, *The Arab Renaissance*. See also Dakhli, *Une génération d'intellectuels arabes*; Khuri-Makdisi, *The Eastern Mediterranean*; al-Muhsin, *Tamathulat al-nahda fi thaqafat al-'iraq al-hadith* [Representations of the nahda in the culture

of modern Iraq], and *Tamthulat al-hadatha fi thaqafat al-'Iraq* [Representations of modernity in Iraqi culture]; Bashkin, *The Other Iraq*; Hamzah, *The Making of the Arab Intellectual*; "Arabic Literature," special double issue of the *Journal of Arabic Literature*; Gonzalez-Quijano, "La renaissance arabe au XIXe siècle"; Di-Capua, *No Exit*; Abu-'Uksa, *Freedom in the Arab World*; and Holt, "Narrating the *Nahda*."

6. Here I tend to agree with Reinhard Schulze's footnote remark in "Was ist die islamische Aufklärung?" [What is the Islamic Enlightenment?], 291n38, about the dearth of studies on the reception of Western thinkers in modern Arab thought, and in which he cites one of the rare reception studies: Centre d'Études françaises, *Actes du colloque "la réception de Voltaire et Rousseau en Égypte."* But one needs to mention the early work of Raif Khoury, *Al-Fikr al-'arabi al-hadith* [Modern Arab Thought]. Since then other studies have appeared, such as Abdelaziz, "Présence de Rousseau dans la Renaissance arabe," "Eine Quelle des zeitgenössischen arabischen Denkens" [A source of contemporary Arab thought], and "Al-ma'rifi wa al-idioloji fi dirasat al-fikr al-gharbi" [The cognitive and the ideological in studies of Western thought]. See also the comments of Nassif Nassar and others in Belqziz, *Al-Ma'rifi wa al-idioloji fi dirasat al-fikr al-'arabi al-mu'asir* [The cognitive and the ideological in contemporary Arab thought], 420–40; the volume contains the proceedings of a conference organized by the Markaz dirasat al-wihda al-arabiyya (Center for Arab Unity Studies). Other studies include Mosbah, "Spinoza et le problème du théologico-politique en Tunisie"; Moghith, "Le darwinisme et la sécularization de la pensée en Égypte"; Elshakry, *Reading Darwin in Arabic*; El Shakry, "The Arabic Freud"; 'Attieh, "Kant wa al-tanwir fi al-fikr al-'arabi" [Kant and tanwir in Arab thought]; al-Tawati, ben Ahmuda, and al-Azm, *Athar al-thawra al-faransiyya fi fikr al-nahda* [The traces of the French Revolution on nahda thought]; and Saleh, *Madkhal il al-tanwir al-urubbi* [Introduction to the European Enlightenment], *Ma'arek al-tanwiriyyin al-usuliyyin fi Urubba* [The battles of the proponents of enlightenment and the fundamentalists in Europe], and *Makhadat al-hadatha al-tanwiriyya* [The processes of enlightenment modernity].

7. On the centrality of nahda thought in contemporary Arab debates, see Kassab, *Contemporary Arab Thought*; see also Kassab, "Summoning the Spirit of Taha Husayn's Enlightenment Project." The centrality of the nahda to the tanwir debates is one of the major topics I develop in this essay. See also Belqziz, "Al-ma'rifi wa al-idioloji fi dirasat al-fikr al-'arabi al-mu'asir [The cognitive and the ideological in contemporary Arab thought]; and the comments of Faisal Darraj and others in Belqziz, *Al-Ma'rifi wa al-idioloji fi dirasat al-fikr al-'arabi al-mu'asir* [The cognitive and the ideological in contemporary Arab thought], 371–84.

8. For a history of the use of the term *tanwir* in the nineteenth- and twentieth-century Arab world, see *Encyclopedia of Mediterranean Humanism*, s.v. "Tanwīr." For a cogent definition of the nahda as a complex cultural, linguistic, political, and press phenomenon, see Dakhli, *La nahda*. The digitalization of the nahda corpus would greatly facilitate the task of tracing the genealogy and transformations of such terms in modern intellectual history.

9. Gran, *The Islamic Roots of Capitalism*. For reviews of the book, see Gabriel Baer, in *Journal of the Economic and Social History of the Orient* 25, no. 2 (1982): 217–22; Charles Issawi, in *Journal of Economic History* 39, no. 3 (1979): 800–1; Roger Owen, in

Economic History Review 33, no. 1 (1980): 150–151; Pierre Cachia, in *Journal of the American Oriental Society* 101, no. 4 (1981): 462–63; Eric Davis, "Egypt's Culture and the Roots of Capitalism," *MERIP Reports* 82 (1979): 24–25; Alexander Schölch, in *Die Welt des Islams* 20, nos: 1–2 (1980): 114–15; Terence Walz, in *International Journal of African Historical Studies* 13, no. 3 (1980): 542–44; and F. De Jong and Peter Gran, "Islamic Roots of Capitalism: Egypt, 1760–1840: A Review Article with Author's Reply," *International Journal of Middle East Studies* 14, no. 3 (1982): 381–99. See also an interview with Peter Gran by two Egyptian historians twenty years after the publication of his book: Gran, "Une Renaissance récusée."

10. Gran, *Judhur al-ra'smaliyya al-islamiyya fi misr* [Roots of Islamic capitalism in Egypt].

11. Reinhard Schulze initiated the debate by inviting readers to reconsider the Islamic eighteenth century in a new historiographical perspective that removes it from the confines of a specificity prejudice and puts it in a larger global history. Schulze, "Das islamische achtzehnte Jahrhundert" [The Islamic eighteenth century]. Schulze then expanded his argument by further clarifying what he meant by his historiographical critique and his use of the term *Aufklärung* (enlightenment), and by giving empirical evidence from the literature of the epoch to support his argument. Schulze, "Was ist die islamische Aufklärung?" [What is the Islamic Enlightenment?]. In this article he also replied to his critics, who had rejected more or less virulently his assumptions and arguments. Here are some of those critical pieces: Peters, "Reinhard Schulze's Quest for an Islamic Enlightenment"; Nagel "Autochthone Wurzeln des islamischen Modernismus" [The native roots of Islamic modernism]; Hagen and Seidensticker, "Reinhard Schulzes Hypothese einer islamischen Aufklärung" [Reinhard Schulze's hypothesis of an Islamic enlightenment]; Radtke, "Erleuchterung und Aufklärung" [Illumination and enlightenment], and *Autochtone islamische Aufklärung im 18. Jahrhundert* [Native Islamic enlightenment in the eighteenth century], the second source reviewed by Rudolph Peters in *Die Welt des Islams* 42 (2002): 135–37; Haarman, "'Ein Missgriff des Geschicks'" ['A skills' error of judgment']; and finally, Reichmuth, "Arabic Literature and Islamic Scholarship in the 17th/18th Centuries." A selection of the main pieces of this debate were published in Wild, "Islamic Enlightenment in the 18th century?," with a foreword entitled "To Our Readers." Khaled El-Rouayheb, Harvard professor of Arabic and of Islamic intellectual history, examines the theses of Gran and Schulze in "Was There a Revival of Logical Studies in Eighteenth Century Egypt?" While documenting a certain renewed activity in logical studies that debunks the idea of a stagnant eighteenth-century Egyptian (and Arab) culture, El-Rouayheb does not think this activity amounted to an enlightenment phenomenon, understood in a substantial way. A more recent historical reconstruction of writings and debates in eighteenth-century reformist Islamic thought argues for the existence of a vibrant intellectual productivity "hardly equaled in any other period of Islamic history." Dallal, *Islam Without Europe*, 19.

12. See the interesting special issue of *Égypte/Monde arabe*, edited by Ghislaine Alleaume. It includes a list of the events and publications that came out in France and Egypt on this occasion. Alleaume, "Agenda."

13. For French critical reviews of the Napoleonic expedition see, for instance, Laurens, *L'expédition d'Égypte*; Raymond, "Les égyptiens et les lumières pendant l'expédition française."

14. Among the first and few Arab-Egyptian historians to argue for the existence of an intellectual life in Egypt before 1798 was Gamal al-Din al-Shayyal (1911–1967). But his 1958 book, *Al-tarikh wa al-mu'arrikhun fi misr fi al-qarn al-tassi' 'ashar* [History and historians in Egypt in the nineteenth century], did not make much of an impact. For a recent history of intellectual activity in Egypt and the Middle East in the seventeenth century, see El-Rouayheb, *Islamic Intellectual History in the Seventeenth Century.*

15. Among the outspoken opponents to the commemorations was Egyptian professor of French civilization at the University of Cairo Laïla Enan. See her essay, Enan, "'Si tu le sais, alors c'est une catastrophe. . . .'" See also the interview conducted by two Egyptian historians with ten professors of history at Egyptian universities: al-Khuli and Isa, "Un bilan controversé." For reflections on commemoration, writing history, and the lack of French-Egyptian dialogue on the 1798 event, see Alleaume, "Des incertitudes de la mémoire aux exigences de l'histoire." And for an ambivalent reading of the event, beyond the expedition versus invasion debate, see Colla, "'Non, non! Si, si!'"

16. For general studies of state formation in the modern Middle East, see Owen, *State, Power and Politics in the Making of the Modern Middle East*; Ayubi, *Over-Stating the Arab State*; and Luciani, *The Arab State*. For studies on the Egyptian state, see Waterbury, *The Egypt of Nasser and Sadat*; and Kienle, *A Grand Delusion*. On the Syrian state, see Kienle, *Ba'th Versus Ba'th*, and *Contemporary Syria*; Perthes, *Syria Under Asad*; Seale, *The Struggle for Syria*; and Wedeen, *Ambiguities of Domination.*

17. For studies of the Islamization of the public sphere in Egypt, see Ismail, "Confronting the Other," and *Rethinking Islamist Politics.*

18. For an earlier formulation of this line of thought, see Kassab, "The Arab Quest for Freedom and Dignity."

1. Secularist, Governmental, and Islamist Tanwir Debates

1. al-Kawakibi, *Taba'i' al-istibdad* [The characteristics of despotism].

2. The government also commissioned Egyptian artist Saleh Enani to produce a large painting representing the hundred years of tanwir in Egypt. *Mi'at 'am min al-tanwir* [Hundred years of enlightenment], 1992.

3. *Al-Hilal* was established in Cairo by Lebanese writer Jurji Zaidan (1861–1914). For excerpts from the celebrations, see the photos under the title "The Centennial Celebrations of Dar al-Hilal" as well as the videos under "Prelude with Speeches of Literary Figures, Parts I & II," Zaidan Foundation, http://zaidanfoundation.org /ZF_Website_Videos_02.html. See also al-Tamawi, *Al-Hilal.*

4. Ghislaine Alleaume, "De la renaissance aux Lumières."

5. Atef al-Iraqi, *Ibn Rush* [Ibn Rushd].

6. For more information on these two opposite campaigns, see the essays of Fauzi M. Najjar, "The Debate on Islam and Secularism in Egypt" and "Ibn Rush (Averroes) and the Egyptian Enlightenment Movement." See also Najjar, "Islamic Fundamentalism and the Intellectuals: The Case of Naguib Mahfouz," and "Islamic Fundamentalism and the Intellectuals: The Case of Nasr Hamid Abu Zayd"; Abaza, "Trafficking with Tanwir (Enlightenment)."

7. Among Asfour's many writings on tanwir, see al-Tanwir yuwajih al-idhlam [The enlightenment faces obscurantism], Mihnat al-tanwir [The crisis of enlightenment], Difa'an 'an al-tanwir [In defense of tanwir], Anwar al-'aql [The lights of reason], and Didd al-ta'assub [Against intolerance]. We will refer to some of them in this section.

8. Muhammad Imarah, Al-Islam bayn al-tanwir wa al-tazwir [Islam between tanwir and falsification].

9. According to a statement at the end of Mourad Wahba's Madkhal ila al-tanwir [Introduction to tanwir], it was the first publication in a series launched by the two publishing houses dedicated to issues of tanwir. The statement goes on to say that the Arab nation has been hampered in its journey to nahda, despite the important tradition that has been shaped by the contributions of giant figures of modern Arab thought. The hindrances are due to the unfinished project of tanwir: thus the need to address this matter in a scientific series ('ilmiyya) written in simple language by major thinkers of our times. The volume by Wahba, according to the series statement, deals with the open question as to whether tanwir in the Arab world is a movement of individuals, a movement of society, or a movement of an epoch. The answer, the statement adds, is left for the reader to gather.

10. For a brief statement of this paradox, see Wahba, "The Paradox of Averroes"; based on a paper he submitted at the 1979 First Conference of Islamic Philosophy on Islam and Civilization in Cairo, which he chaired.

11. Wahba, "Al-asala wa al-hadatha fi al-'alam al-thaleth" [Authenticity and modernity in the third world], in Madkhal ila al-tanwir, 103–16.

12. The proceedings were edited by Mourad Wahba and Mona Abousenna in a bilingual English-Arabic volume titled Enlightenment and Culture. Wahba's contribution was reprinted in Madkhal ila al-tanwir as "Ishkaliyyat al-tanwir wa al-thaqafah" [The problematic of enlightenment and culture], 187–200.

13. Wahba and Abousenna, Enlightenment and Culture, 13. For the Arabic version, see Wahba, Madkhal ila al-tanwir, 200.

14. Wahba, Madkhal ila al-tanwir, 159.

15. Wahba reiterates the same criticisms in his 2011 book Ruba'iyyat al-dimuqratiyya [The democracy quartet], 36 and 48.

16. Antun, Ibn Rushd wa falsafatuhu [Ibn Rushd and his philosophy]. Wahba relates the story of this publication in his article "Iqalat al-duktur Ahmad Mujahid" [The dismissal of Ahmad Mujahid].

17. Wahba, "Rifa'a wa al-tanwir" [Rifa'a and the tanwir], in Madkhal ila al-tanwir, 160–67.

18. Atef al-Iraqi, Ibn Rushd mufakkiran 'arabiyyan wa ra'idan li al-ittijah al-'aqli [Ibn Rushd: Arab thinker and pioneer of the rational orientation]. Al-Iraqi's writings have been criticized for their lack of depth, as in Hiwar hawla Ibn Rushd [Dialogue

about Ibn Rushd], edited by Mourad Wahba and commissioned by the Supreme Council of Culture and devoted to discussing the aforementioned Averroes volume edited by al-Iraqi. Wahba, *Hiwar hawla Ibn Rushd*. The harshest criticism came from Hassan Hanafi and Fouad Zakariyya. The latter also criticized Wahba's Averroes paradox by pointing out that enlightenment trends in the West also had to deal with formidable obstacles and opposition.

Among the other writings of al-Iraqi, see *Al-falsafa al-'arabiyya wa al-tariq ila al-mustaqbal* [Arab philosophy and the way to the future], *Al-faylasuf Ibn Rushd wa mus-taqbal al-thaqafa al-'arabiyya* [The philosopher Ibn Rushd and the future of Arab culture], and *Al-'aql wa al-tanwir fi al-fikr al-'arabi al-mu'asir* [Reason and enlightenment in contemporary Arab thought].

19. Wahba and Abousenna, *Averroes and the Enlightenment.*

20. Wahba, "Al-tanwir wa rajul al-shari'" [Enlightenment and the man on the street], in *Madkhal ila al-tanwir*, 88–101.

21. Wahba, 17–74.

22. See Wahba, *Ruba'iyyat al-dimuqratiyya* [The democracy quartet].

23. See the magazine's identity statement in Arabic and English: http://www .civicegypt.org/?page_id=5.

24. For his analyses of fundamentalism, see Wahba, *Al-usuliyya wa al-'almaniyya* [Fundamentalism and secularism], and *Mullak al-haqiqa al-mutlaqa* [The owners of absolute truth].

25. In Wahba's intellectual autobiography, he relates his lifelong struggles and endeavors: see Wahba, *Masar Fikr* [Thought journey], part 1.

26. Among Wahba's numerous recorded debates and public appearances, I suggest the following: Interview by Taha Elkorany, March 4, 2013, https://www .youtube.com/watch?v=OhIosRs-P9c; "Hiwar al-yawm: Special Encounter with Dr. Mourad Wahba, Philosophy Professor from Ain Shams University" [in Arabic], posted September 10, 2014, https://www.youtube.com/watch?v=O-H1W4CvPxI; *Jusur min al-Qahira* program [in Arabic], episode 16, part 1, posted September 24, 2012, https://www.youtube.com/watch?v=VyDnGAaUGsk; and "Liqa' ham ma' al mufakkir wa al-faylasuf Mourad Wahba" [Important encounter with the thinker and philosopher Mourad Wahba], posted January 10, 2012, https://www.youtube .com/watch?v=b2B9JSop6ww.

27. See, for instance, Wahba, "Al-muthaqqafun sabab nakbat hadha al-balad" [The intellectuals are the cause of this country's catastrophe].

28. See for instance, Wahba, "Al-Sisi wa al-haqiqa al-mutlaqa" [Sisi and the absolute truth].

29. For a scathing criticism of his statements in this interview, see Louis, "Murad Wahba." For Louis, Wahba's positions demonstrate a total absence of ethical thinking and are symptomatic of the whole Arab tanwir discourse.

30. For a recent extensive interview with Wahba, see "Mourad Wahba . . . tahrir al-'aql: Al-muharramat al-thaqafiyya wa sujun al-madi" [Mourad Wahba . . . liberation of reason: The cultural taboos and the prisons of the past], interviewed by Hanan 'Aqil, *al-Jadid*, December 2015, http://aljadeedmagazine.com/?id=1139; and for comments on this interview, see Abu Bakr al-'iyadi, "Mourad Wahba wa al-ta'min al-mukhill bi al-haqiqa" [Mourad Wahba and the generalization that

disturbs the truth], *al-Jadid*, December 2015, http://aljadeedmagazine.com/?id=1141; and Abdel Rahman Bsiso, "Al-as'ila al-maraya wa idlaqiyyat al-ajwiba . . . mustahall hiwar ma' al-mufakkir Mourad Wahba" [Mirror questions and absolute answers . . . preface to a dialogue with the thinker Mourad Wahba] *al-Jadid*, January 2016, http: // www.aljadeedmagazine.com/?id=1185.

31. This is part of my work in progress. Some of my early findings are presented in Kassab, "Critics and Rebels."

32. See, for instance, Shoair, "Suqut muthaqqaf misri" [The fall of an Egyptian intellectual]; Saleh, "Hal akhta'a Gaber Asfour?" [Did Gaber Asfour make a mistake?]; Dib, "Mufaraqat Gaber Asfour" [The paradoxes of Gaber Asfour]; Nasser, "Limadha ya Gaber Asfour" [Why oh Gaber Asfour]. See also Colla, "State Culture, State Anarchy."

33. See, for instance, his interview with prominent anchor Hafiz al-Mirazi on al-'Arabiyya television, uploaded February 12, 2011, https://www.youtube.com/watch?v=otkViGvAIm4. See also Asfour's justificatory article "Gaber Asfour yakshuf asrar tawzirihi" [Gaber Asfour unveils the secrets of his appointment as minister].

34. Indeed, his weekly *al-Ahram* article published on January 24, 2011, on the eve of the revolution, expressed deep pessimism about the state of the country, especially regarding its socioeconomic and political situation. It was titled "Wa madha 'an al-mustaqbal al-wa'id" [And what about the promising future?].

35. On this vision, see his interviews: Asfour, " 'Like Water and Air,' " "Renewing Discourse," and "Gaber Asfour waziran li al-marra al-thaniya" [Gaber Asfour minister for the second time].

36. See, for instance, al-Sirgani " 'Azizi d. Gaber Asfour:" [Dear Dr. Gaber Asfour]; and Asfour's explanation for involving Sayyed Yassin in *Akhbar al-Adab*, July 29, 2014.

37. See for instance, damning reports by Amnesty International such as "Facts and Figures. Egypt: Roadmap to Repression—No End in Sight for Human Rights Violations," January 23, 2014; and by UK director of Human Rights Watch David Mepham, "Repression Unbound." For harsh criticisms of Asfour, see al-Qimhawi, "Farouk Hosni akher wazir thaqafa li misr" [Farouk Hosni, last culture minister for Egypt]; Zakariyya, "Gaber Asfour" [Gaber Asfour]; al-Biyari, "Gaber Asfour yakhda' nafsahu mujaddan" [Gaber Asfour deluding himself again].

38. Asfour, interview by Al-Baha' Husayn, August 28, 2011. The webpage also includes excerpts from the videotaped interview: http://gate.ahram.org.eg/News /109615.aspx.

39. See his article from October 25, 2010: Asfour, "Al-thaqafa al-misriyya fi karitha" [Egyptian culture in catastrophe]. On October 28 he gave an interview in *al-Masry al-yawm* on the same topic, this time in connection with the book he had recently published, *Naqd thaqafat al-takhalluf* [Critique of the culture of backwardness]. On the predicament of intellectuals caught between religious fundamentalism and political state despotism, see also Asfour, "Undhur hawlak fi ghadab" [Look around you in anger].

40. Asfour, interviewed by Hamdi Rizk, al-Balad television, June 19, 2014, part 1, https://www.youtube.com/watch?v=j6lTW6WXddI, and part 2, https://

www.youtube.com/watch?v=kguffftcZFg. The first part is more relevant for our purposes.

41. Asfour, "Tatwir al-mandhuma al-thaqafiyya li al-dawla" [Developing the cultural system for the state].

42. Gaber would leave the ministry in March 2015, before the elections, as a result of a governmental shuffle. The first parliamentary elections under Sisi took place in fall 2015.

43. Asfour, *Manarat* program, al-Arabiyya television, posted June 23, 2015, https://www.youtube.com/watch?v=mrmok_eoGRc.

44. This is reminiscent of Sadeq al-Azm expressing his shock at the 1967 defeat and the ensuing realization that all the alleged accomplishments of the nahda were in reality fragile aspirations that could not be relied or built upon, that everything remained to be done, starting with the basics of modernity. See al-Azm, "An Interview with Sadik al-Azm."

45. Asfour, "Min al-tanwir ila al-idhlam" [From enlightening to obscuring], in *Hawamish 'ala daftar al-tanwir*, 249–90. The following year, in 1993, he published a book with a similar title: *al-Tanwir yuwajih al-idhlam* [Enlightenment faces obscurantism].

46. See also Asfour, 177–85.

47. Asfour, "Limadha yantakis al-tanwir?" [Why does tanwir suffer setbacks?], in *Hawamish 'ala daftar al-tanwir*, 291–325.

48. A few years earlier, Egyptian historian Ghali Shukri (1935–1998) had argued along the same lines, saying that if at the time of the nahda the conciliatory strategy had been useful, it could no longer play a positive role nowadays, when what is needed is the revolutionizing of culture. See Shukri, *Diktatoriyyat al-takhalluf al-arabi* [The dictatorship of Arab backwardness]. See also Kassab, "Critique of the Conciliatory Pattern of Thinking," in *Contemporary Arab Thought*, 253–69.

49. To hear el-Houdaiby elaborate on this aspect of Muhammad Abduh's thought, see his television interview with Bilal Fadl, *'Asir al-Kutub* program [in Arabic], al-'Arabi television, episode 21, posted October 30, 2015, https://www.youtube.com/watch?v=rT5UGt_-Oes. Trained in political science and Islamic studies in Cairo, he was pursuing a doctoral degree in political science at Columbia University at the time of the interview.

50. Asfour, "Mihnat al-tanwir" [The crisis of tanwir], in *Hawamish 'ala daftar al-tanwir*, 327–60.

51. On Egyptian cultural policies and practices in the second half of the twentieth century, see Gonzalez-Quijano, *Les gens du livre*.

52. Taher, *Abna' Rifa'a* [The Sons of Rifa'a].

53. See, for instance, a collection of his essays on these cases in Asfour, *Didd al-ta'assub* [Against intolerance].

54. Imarah, preface to *Al-Islam bayn al-tanwir wa al-tazwir* [Islam between tanwir and falsification], 5–33.

55. In an extended television interview on the subject of tanwir, Imarah speaks of a "fury" (*howja*) of tanwir dominating Egypt in the early 1990s and presents many of his theses developed in *Al-Islam bayn al-tanwir wa al-tazwir*. Imarah, "Al-tanwir fi al-mafhum al-islami wa al-gharbi" [Tanwir in the Islamic and Western

understanding], in *al-Muntada* program [in Arabic], Azhar satellite television, posted December 18, 2012, https://www.youtube.com/watch?v=6MlV5rgt4lM.

56. Imarah, *Al-Islam bayn al-tanwir wa al-tazwir* [Islam between tanwir and falsification], 19.

57. Imarah, 27.

58. Imarah, 225–27.

59. Imarah, 184.

60. Imarah, 186–87.

61. Imarah, 37.

62. Abdel Raziq, *Al-Islam wa usul al-hukm* [Islam and the principles of governance].

63. For a review of the debates regarding the reestablishment of the caliphate after its abolishment in Turkey in 1924, see M. Haddad, "Arab Religious Nationalism in the Era of Colonialism."

64. Imarah, *Al-Islam bayn al-tanwir wa al-tazwir* [Islam between tanwir and falsification], 39.

65. Imarah, 166.

66. Imarah, 59–65.

67. Imarah, 88.

68. Husayn, *Mustaqbal al-thaqafa fi Misr* [The future of culture in Egypt].

69. Husayn, *Fi al-shi'r al-jahili* [On Jahili poetry].

70. Moussa, *Al-yawm wa al-ghad* [Today and tomorrow].

71. Imarah, *Al-Islam bayn al-tanwir wa al-tazwir* [Islam between tanwir and falsification], 97. He also wrote a series of articles in *al-Hayat* on Salama Moussa and then collected his views in a booklet entitled *Salama Moussa: Ijtihad khati' am 'amala hadariyya?* [Salama Moussa: Mistaken interpretation or civilizational betraying agency?].

72. Imarah, 109, 111, 112, 114, 117, 127, 128, 138, 148, 149, 151.

73. Imarah, 100.

74. Charif, "Musahama fi al-jadal al-rahin hawl al-tanwir" [A contribution to the current dialogue on tanwir]; Imarah's article appeared in *Al-Hayat*, May 15, 1994. On Salama Moussa's positions in the nahda context viewed from the late twentieth century, see Shukri, *Salama Moussa wa azamat al-damir al-arabi* [Salama Moussa and the crisis of Arab conscience]; and Abdel Latif, *Salama Moussa wa ishkaliyyat al-nahda* [Salama Moussa and the problematic of the nahda].

75. Charif, "Musahama fi al-jadal al-rahin hawl al-tanwir" [A contribution to the current debate on tanwir], 176.

76. Charif, 166–67. For more Maher Charif essays on the nahda, see *Rihanat al-nahda fi al-fikr al-arabi* [The stakes of the nahda in Arab thought].

77. See Abu Fakhr and al-Azm, "Al-tanwir wa al-'almaniyya wa al-salafiyya" [Tanwir and secularism and salafism], in *Hiwar ma' Sadeq Jalal al-Azm* [Conversation with Sadeq Jalal al-Azm], 56; Eid, *Yas'alunak 'an al-mujtma' al-madani"* [They ask you about civil society]; and particularly Eid, "Madkhal li qira'at al-ta'addudiyya fi surya" [Introduction to a reading of pluralism in Syria], originally published in *Huquq al-Insan wa al-dimuqratiyya fi surya* [Human rights and democracy in Syria].

78. Imarah, *Al-Islam bayn al-tanwir wa al-tazwir* [Islam between tanwir and falsification], 226, 245.

79. Imarah, 227.

80. Imarah, 230–35.

81. Imarah, 237.

82. Imarah, 239–52.

83. Imarah, 259–66. This policy of publishing truncated texts, as we saw earlier in the case of Farah Antun's work, pointed out by Mourad Wahba, shows the extent to which the tanwir publication campaign served political agendas rather than the scholarly cultivation of an intellectual heritage. In fact, Yves Gonzalez-Quijano compares the Muwajaha campaign to that of the Nasserite publishing campaign, aimed at disseminating socialist doctrines. See Gonzalez-Quijano, *Les gens du livre*, 69.

84. Mabruk, *Muwajahat al-Muwajaha* [Confrontation of the confrontation].

2. The Deconstruction of the 1990s Egyptian Tanwir Debates

1. To document and discuss that work is part of my larger project on the Arab uprisings and Arab contemporary thought.

2. On the sociology of knowledge, see Abaza, "Social Sciences in Egypt," and *Debates on Islam and Knowledge in Malaysia and Egypt*. On the cultural scene, see Abaza, *Twentieth Century Egyptian Art*, and "Walls, Segregating Downtown Cairo and the Mohammed Mahmud Street Graffiti."

3. Among her most recent pieces on the revolution, see Abaza, "Is Cairene Graffiti Losing Momentum?," and "Egypt."

4. Abaza, "Tanwir and Islamization," and "Trafficking with Tanwir (Enlightenment)."

5. I prefer to use this more widespread transliteration of the name Muhammad Imarah, rather than the one used by Abaza, " 'Immara."

6. On the significance and influence of the journal, see Dudoignon, Hisao, and Yasushi, *Intellectuals in the Modern Islamic World*; in particular, contributions by M. Haddad, "The Manarists and Modernism"; and Yasushi, "*Al-Manar* Revisited."

7. Abaza, "Tanwir and Islamization," 95.

8. Abaza, 97.

9. Abaza, 97.

10. Kepel, "Les oulémas, l'intelligentsia et les islamistes en Égypte."

11. Kepel, 427.

12. For a longer analysis of the rise of the Islamists in Egypt, see Kepel, *Le prophète et Pharaon*.

13. For the centennial celebrations of *Dar al-Hilal*, see the photos under the title "The Centennial Celebrations of Dar al-Hilal" as well as the videos under "Prelude with Speeches of Literary Figures, Parts I & II," Zaidan Foundation, http://zaidan foundation.org/ZF_Website_Photos_CentennialCelebrations.html.

14. See al-Bishri, *Al-Hiwar al-islami al-'almani* [The Islamic secular dialogue].

15. See Nasr Hamid Abu Zayd's critical comments on Imarah's turn in assessing Ali Abdel Raziq's thought in Abu Zayd, "Mawqif Imarah min Ali Abd el Raziq" [Imarah's position regarding Ali Abd el Raziq].

16. Quoted in Abaza, "Tanwir and Islamization," 103.

17. Imarah, *Taha Husayn*. The book was distributed with the monthly *al-Azhar* magazine, edited by Imarah.

18. Dab', *Taha Husayn*. The book's title refers to a series of articles that Taha Husayn published in 1933 and 1934 in the Egyptian magazine *al-Risala*.

19. For a brief summary of the debate, see 'Asem, "Hal yuhawil al-islamiyyun musadarat Taha Husayn ba'd 41 'aman 'ala rahilihi?" [Are the Islamists trying to confiscate Taha Husayn 41 years after his departure?].

20. Abaza, "Tanwir and Islamization," 98.

21. Abaza, "Trafficking with Tanwir (Enlightenment)," 32.

22. Mehrez, "Take Them Out of the Ballgame." For the effects of this interface between politics and culture in censoring cinema, see Mehrez, "The New Kid on the Block: *Bahibb issima* and the Emergence of the Coptic Community in the Egyptian Public Sphere," in *Egypt's Culture Wars*, 188–207. For the impact on the visual arts, see Mehrez, "*Found in Cairo*: The Limits of Representation in the Visual Field," in *Egypt's Culture Wars*, 208–28. See also Ghazoul, "The Artist vs the Commissar"; Ferial Ghazoul is professor of English and comparative literature at the American University of Cairo and founding editor of *Alif: Journal of Contemporary Poetics*. For literature and censorship in Egypt, see Jacquemond, "Les limites mouvantes du dicible dans la fiction égyptienne"; and al-Ahnaf, "L'affaire Haydar Haydar." See also Jacquemond, "The Shifting Limits of the Sayable in Contemporary Egyptian Fiction."

23. The Kifaya movement came together in 2004 to warn against the regime's intention to hand over power to the president's son, Gamal Mubarak, and to protest against corruption.

24. Salam, "Egyptian Culture Minister, Imaginary and Fabricated Battles."

25. The text appeared under the first title in *Akhabar al-Adab* 18 (February 2001) and under the second title in *Akhbar al-Adab* (2005).

26. These slogans returned when President Mohamed Morsi was ousted and Field Marshal Abdel Fatah el-Sisi took over in July 2013.

27. Abu Zayd also used this formulation in a speech at the 2008 Cairo meeting of the Egyptian Philosophical Society entitled "Al-mufakkir haris qiyam . . . la kalb hirasa" [The thinker, a guardian of values . . . not a watchdog"], http://civicegypt.org/?p=16420.

28. For more on Mohammed Arkoun's work and on the brief exchange between him and Abu Zayd, see Kassab, *Contemporary Arab Thought*, 173–94.

29. Due to the unavailability of an online search of the archives of *Akhbar al-Adab* I am unable to give the exact page of this quotation. However, here is the link to the article in the Abu Zayd online archive: Abu Zayd, "Suqut al-tanwir al-hukumi" [The fall of the governmental tanwir], 2005, posted April 11, 2009, https://rowaqnasrabuzaid.wordpress.com/2009/04/11/. See also Abu Zayd's interview with his publisher in his book *Al-khitab wa al-ta'wil*, 232–37. All translations from Arabic texts are mine unless otherwise indicated.

30. Abu Zayd, "Ishkaliyyat al-muthaqqaf wa al-dawla/al-sulta" [The problematic of the intellectual and the state/power].

31. Abu Zayd.

32. Abu Zayd, "Ishakaliyyat al-ʻilaqa bayna al-ʻaql wa al-wahi" [The problematic between reason and revelation].

33. Abu Zayd.

34. Abu Zayd.

35. Abu Zayd, "Al-fazaʻ min al-ʻilmaniyya" [The fear from secularism].

36. Abu Zayd.

37. Abu Zayd, "Ladayna duʻat tanwir wa laysa sunnaʻ tanwir, wa hunaka farq bayna an tadʻu li al-tanwir wa bayna an tassnaʻahu" [We have preachers of tanwir, not makers of tanwir, and there is a difference between preaching tanwir and making it]. The interview is undated, but from the information given at the beginning it must have been from 2009. In it Abu Zayd affirms that attempts at reforming and renewing religious thought have been going on since Muhammad Abduh and mentions the works of Tayyib Tizini, Muhammed Abed al-Jabiri, and Hasan Hanafi, but he laments the difficulty of disseminating new ideas under political repression.

38. See Abu Zayd, *Naqd al-Khitab al-Dini* [The critique of religious discourse].

39. Abu Zayd, introduction to *Dawaʼir al Khawf* [The circles of fear], 6. For a brief presentation of his oeuvre, see Kassab, "The Historicity of Revelation and the Struggle for Thought in the Time of Anathema: Nasr Hamid Abu Zayd," in *Contemporary Arab Thought*, 183–94.

40. Hanafi, "Al-tanwir am al-tathwir?" [Enlightenment or revolutionizing?]. This is a modified version of an earlier article he wrote in two parts for the Kuwaiti daily *al-Jarida*, June 23 and 30, 2008.

41. Hanafi.

42. For more on Hanafi's "Islamic left" project, see the section on his work in Kassab, *Contemporary Arab Thought*, 200–7.

43. Hanafi, "Al-salafiyya wa al-ʻalmaniyya" [Salafism and secularism].

44. Hanafi, "Tanwir aw Tazwir?" [Enlightening or faking?].

45. Hanafi, "Nahnu wa al-tanwir wa al-ʻaql" [We and the enlightenment and reason], "Nahnu wa al-tanwir . . . al-huriyya wa al-insan" [We and the enlightenment . . . freedom and the human], "Nahnu wa al-tanwir . . . wa iktishaf al-tabiʻa" [We and the enlightenment . . . and the discovery of nature], "Nahnu wa al-tanwir . . . wa thaqafat al-mujtamaʻ" [We and the enlightenment . . . and the culture of society], and "Nahnu wa al-tanwir . . . wa al-waʻi al-tarikhi" [We and the enlightenment . . . and historical awareness].

46. Louis, "Dhulumat al-tanwir al-masri" [The manifold darkness of Egyptian tanwir].

47. Abd Rabou, "ʻAn asatir al-tanwir."

48. See Younis, *Masarat al-thawra* [The courses of the revolution]. Indeed, after having been a clear, albeit critical, supporter of the revolution, Sherif Younis sided with the Sisi regime after the ousting of Morsi. His critique vis-à-vis the revolutionary turned into an attack, and his rejection of the Islamists, the Muslim Brotherhood in particular, became absolute. Many of his colleagues and former fellow

revolutionaries remain perplexed by his change of attitude, and his Facebook followers are baffled by his bellicose comments. This perplexity is well articulate by a young Egyptian dentist, poet, and writer, Ahmad Nada, in "Nisf Sherif Younis al-akhar" [The other half of Sherif Younis]. In it Nada wonders how Younis could support a regime and a state ideology so similar to the ones he deconstructed and condemned in his insightful analyses of the Nasser era.

49. *Al-Kitaba al-ukhra* was launched in May 1991 and sustained to a great extent by the persistant efforts of Hisham Qashta, its editor and manager, who produced twenty-four issues. After that it stopped publishing for lack of funds and reemerged in 2010. See Mahmoud, "'Al-Kitaba al-ukhra' khadat ma'rakat al-thaqafa al-muhammasha" [Al-Kitaba al-ukhra led the battle for the marginalized culture]; and Jacquemond, *Conscience of the Nation*, 170–71.

50. Younis, *Su'al al-huwiyya* [The question of identity].

51. Younis, *al-Zahf al-Muqaddas* [The holy march].

52. Younis, *Nida' al-sha'b* [The call of the people].

53. Younis, *al-Bahth 'an al-khalas* [The search for salvation].

54. Younis, *Sayyed Qutb wa al-usuliyya al-islamiyya* [Sayyed Qutb and Islamic fundamentalism], 19–27.

55. Younis, 11–18.

56. Power (*sulta*) here meaning the power of the ruler.

57. "Awham al-tanwir" was published in *Adab 21*, March 1996, in the town of al-Mansura; "Ma'zaq al-tanwir ma bayn al-sulta wa al-usuliyya al-islamiyya" appeared in the journal *Al-kitaba al-ukhra* [The other writing] 10, no. 11 (April 1995); and "Al-wida' al-akhir li al-haras al-qadim: Azamt al-intelligentsia al-misriyya wa idilyolojiyyat al-huwwiyya" also appeared in *Al-kitaba al-ukhra* 14, no. 15 (May 1996).

58. The book was published in 1999 in Cairo by the publishing house Merit. I will be quoting from the book for the convenience of pagination; the book is unfortunately no longer in print, but available online.

59. The first article appeared as "Limadha fashila mashrou' al-tanwir?" [Why did the tanwir project fail?], September 20, 2002, http://www.ahewar.org/debat/show.art.asp?aid=3056. The second article appeared January 17, 2003, http://www.ahewar.org/debat/show.art.asp?aid=2982. And the third one appeared December 10, 2002, http://www.ahewar.org/debat/show.art.asp?aid=4295. The journal won the 2010 Ibn Rushd prize for free thought: al-Hewar al-Mutamaddin, last accessed October 17, 2018, http://ahewar.org/ibn-rushdAward/index.html. See also the press release announcing the prize: "The Ibn Rush Fund for the Freedom of Thought Announces the Ibn Rush Award 2010 Goes to the Arab Internet Forum al-Hewar," http://www.ibn-rushd.org/typo3/cms/fileadmin/Ibn_Rushd/awards/2010/pressRelease-en.html. The Ibn Rushd Fund was established in Germany "in 1998 in commemoration of the 800th anniversary of Ibn Rushd's (Averroes') death and on the 50th anniversary of [the] Universal Declaration of Human Rights." It is awarded yearly in Berlin, and its aim is to foster "freedom of thought and democracy in the Arab world."

60. Sherif Younis, *Su'al al-huwwiyya*, 36.

61. As an eloquent illustration of this phenomenon, see the recent interview of Sonallah Ibrahim, "Sonallah Ibrahim."

62. Ibrahim, 41.

63. Ibrahim, 29.

64. Ibrahim, 32–33.

65. On the subservience of the medical establishment to the state since the beginning of the modern Egyptian state, see Fahmy, "Dissecting the Modern Egyptian State."

66. Younis, *Sayyed Qutb wa al-usuliyya al-islamiyya* [Sayyed Qutb and Islamic fundamentalism], 12.

67. For a brief review of this early elite and its claim to speak in the name of the people, see Moghith, "Au nom du peuple."

68. For a recent discussion of the relation of liberals and Islamists to the Egyptian state, see Abdel Meguid and Faruqi, "The Truncated Debate," Abou el-Fadl, "Egypt's Secularized Intelligentsia and the Guardians of Truth," and Fahmy and Daanish, "Egyptian Liberals, from Revolution to Counterrevolution."

69. Abdel Meguid and Faruqi, 59–60.

70. For a study of the fate of Egyptian Marxism under Abdel Nasser, see Younis, "Marxisme et patriotisme dans les régimes militaires de libération nationale."

71. Younis, 85.

72. Roussillon, "Intellectuels en crise dans l'Égypte contemporaine."

73. Mohamed Hassanein Heikal edited the various contributions in *Azamat al-muthaqqafin* [The crisis of the intellectuals].

74. Abdel Malek, "La 'crise des intellectuels.'" While the Egyptian literary field of the second half of the twentieth century has received considerable attention, the intellectual field, including the animated debates on thought, culture, and politics, has not been explored sufficiently. An intellectual history of this period remains to be written. The ideas of thinkers such as Ghali Shukri (1935–1998), Louis Awad (1915–1990), and Magdi Wahba (1925–1991) deserve close examination. In connection with this, it is worth mentioning the documentary work of Shafi' Shalabi, the Egyptian media anchorman, filmmaker, and political activist who in 1981 founded the National Center for Documenting Egypt's Revolution and Renaissance and in the early 2000s the People and Earth Network (PENtv): https://www.youtube.com/playlist?list=PL195EA62CC0F59BFC&feature=mh_lolz.

He has hours of interviews with, and films on, Egyptian intellectuals of the period that document important debates of the time. The films are part of a collection he calls *Mawsu'at a'lam min al-qarn al-'ishrin* [Starts from the twentieth century], meant to preserve the cultural and intellectual memory of twentieth-century Egypt. One on Louis Awad, entitled *Awraq al-'umr* [The sheets of life], takes its name from the title of Awad's autobiography, published in Cairo in 1989 by Maktabat Madbuli. I wish to thank Mr. Shalabi for the private screening of the film he offered me during one of my visits to Cairo.

Many of his films have not been released yet, as he wants them to be sponsored by people's associations and an independent people's channel aiming to emancipate the mind (*tahrir al-'aql*) by emancipating the Nile communication satellite: https://www.youtube.com/user/2010pentv. In the meantime, he has posted brief excerpts of some films on YouTube, such as *Awraq al-'umr*, last updated July 10, 2017, https://www.youtube.com/playlist?list=PLvjKZrK7PdgHSEK6KNNweOVVju

bdfJypf; and his documentary on Egyptian philosopher Zaki Naguib Mahmoud (1905–1993), *Ayna 'aqli?* (Where is my reason?), posted August 2, 2014, https://www.youtube.com/watch?v=iKfQwfmCHss&list=PLvjKZrK7PdgG_72SFIkWMC9ai7LDA8fg3.

75. For an informative history of Cairo University, including the Nasser era, see Reid, *Cairo University and the Making of Modern Egypt*.

76. See Roussillon "Sociologie et société en Égypte." See also Abaza "Social Sciences in Egypt."

77. *Al-Ahram al-iqtisadi* (October–December 1982); Roussillon, "Sociologie et société en Égypte," 134. See also Reid, *Cairo University and the Making of Modern Egypt*, 217–18.

78. Roussillon, "Sociologie et société en Égypte," 129, 133, 138, and "Intellectuels en crise dans l'Égypte contemporaine," 237.

79. al-Ahnaf, "Débats intellectuels et intellectuels en débat."

80. Kandil, "On the Margins of Defeat."

81. Kassab, *Contemporary Arab Thought*. My conclusion discusses the views of a number of Arab intellectuals interviewed around the mid-2000s about their work and role in their societies.

82. From the vast literature on the German Aufklärung, see Schmidt, *What Is Enlightenment?* His introduction to the anthology gives an informative background on both the eighteenth- and twentieth-century debates.

83. For a detailed presentation of the debate about Spinoza's philosophy and atheism, known as the "Pantheism controversy," see Beiser, *The Fate of Reason*, especially chapters 2, 3, and 4. Most interesting in this respect is the reception of Spinoza's philosophy by modern Arab philosophers, such as Egyptians Hasan Hanafi and Fouad Zakariyya. Zakariyya published a book on Spinoza in 1962 and in the 1983 edition added a long preface presenting Spinoza's philosophy as a counter-view to the obscurantism of the Islamic fundamentalists and the revolutionary despotism of Nasser. He presented Spinoza's philosophy as a defense of rationalism and secularism. Zakariyya's pioneering book was followed by Hasan Hanafi's 1971 translation of Spinoza's 1670 *Tractatus Theologico-Politicus* (*Theologico-Political Treatise*). For more on Spinoza's reception in Tunisia, see Mosbah, "Spinoza et le problème du théologico-politique en Tunisie."

84. See Beiser, *Enlightenment, Revolution, and Romanticism*, 1–56.

85. On the subject of education and elitism in the Enlightenment, I refer to Zygmunt Bauman's *Legislators and Interpreters*, particularly chapter 5.

3. Tanwir Debates in Syria in the 1990s

1. On power struggles in Syria in the 1950s and 1960s, see Seale, *The Struggle for Syria*.

2. On the social background of Syria's ruling military at the time, see Batatu, "Some Observations." See also the two-part documentary produced by *Al Jazeera* satellite television, *Mamlakat al-samt* [The kingdom of silence], written and directed

by Suheib Abu Dawla, https://www.youtube.com/watch?v=GF9TpudTvaU (posted March 11, 2015), and https://www.youtube.com/watch?v=RWTTLz8xqu4 (posted March 3, 2014).

3. For an overview of Syrian politics, economy, and culture from the Ottoman period to the late 1970s, see Raymond, *La Syrie d'aujourd'hui.*

4. For details on this and following waves of protests and their repression by the governing powers, see Syrian sociologist Khouloud Zghayar, "Suria fi mu'taqal al-Baath/al-Assad—Qissat watan" [Syria in the captivity of the Baath/Assad—Story of a homeland], parts 1 and 2, Souria Houria (Syrian opposition website), March 18 and April 28, 2012, part 2 available online, https://souriahouria.com /سوريا-في-معتقل-البعثالأسد-قصة-وطن-2/.

5. On the elite, the army, and sectarianism in Syria under Assad the father, see Van Dam, *The Struggle for Power in Syria.* On the formation of the Baath state, see Hinnebusch, *Authoritarian Power and State Formation in Ba'thist Syria.*

6. On the political economy of Hafez al-Assad in the 1970s and 1980s, see the classic work of Volker Perthes, "Stages of Economic and Political Liberalization." See also Perthes, "The Syrian Private Industrial and Commercial Sectors and the State," "A Look at Syria's Upper Class," and *The Political Economy of Syria Under Asad.* See also Eberhard Kienle, "The Return of Politics?" For an overview of the private sector under the two Assad regimes, see B. Haddad, "Enduring Legacies."

On the corruption that accompanied Assad's economic policies and its role in his political power, see Sadowski, "The Eighth Regional Congress of the Syrian Baath." See also Sadowski, "Patronage and the Ba'th," and "Ba'thist Ethics and the Spirit of State Capitalism."

7. On the end of political parties in Syria, see Picard, "Fin de partis en Syrie"; and on the Syrian parliamentary elections of 1990, see Perthes, "Syria's Parliamentary Elections."

8. See Zghayar, "Suria fi mu'taqal al-Baath/al-Asad" [Syria in the captivity of the Baath / Asad], part 2.

9. American scholar of comparative literature Miriam Cooke analyzes this blurred but effective cultural censorship by the regime, arguing that the regime would even "commission critique" while keeping the power to dispose of its products. See Cooke, *Dissident Syria.* For her work on art and the revolution after the Syrian uprising, see Cooke, *Dancing in Damascus.*

10. American political scientist Lisa Wedeen analyzes the workings and effects of such a repressive cult of personality in *Ambiguities of Domination.* She argues that the system forces people to behave as if they loved and were obedient to the leader. People's awareness of their being forced to express what they don't believe in, is, according to her, the ultimate show of power by the regime. On page 131 she writes:

> Because organized opposition is not tolerated, language and the courage it takes to speak with others establish the foundation of what might ultimately eventuate in organized opposition. But a joke, a movie line, or a cartoon is politically relevant not only insofar as it may have consequences for or help define the parameters of future political upheavals; in the moment when a joke is told, when laughter resounds in the room, people are also cancelling the isolation

and atomization manufactured by a politics of "as if." People are affirming with each other that they are unwilling conscripts, that the cult is both unbelievable and powerful.

And yet, paradoxically, it is precisely this shared acknowledgement of involuntary obedience that also makes the cult so powerful. Or to put it differently, Asad's cult is powerful, in part, because it is unbelievable. These acts of transgressing might counteract the atomization and isolation a politics of "as if" produces, but they also shore up another of the cult's mechanisms of discipline, namely, the ways in which the cult relies on an external obedience produced through each citizen's unbelief. If Asad's cult disciplines citizens by occasioning continual demonstrations of external obedience, and if external obedience relies on a self-conscious submission to authority, then recognizing the shared conditions of unbelief reproduces this self-consciousness without which a politics of "as if" could hardly be sustained.

See also her article on the subject, "Acting 'As if.'" In a more recent interview ("New Texts Out Now") on her 2013 article "Ideology and Humor in Dark Times," dealing with reactions to power under the new president, she summarizes the argument of *Ambiguities of Domination* in the following way:

For much of Asad's rule (1970–2000) his image was omnipresent. In newspapers, on television, and during orchestrated spectacles, Asad was praised as the "father," the "gallant knight," even the country's "premier pharmacist." Yet most Syrians, including those who created the official rhetoric, did not believe its claims. *Ambiguities* asked: Why would a regime spend scarce resources on a cult whose rituals of obeisance are transparently phony? The book concluded that Syria's cult of Hafiz al-Asad operated not to produce belief or emotional commitment—which the concept of Weberian legitimacy presupposes—but to specify both the form and content of civic obedience. Beyond the barrel of the gun and the confines of the torture chamber, Asad's cult served as a disciplinary device, generating a politics of public dissimulation in which citizens acted *as if* they revered their leader. By inundating daily life with instructive symbolism, the regime exercised a subtle yet effective form of power. The cult worked to enforce obedience, induce complicity, isolate Syrians from one another, and set guidelines for public speech and behavior.

11. On Syria's Islamists—their history, ideology, and confrontation with the state and its secular ideology—see Lobmeyer, "Islamic Ideology and Secular Discourse"; see also Batatu, "Syria's Muslim Brethren."

12. On the manipulation of the judiciary for repression, see Leenders, "Prosecuting Political Dissent."

13. On the state of the opposition in the early 1990s, see Lobmeyer, "Al-dimuqratiyya hiyya al-hall?"

14. Barqawi, "Ma al-tanwir?" [What is enlightenment?].

15. Barqawi, 5.

16. They were posthumously published in Seurat, *L'état de barbarie*, 15–34, 35–52.

17. See Thomas Pierret, "Syrie: État sans nation ou nation sans état?," 185. For a more recent study of the effects of this rule of systematic violence, see Ismail, *The Rule of Violence*.

18. On his ordeal, see the documentary film by Syrian filmmaker Omar Amiralay, *Fi yawm min ayam al-'unf al-'adi, mata sadiqi Michel Seurat* [On a day of ordinary violence, my friend Michel Seurat died] (France/Lebanon, 1995), part 3 available on YouTube, https://www.youtube.com/watch?v=gRZe3Pslm08. On Seurat's book, see also the television program *Muni'a min al-nashr* [Forbidden from publication], Orient (Syrian opposition TV channel), "Suria . . . al-dawla al-mutawahhisha: al-Kitab al ladhi awda bi hayat mu'allifihi" [Syria . . . the barbaric state: The book that led to the death of its author], posted October 18, 2017, https://www.youtube.com/watch?v=4_1fl8QXphg. Al Jazeera television also produced a two-part film in its documentary series *Kharej al-nass, Michel Seurat yakshuf al-dawla al-mutawahhisha fi Suria* [Michel Seurat uncovers the barbaric state in Syria], part 1, https://www.youtube.com/watch?v=5O5C3DkPud8 (broadcast and posted March 11, 2018), and part 2, https://www.youtube.com/watch?v=fybcCAfLHG8 (broadcast and posted March 18, 2018).

19. For a history of the Syrian writers' union, which started in 1951 as the Syrian Writers Collective and became the Union of Arab Writers in Syria in 1954, see Firat, "Cultural Battles on the Literary Field." Firat discusses the union's literary, ideological, and ultimately political battles between the 1950s and the 1970s. She shows how some writers perceived the call to abide by social realism as a call to obey authoritarianism, and how many writers after 1967 became more self-reflective and autonomous and less inclined to view the function of literature as primarily social. On the founding congress of 1954, see Baldissera, "The Founding Congress of the League of Arab Writers."

20. Michel Kilo, recording of his speech at the Conference of the Arab Writers' Union, Damascus, 1981, posted July 1, 2011, https://www.youtube.com/watch?v=Hx9rxdNPqwE. Mamdouh Adwan, recording of his speech at the Conference of the Arab Writers' Union, Damascus, 1981, posted July 1, 2011, https://www.youtube.com/watch?v=Zb1dbHuSgv8. Although the recording says 1981, the conference actually took place in 1979.

21. Between the mid-1990s and mid-2000s Kilo wrote abundantly in the Lebanese daily *an-Nahar*, which had opened its opinion pages and cultural supplement to Syrian oppositional figures. This was an act of courage by its owner and editor, Ghassan Tueni (1926–2012), himself a prominent Lebanese journalist and diplomat, as Lebanon in that period was under Syrian control. His son, Gebran Tueni (1957–2005), continued the same political line as head of *an-Nahar* between 2000 and his death in 2005. He was assassinated in a car explosion, presumably by the Syrian authorities, in response to his anti-Assad politics. The articles published during that decade by numerous Syrian writers still await compiling and studying.

22. On the circumstances of Kilo's joining and leaving the Syrian National Coalition, see his article "Limadha taraktu al-i'tiliaf?" [Why did I leave the coalition?].

23. Adwan, *Haywanat al-insan* [The animalization of the human]. In Adwan's play *Al-ghoul* [The ghoul], for instance, he elaborated on the phenomenon of despotism

by referring to the brutal Ottoman governor Djemal Pasha, who ruled over the Syrian provinces between 1915 and the end of World War I.

24. Adwan, *Difa'an 'an al-junun* [In defense of madness].

25. Adwan, *Haywanat al-insan* [The animalization of the human], 16.

26. Syrian digital artist Nihad Nadam transformed a photo of Abdel Wahhab: *Ana insan mani haywan* [I am a human, not an animal], September 1, 2012, http://www.creativememory.org/?p=99273. See also the artist's website: http://www.nihad.me/.

27. Here is a selection from this literature: Syrian leftist political thinker and medical doctor Yassin Haj Saleh, *Bil Khalas ya shabab!* [Hopefully out my friends!].

Syrian leftist political activist Aram Karabet, *Al-rahil ila al-majhul* [Journey to the unknown].

Leftist Syrian activist and writer and medical doctor Rateb Shabo, *Madha wara' hadhihi al-judran* [What is there behind those walls?]. For more about the author's life, prison experience, and political analysis, see his interview on the Arabic France 24 program *Daif wa masira* [Guest and journey], posted March 8, 2016, https://www.youtube.com/watch?v=WIfJu7oZN6o.

Biology lecturer at City Colleges of Chicago Bara al-Sarraj, *Min Tadmur ila Harvard* [From Tadmur to Harvard]. Al-Sarraj was accused of having Islamist sympathies. For connections between his prison experiences and the violent state reaction to the revolution, see his interview on a program devoted largely to the prison experiences of Syrians, *Ya hurria* [Oh freedom], Syria TV (opposition channel), posted July 12, 2018, https://www.youtube.com/watch?v=dgf5S3OXSvk&feature=youtu.be.

Syrian leftist political activist and publisher Louay Hussein, *Al-Faqd* [The loss].

Syrian leftist activist and novelist Mustafa Khalifeh, *Al-Qawqa'a* [The shell]. For excerpts from the novel in English, see https://arablit.org/2013/10/12/mustafa-khalifas-the-shell-memoires-of-a-hidden-observer/ and http://muftah.org/mustapha-khalifa-and-arabic-prison-literature/#.V4pSoa60RDT. See also Taleghani, "A Memoir Novel of Tadmur Military Prison." For more on his novel, prison experience, and thoughts on the regime and the ongoing uprising, see his interview with Syrian writer Dima Wannous on her program *Ana min Hunak* [I am from there], Orient (Syrian opposition TV channel), posted July 19, 2015, https://www.youtube.com/watch?v=48oaSadCQWc. Hear also his radio interview with Jaber Bakr on the opposition radio channel Alwan.fm, posted January 19, 2015, https://www.youtube.com/watch?v=oRjXx_bHKos. For a more general study of Syrian prison literature, see Taleghani, "Vulnerability and Recognition in Syrian Prison Literature."

Syrian leftist political activist, poet, and novelist Faraj Bayraqdar, *Khiyanat al-lugha wa al-samt* [The betrayals of language and silence], and *Al-Khuruj min al-kahf* [Exit from the cave]. For more on his life, imprisonment, and writing, see his two-part interview "Taghribat al-shi'r al-ula: Faraj Bayraqdar" [Poetry's first exile: Faraj Bayraqdar], *Taghayarna* [We changed], Orient TV, part 1, https://www.youtube.com/watch?v=of8hOcgF5s4 (posted March 19, 2015), and part 2, https://www.youtube.com/watch?v=D_s2dOorgYg (posted May 8, 2015).

Syrian leftist playwright Ghassan Jaba'i, *Asabi' al-mawz* [Finger bananas]. On Jaba'i's work, including his writings on prison, see Cooke, "Ghassan al-Jaba'i."

Leftist Syrian short story writer Ibrahim Samu'il, *Ra'ihat al-khatw al-thaqil* [The stench of heavy steps]. In the rest of his writings he often showed the parallels between fear and oppression in prison and in the country, or the "bigger prison," as it is often called by prison survivors. See, for instance, his other collections of short stories, *Al-nahnahat* [Light coughs] and *Al-Manzil dhu al-madkhal al-wati'* [The house with the low entrance].

Syrian leftist political activist and feminist Hasiba Abdel Rahman, *Al-Sharnaqa* [The cocoon]. See her 2005 interview "Hiwaran ma' al-riwa'iyya Hasiba Abdel Rahman" [A conversation with novelist Hasiba Abdel Rahman], *al-Hiwar al-Mutamaddin*, July 21, 2005, http://www.m.ahewar.org/s.asp?aid=41556&r=0.

Hiba al-Dabbagh is one of two members of her family to survive the Hama massacre: she was in jail, and her brother was outside the country. Her book *Khams daqa'q wa hasb* [Five minutes only] is among the earliest Syrian prison memoirs.

Syrian novelist Rosa Yassin Hassan's *Nigativ* [Negative] is a documentary based on the experiences of leftist and Islamist women political prisoners in the 1990s.

On Michel Kilo's experiences with Syrian prisons, see Kilo, "Qisas ukhra min 'alam al-ashbah" [Other stories from the world of ghosts].

On the Tadmur prison memoirs, see Taleghani, "Breaking the Silence of Tadmor Military Prison," and "The Cocoons of Language, the Betrayals of Silence." For the experience of a Lebanese detainee in Tadmur prison, see Abu Dehn *'Aid min jahannam* [A returnee from hell], and, about his experience and his book, "Sujana' al-Ra'I al-lubnaniyyinfi al-Sujun al-Suriyya" [The Lebanese opinion prisoners in the Syrian prisons], interview by Dima Wannous and Lokman Slim, *Ana min Hunak*, posted April 25, 2016, https://www.youtube.com/watch?v=w49BI5bYWI0. For a film on the Tadmur prison as experienced by some of its survivors, see Monika Borgmann and Lokman Slim, *Tadmor* (Lebanon, 2016), https://www.tadmor-themovie.com/trailer. For a documentary film revisiting Tadmur prison with Yassin Haj Saleh, Faraj Bayraqdar, and Syrian playwright Ghassan Jbai, see Hala Mohammad, *Rihla il al-dhakira* [Journey into memory] (2006), posted August 1, 2012, https://www.youtube.com/watch?v=oKeZyoCy1yk.

On the impact of long-term imprisonment on the family of prisoners, see Mohammad Atassi, "The Other Prison." His father, Noureddin Atassi, president of Syria between 1966 and 1970, was arrested and sent to jail by Hafez al-Assad as Assad took power. Noureddin Atassi was released twenty-two years later and died a few months after that in Paris, where he was flown to receive urgent medical treatment. See also al-Turk, "Riad al-Turk."

Riad al-Turk (born 1930) is a prominent Syrian oppositional figure who has been jailed several times since 1952, the last time in 2002, and for the longest stretch, between 1980 and 1998, was mostly in solitary confinement. He was the general secretary of the Syrian Communist party, a section of which refused to give allegiance to Hafez al-Assad. See Mohammad Ali Atassi's 2001 film *Ibn el-'amm* [The cousin], posted August 23, 2012, https://www.youtube.com/watch?v=htdoCxAFf9c. For more on Turk, see L. Haddad, *Riad al-Turk*.

On Syrian prison literature in general, see Sakr, "'We Would Meet Them One Day'"; and Cooke, "The Cell Story."

For the Syrian regime's torture and killing of people associated with the 2011 revolt, see "Syria: Stories Behind Photos of Killed Detainees," Human Rights Watch, December 16, 2015, https://www.hrw.org/news/2015/12/16/syria-stories-behind -photos-killed-detainees, on the 2015 Human Rights Watch report *If the Dead Could Speak: Mass Deaths and Torture in Syria's Detention Facilities*; and the book based on it, Le Caisne, *Opération César* [Operation Cesar]. See Garance Le Caisne, interview by Anas Azraq, *Al-Mun'ataf* [The turn], Syria TV, posted August 7, 2018, https://www .syria.tv/content/لوكين-غرانس-الفرنسية-الصحفية-مع-عليها-الحصول-وتفاصيل-قيصر-صور. See also the Amnesty *International campaign about* the Saydnaya prison, https://www.amnesty.org /en/latest/campaigns/2016/08/syria-torture-prisons/. See also *Report from Amnesty International to the Government of the Syrian Arab Republic* (London: Amnesty International, 1983), https://www.amnesty.org/en/documents/mde24/004/1983/en/.

28. Haj Saleh, "Michel Kilo wa wiladat al-muthaqqaf al-suri" [Michel Kilo and the birth of the Syrian intellectual].

29. This also corresponds to Kilo's understanding of the intellectual. See Kilo, "Al-Muthaqqafun al-suriyyun laysu hizban" [The Syrian intellectuals are not a party].

30. See Kilo, "Muthaqqaf al-taghyir" [The intellectual of change].

31. The regime of silence affected all forms of expression, including literature. In "The Silences of Contemporary Syrian Literature," Syrian-American poet and writer Mohja Kahf writes the following:

> Contemporary Syrian literature is created in the crucible of a tenacious authoritarianism. Manifold silence, evasion, indirect figurative speech, gaps and lacunae are striking features of Syrian writing, habits of thought and wary writerly techniques that have developed during an era dominated, in Syria more overwhelmingly than in other Arab countries excepting Iraq and perhaps Libya, by authoritarian governments with heavy-handed censorship policies and stringent punitive measures. Idilbi's silences are sweet and sad; Maghut's are bitter, sarcastic, choked; and silence that is at once terrified, mesmerized, and complicit is Tamer's specialty. Syrian literature today is jittery with what it cannot say, and that is its genius. The ultimate silence of contemporary Syrian literature is its collective silence about the Hama massacre of 1982, "a bloodbath without parallel in the history of modern Syria," according to the late Hanna Batatu, a sober and distinguished Syria scholar. . . . That a trauma of the magnitude of the Hama massacre is nowhere to be found in contemporary Syrian literature is stunning and, of course, impossible; Hama, being nowhere in Syrian literature, can be read in it everywhere. (235)

On the theme of silence and roar, see the novel written by the Aleppine writer Nihad Sirees, *Al-Samt wa al-Sakhab*, depicting, on the one hand, the silence imposed by the regime on the will of the people to participate in public affairs, and on the other, the forced roar created by the regime to celebrate itself through loud "popular" demonstrations. In an interview on Al Jazeera television, the author says that he was inspired to write this novel in the aftermath of the clampdown on the Damascus Spring. The novel was published in Beirut in 2004, then translated into several languages, including English. Nihad Sirees, interview, *Kharij al-nass* [Outside the text], Al Jazeera, posted March 20, 2017, https://www.youtube.com/watch?v=bjUD7zM0RV8.

On the lingering effects of the Hama massacre and the ensuing prison experiences, see Ismail, *The Rule of Violence*. For a recent literary articulation of the effects of the violent repression after decades of silence, see Khalifa, *La sakakina fi matabikh hadhihi al-madina* [No knives in this city's kitchens]. Khaled Khalifa, a novelist and screenwriter born in Aleppo in 1964, depicts the social and physical damage caused by the Assad regime in his hometown through the saga of a family that experiences fanaticism, violence, shame, and humiliation. The book won the 2013 Naguib Mahfouz Prize. Hear him speak about it: Khaled Khalifa, "Awwal ra'is Baathi awha li bi 'unwan riwayati al-akhira" [The first Baathi president inspired me with the title of my latest novel], *al-Araby*, posted May 11, 2014, https://www.youtube.com/watch?v=9oKdXQG45LQ. For his attitude toward the revolution, see Khaled Khalifa, "Silence Is Disgraceful Too," interview by Anders Hastrup, Louisiana Channel (Internet channel), Louisiana Museum of Modern Art, posted September 2, 2013, https://www.youtube.com/watch?v=ciCkcAUg7lI. See also his interview with Anas Azraq in *Al-mun'ataf* [The turn], Syria TV, posted May 30, 2018, https://www.youtube.com/watch?v=C3LVfVjSzAQ. His previous novel, *Fi madih al-karahiyya* [In praise of hatred], also dealt with the Assad repression of the 1980s and its effects on an Aleppo family. It was shortlisted for the International Prize for Arabic Fiction in 2008 and then banned from Syria and republished in Beirut by Dar al-Adab in 2010. The two novels were translated into English and other European languages, including French, Italian, and Dutch.

32. See Hafiz's collected works, *al-A'mal al-kamila li Yassin al-Hafiz*. On his critical revisiting of ideologies, see for instance Frangie, "Historicism, Socialism and Liberalism After the Defeat"; al-Juba'i, "Yasin al-Hafiz mu'asiran" [Yasin al-Hafiz as a contemporary]; and Nachar, "'An Yasin al-Hafiz al-shab wa zamanihi 'al-thawri'" [On the young Yasin al-Hafiz and his "revolutionary" time].

33. For Ghalioun's analysis of Syrian realities, especially regarding the promises and challenges of democracy, see his long dialogue with Syrian publisher and activist Louay Hussein, *Al-Ikhtiyar al-dimuqrati fi suria* [The democratic option in Syria]. Hussein also published a number of dialogues with other Syrian intellectuals on issues of Syrian nationalism and politics in *Hiwarat fi al-wataniyya al-suriyya* [Dialogues on Syrian nationalism], including Sadeq Jalal al-Azm, Georges Tarabichi, Fayez Ezzeddine, Tayyeb Tizini, Jawdat Said, Muwaffaq Nyrabia, and Jamal Barout.

34. Ghalioun, *Bayan min ajl al-dimurratiyya* [Manifesto for democracy]. I refer to the fifth edition. For information on Ghalioun's writings and activities, check his personal website: http://burhan.burhanghalioun.net/.

35. Ghalioun further analyzed this antagonism between state and society in the Arab world in his book *Al-Mihna al-arabiyya* [The Arab crisis].

36. Ghalioun, *Ightiyal al-'aql* [Assassination of reason].

37. Ghalioun devoted his book *Mujatama' al-nukhba* [The elite society] to the analysis of this elite problematic.

38. Ghalioun, *Bayan min ajl al-dimurratiyya* [Manifesto for democracy], 13–14.

39. For Ghalioun's reflections on his political experience as an intellectual, see his interview "Fi al-qadiyya al-suriyya wa al-hadatha al-mushawwaha ma' Burhan Ghalioun" [On the Syrian cause and the distorted modernity with Burhan Ghalioun], *Hadith al-Arab* [The talk of the Arabs], Sky News Arabiyya, posted February 19, 2016, https://www.youtube.com/watch?v=2n-l0lf0I5E&feature=share; see also Burhan Ghalioun, "Limadha dakhala Burhan Ghalioun 'alam al-siyasa? Wa hal yaqbal bi hukm al-islamiyyin?" [Why did Burhan Ghalioun go into politics? And does he accept the rule of the Islamists?], interview by Anas Azraq, *al-Mun'ataf* [The turn], Syria TV, posted June 19, 2018, https://www.syria.tv/content لماذا-دخل-برهان-غليون-عالم-السياسة؟-وهل-يقبل-بحكم-الإسلاميين؟/.

40. See Abdel Raziq, *Al-Islam wa usul al-hukm* [Islam and the principles of governance]. For an English translation of some brief but crucial passages, see Donohue and Esposito, *Islam in Transition*, 29–37. See also al-Kawakibi, *Taba'i' al-istibdad wa Masari' al-isti'bad* [The characteristics of despotism and the deaths of enslavement]. For the English translation of a short excerpt, see Kurzman, *Modernist Islam*, 152–57.

41. Eid, *Azamat al-tanwir* [The crisis of tanwir]. I refer here to the two introductory sections, "Muqaddima," 5–8, and "Bi mathabat tamhid: Azamat tanwir," 9–30.

42. Al-Jabiri, *Bunyat al-'aql al-arabi* [The structure of Arab reason]. For a brief excerpt from his work in English, see al-Jabiri, *Arab-Islamic Philosophy*.

43. "Al-tanwir wa al-'almaniyya wa al-salafiyya" [Tanwir and secularism and Salafism], in Fakhr, *Hiwar ma' Sadeq Jalal al-Azm* [Dialogue with Sadeq Jalal al-Azm], 53–66.

44. Many of al-Azm's essays and articles are now available in English through the Gerlach Verlag. See, for instance, al-Azm, *Collected Essays*.

45. This is also the position of Syrian historian Aziz al-Azmeh (born 1947). See, for instance, his book *Al-'almaniyya min mandhour mukhtalif* [Secularism from a different perspective].

46. Tizini, *Bayan fi al-nahda wa al-tanwir al-arabi* [Manifesto on the Arab nahda and tanwir].

47. Tizini, 156.

48. Tizini, *Min al-turath ila al-thawra* [From tradition to revolution]. In 1978 Lebanese Marxist thinker Husayn Muruwweh (1908–1987) published a major work entitled *Al-Naza'at al-maddiyya fi al-falsafa al-arabiyya al-islamiyya* [The material tendencies in Arab-Islamic philosophy]. For a discussion of his study, see Jurdi Abisaad, "Deconstructing the Modular and the Authentic." On Muruwweh's complex intellectual project, see Di-Capua, "Homeward Bound."

49. Tizini, "Al-mufakkir al-suri Tayyeb Tizini" [The Syrian thinker Tayyeb Tizini].

50. Kilo, "Tayyeb Tizini aw faylasuf al-'asr!" [Tayyeb Tizini or the epoch's philosopher!].

51. Syrian philosopher and translator Elias Murqus collaborated with Yasin Hafiz in adapting Marx's ideas to Arab realities. He was among the first Arab thinkers to elaborate on the notion of "civil society" without minimizing the importance of the state. However, he criticized the despotism and corruption of the

existing states. In his numerous writings he wanted to integrate the humanist values of freedom and reason with those of Marxist social justice and pan-Arab nationalism. See, for instance, Murqus, *Al-ʿAqlaniyya wa al-taqaddum* [Rationality and progress], with an introduction by Moroccan philosopher Kamal Abdul Latif, and *Naqd al-ʿaqlaniyya al-arabiyya* [Critique of Arab rationalism]. See also the posthumously published conversations with him: Neʿmeh, *Elias Murqus*; and al-Jabaʿi, *Hiwar al-ʿumr* [The life conversation].

52. Tizini, *Min thulathiyyat al-fasad ila qadaya al-mujtamaʿ al-madani* [From the trilogy of corruption to the issues of civil society].

53. Many of the articles in Tizini's book were part of a controversy he had with Michel Kilo. For Kilo's responses, see, for instance, his piece in *an-Nahar* entitled "ʿAn al-sulta wa al-dawla wa ʿal-mujtamaʿ al-madani'" [On power and the state and "civil society"].

54. See a recording of his speech at https://www.youtube.com/watch?v=I6Z3xh3_HoQ.

55. According to a collaborator on the journal, Muhammad Jamal Barut, its funding was facilitated by the Popular Front for the Liberation of Palestine, through George Habash. See Barut and al-Kilani, *Suria bayn ʿahdayn* [Syria between two epochs], 37.

56. Darraj, "Faysal Darraj."

57. Here are themes for the six volumes of *Qadaya wa-shahadat*. Vol. 1 (Spring 1990): rationalism, democracy, and modernity; vol. 2 (Summer 1991): the nahda, and modernization then and now; vol. 3 (Winter 1991): nationalism, the culture of difference, and the modernity of others; vol. 4 (Fall 1991): dependency and *turath*; vol. 5 (Spring 1992): reason, the nation, and universality; vol. 6 (Winter 1992): literature, reality, and history. On average, each volume was four hundred pages long.

58. Scott, "The Aftermaths of Sovereignty."

59. My own translation, kindly edited by Max Weiss.

60. For a representation of Sisyphus in modern Syrian art, see the 2012 animation by Iraqi artist Sadik Kwaish Alfraji, *Sisyphus Goes on Demonstration*, video, posted October 14, 2012, https://vimeo.com/51407903.

61. For more on the journal and its work reconnecting with the nahda, see Elizabeth Suzanne Kassab, "Summoning the Spirit of Enlightenment: On the Nahda Revival in *Qadaya wa-shahadat*," in Hanssen and Weiss, *Arabic Thought Against the Authoritarian Age*, 311–35.

62. Wannous's writings are published in a three-volume collection, *Al-Aʿmal al-kamila* [The complete works]. Volume 3 contains a detailed biography of Wannous as well as a bibliography of his writings that includes information about translations and performances of his plays.

63. For more on Wannous's work, see Kassab, "The Existential Dramatization of Critique the Day After the Defeat: Saadallah Wannous' Theatrical Oeuvre," in *Contemporary Arab Thought*, 48–65. On his theater, see Jalabi-Wellnitz, *Spectateurs en dialogue*. To hear Wannous on culture, theatrical freedom of expression, and democracy, see two excerpts of a rare, but unfortunately undated, television interview with him: Saadallah Wannous, "Al-kateb a-kabir Saadallah Wannous yatahaddath maʿ Sufian Jabr ʿan al-dimuqratiyya wa al-hurriyy wa al-thaqafa" [The great writer

Saadallah Wannous speaks with Sufian Jabr on democracy, freedom, and culture], interview by Sufian Jabr, https://www.youtube.com/watch?v=cSkxpWJWs0c (posted March 6, 2011), and "Saad Wannous yatahaddath 'an masrah al-tassyis wa al-masrah al-siyasi" [Saad Wannous speaks about the politicizing theater and on political theater], https://www.youtube.com/watch?v=su_E12daqDI (posted July 18, 2013).

64. *Wa hunak ashia' kathira kana yumkin an yatahaddath al-mar' 'anha* [There are still so many things one could talk about], directed by Omar Amiralay (La Sept/ARTE and Les Films Grain de Sable, 1997), https://www.youtube.com/watch?v=cdFFUdP2aUU. Wannous and Amiralay collaborated in the 1960s on documentaries of real life in Syria, especially in the rural areas; for instance, *Al-Hayat al-yawmiyya fi qarya suriyya* [Daily life in a Syrian village] (1971), which was banned by the Syrian authorities, who were apparently not interested in depictions of reality. Amiralay made a documentary about one of the remote villages in the Euphrates valley, depicting the Syria that was created by the forty years of Assad rule. *Tufan fi bilad al-baath* [Flood in the Baath country], directed by Omar Amiralay (France: AMIP-ARTE, 2003), posted July 29, 2011, https://www.youtube.com/watch?v=GWAu22K8uuE.

65. Saadallah Wannous, "Hawl al-samt . . . wa mas'uliyyat al-muthaqqafin" (On silence . . . and the responsibility of intellectuals), *Al-A'mal al-kamila* 3:447–60.

66. Saadallah Wannous, "Al-Ju' ila al-hiwar" [The hunger for dialogue], *Al-A'mal al-kamila* 1:39–44.

67. Saadallah Wannous, "In Lieu of an Introduction," *Qadaya wa-shahadat* 1 (Winter 1990): 19.

68. Wannous, 5.

69. Wannous, 5.

70. Wannous, 5. For a review of this first volume, see Syrian historian Muhammad Jamal Barut's "Muthaqqafun dimuqratiyyun yu'idun istikshaf Taha Husayn." Barut wrote a history of the tanwir movement in Aleppo, focused on the work of Francis Marrash (1836–1873) and Abd al-Rahman al-Kawakibi, *Harakat al-tanwir al-arabiyya fi al-qarn al-tasi' 'ashar* [The Arab tanwir movement in the nineteenth century].

71. Wannous, "In Lieu of an Introduction," 13.

72. Wannous, 6.

73. Wannous, 6.

74. Wannous, 8.

75. Wannous, 8.

76. Wannous, "Bayn al-hadatha wa al-tahdith" [Between modernity and modernization].

77. Wannous, 21.

78. Wannous, 21–22.

79. Wannous, "Al-thaqafa al-wataniyya wa al-wa'i al-tarikhi" [National culture and historical awareness].

80. For more on this conference and similar ones dealing with the post-1967 cultural malaise, see Kassab, *Contemporary Arab Thought*, 116–72.

81. Wannous, "Al-thaqafa al-wataniyya wa al-wa'i al-tarikhi" [National culture and historical awareness], 21.

82. Wannous, 27–28.

83. Wannous, 12–19.

84. Wannous, 37.

85. Wannous, "Hiwar ma' Antoun Maqdisi hawl al-hadatha wa al-tahdith" [Dialogue with Antoun Maqdisi on modernity and modernization].

86. Wannous, 7.

87. Wannous, 9.

88. Wannous, 10.

89. Samar Yazbek, "Scenario Camera."

90. On the Sisyphean and Promethean figures in modern Arab literature and art, particularly the sculptural art of Kuwaiti artist Sami Mohammad, see Hussein Ali, "The Prometheus Myth."

91. For Faysal Darraj's analysis of defeat in Palestinian and Arabic literature, see *Bu's al-thaqafa fi al-mu'assassa al-filastiniyya* [The misery of culture in the Palestinian establishment]. For his study of the Arabic novel, see *Al-Dhakira al-qawmiyya fi al-riwaya al-arabiyya* [National memory in the Arab novel]. For his analysis of Palestinian literary figures, see *Dhakirat al-maghlubin* [The memory of the defeated]. On the specific themes of progress, see *Riwayat al-taqaddum wa ightirab al-mustaqbal* [The story of progress and the estrangement of the future]. For Darraj's views on the state of culture and the intellectual in the Arab world, including his reflections on his experience with *Qadaya wa-shahadat*, see his interview with Mazen Mustafa in *Riwaq al-Ma'rifa* [The walk of knowledge], Hiwar TV, posted October 25, 2010,https://www.youtube.com/watch?v=VFnhUFTRzk4.

92. Darraj, "Al-kawni wa al-'alami wa al-thaqafa al-wataniyya" [The universal and the worldwide and national culture], 20–21.

93. Darraj, 16–20.

94. Faysal Darraj, "Al-sheikh al-taqlidi wa al-muthaqqaf al-hadith" [The traditional sheikh and the modern intellectual], and *Al-Hadatha al-mutaqahqira* [Vanquished modernity].

95. Faysal Darraj, "Al-kawni wa al-'alami wa al-thaqafa al-wataniyya" [The universal and the worldwide and national culture].

96. We will be looking at Darraj's essays "Difa'an 'an al-fikr al-'arabi" [In defense of Arab tanwir thought]; "Al-muthaqqafun wa-suq al-afkar" [The intellectuals and the market of ideas]; "Masir al-muthaqqaf bayn al-naqd wa al-hija'" [The fate of the intellectual between critique and derision], part of a special thematic dossier in this journal issue devoted to the "death of the intellectual"; and "Fi ma'na al-tanwir" [On the meaning of tanwir].

97. The essay is included in his later book on Husayn and Adonis, *Al-Hadatha al-mutaqahqira* [Vanquished modernity], 15–35.

98. Husayn, *Al-Ayyam* [The days].

99. Darraj, "Al-sheikh al-taqlidi wa al-muthaqqaf al-hadith" [The traditional sheikh and the modern intellectual], 26–28. With regard to the question of Husayn's elitism, it is worth referring here to the panel debate he had in Beirut in 1955 with Lebanese Marxist thinker Raif Khoury (1913–1967) on the question "To whom does the writer write, to the elite or to the common people?" ("Liman yaktub al-adib, li al-khassa am li al-kaffa?"). Husayn's and Khoury's talks were first published in

al-Adab, spring issue of 1955. Its editor, Suhayl Idriss, initiated the idea of the debate. The talks were later published in Khoury, *Al-adab al-mas'ul* [The responsible literature]. In this panel debate, Khoury defended the idea of a committed literature—in vogue at the time in Arab intellectual circles, under the influence of French existentialism. Khoury believed literature should address the concerns of the people and not limit itself to elite interests and tastes. Husayn criticized the question and expressed his misgivings about imposing theories and ideologies on writers and writings. Writers, he asserted, should be free to produce what they would like to produce, and readers should be free to read, interact, and judge whatever they read. In reality, he said, writers write to those who can read them, who could be few or many. If anything, he believed, literature should not go "down" to the people, but help people rise up to it; and this applied to science and knowledge in general as well.

100. Darraj, "Al-sheikh al-taqlidi wa al-muthaqqaf al-hadith" [The traditional sheikh and the modern intellectual], 43–45.

101. Darraj, 26.

102. Darraj, 30–33.

103. Darraj, 39–45. For an eloquent summary of Darraj's characterization of Husayn's project of rebellion and tanwir, see Darraj *Al-Hadatha al-mutaqahqira* [Vanquished modernity], 229–34, and for a comparison with Adonis's project, 236–38.

104. Faysal Darraj, "Al-kawni wa al-'alami wa al-thaqafa al-wataniyya" [The universal and the worldwide and national culture], 22–23.

105. See also Darraj, 24–25. For more on these thinkers, see Kassab, *Contemporary Arab Thought*, 200–7, 243.

106. Darraj, "Al-kawni wa al-'alami wa al-thaqafa al-wataniyya" [The universal and the worldwide and national culture], 59.

107. Hasan Hanafi coined this phrase to refer to the psychology of people impregnated with Islam, and he called for it to be considered in the design of a philosophy that advocates social justice and liberation—in his case, that of the Islamic Left. For more on this, see Kassab, *Contemporary Arab Thought*, 204–5.

108. Darraj, "Al-sheikh al-taqlidi wa al-muthaqqaf al-hadith" [The traditional sheikh and the modern intellectual], 58.

109. Darraj, 32–33, 59.

110. Shukri, *Diktaturiyyat al-takhalluf al-arabi* [The dictatorship of Arab backwardness], 75.

111. Shukri, 84.

112. Shukri, 63.

113. Shukri, 64.

114. Darraj, "Al-kawni wa al-'alami wa al-thaqafa al-wataniyya" [The universal and the worldwide and national culture], 20.

115. Darraj, 5. See also Darraj, "Al-muthaqqafun wa-suq al-afkar" [The intellectuals and the market of ideas], 3.

116. Darraj, "Al-muthaqqafun wa-suq al-afkar," 2.

117. Darraj, 2.

118. Darraj, 7.

119. Darraj, 3–4.

120. Faysal Darraj, "Masir al-muthaqqaf bayn al-naqd wa al-hija'" [The fate of the intellectual between critique and derision], 65–66.

121. Darraj, 70.

122. Darraj, Al-Hadatha al-mutaqahqira [Vanquished modernity], 7–9, 125.

123. Darraj, 135–36.

124. Darraj, 127.

125. Darraj, 140–41, 234.

126. Darraj, 207–27.

127. Darraj, 229–38.

128. Darraj, 12.

129. Abu Zayd's remarks come in his review of Zaki Naguib Mahmoud's (1905–1993) autobgraphy. Mahmoud was an Egyptian philosophy professor, advocate of logical positivism, and sharp critic of metaphysics in the early part of his career. He later softened his critique and retreated to positions friendlier to religious tradition. See Abu Zayd, "Zaki Naguib Mahmud, Ramz al-tanwir, Symbol of the Tanwir," in Abu Zayd, Al-khitab wa al-ta'wil [The discourse and the interpretation].

130. Darraj, "Fi ma'na al-tanwir" [On the meaning of tanwir].

131. Muhammad Salim al-'Awa, "Ta'qib" [Comment].

4. Tanwir and the Damascus Spring

1. Hinnebusch, "Calculated Decompression as a Substitute for Democratization." See also Hinnebusch, "Syria," especially 97–98.

2. Ismail, "Changing Social Structure," especially 13–24.

3. Perthes, Syria Under Bashar al-Asad.

4. Lust-Okar, "Reform in Syria."

5. Heydemann, "Upgrading Authoritarianism in the Arab World."

6. Heydemann and Leenders, "Authoritarian Learning and Authoritarian Resilience." See also Heydemann and Leenders, "Popular Mobilization in Syria," and Middle East Authoritarianisms.

7. Heydemann, "Syria and the Future of Authoritarianism," 61.

8. Hinnebusch, "Syria," 112:

The consolidation of the Syrian Ba'ath regime under Hafiz al-Asad had built-in flaws, notably its sectarian core and the resentment of the moneyed classes, with a consequent dependence on unsustainable rent. Yet Bashar al-Asad's authoritarian upgrading, intended to address these shortcomings, was itself fatally flawed. The most dangerous juncture for an authoritarian regime is when it seeks to 'reform', particularly when the path of reform combines neo-liberalism and crony capitalism. In Syria after 2000 the overconcentration of power and patronage in the ruling clan debilitated the clientelist networks that connected the regime to society. The spread of electronic media allowed political mobilization to take place as the party's incorporative capacity weakened and in the absence of an alternative integration of youth into jobs that would give them a stake in the status quo. Economic liberalization and the change in the regime's social base advanced too far beyond political adaptation: the Ba'ath Party was gravely weakened but no bourgeois party arose to organize supporters of neo-liberalism, nor were any safety-valve political parties for the secular and Islamic oppositions allowed to compete in freer elections. Although a regime so dependent on a minority Alawi core could never fully accept a majoritarian electoral system without surrendering power, especially once its cross-sectarian Ba'ath Party was debilitated, key elements of authoritarian upgrading deployed elsewhere could have produced a hybrid regime more congruent with the changes in the regime's development strategy and ruling coalition. Given the resistance of the remnants of the regime old guard, this political rigidity was perhaps inevitable, but Asad's strategies exacerbated the risks: the too rapid jettisoning of the regime's rural and peripheral constituency sowed the seeds of rebellion and the violent reaction of the regime to the opposition challenge provided copious irrigation.

9. Wieland, *A Decade of Lost Chances*, especially chapters 3 and 7.

10. Ismail, "Changing Social Structure," 24–27.

11. Pierret and Selvik, "Limits of 'Authoritarian Upgrading' in Syria." In their conclusion they write:

There are thus clear limits to the strategy of 'authoritarian upgrading' in Syria. The Ba'th regime does not possess the material and symbolic resources that could make development of private welfare politically risk free by allowing for direct state control over the social dynamics underpinning charitable activities. The private sector's most reliable sources of funding are small- and medium-sized, noncrony entrepreneurs. These businessmen predominantly give their money to Muslim scholars whose popularity derives from their independent political stance as well as from more strictly religious causes. The most efficient private welfare providers, in other words, are those over whom the government has the least political control.

. . . The wider impact of this process is ambivalent: it stabilizes the unsteady Syrian authoritarian system by alleviating its religious legitimacy problem as well as by absorbing poverty-related tensions in a politically critical social segment but brings unreliable elements into the state-supporting elite coalition. (610–11)

See also Pierret, "Sunni Clergy Politics in the Cities of the Ba'thi Syria"; "The State Management of Religion in Syria: The End of 'Indirect Rule'?," in Heydemann and Leenders, *Middle East Authoritarianisms*, 83–106; and "Merchant Background, Bourgeois Ethics." See also Stenberg, "Muslim Organizations in Bashar's Syria"; Pinto, "God and Nation"; Khatib, *Islamic Revivalism in Syria*.

For an insightful reading of the shift in state-society relations, the opening of the civic arena, and economic liberalization under Bashar al-Assad through the lens of charities and NGOs, see Ruiz de Elvira and Zintl, "The End of the Ba'thist Social Contract in Bashar al-Asad's Syria." On Christian charities more specifically, see Ruiz de Elvira, "Christian Charities and the Ba'thist Regime in Bashar al-Asad's Syria."

12. On Christian political participation in the region, see McCallum, "Religious Institutions and Authoritarian States," and "Christian Political Participation in the Arab World."

13. This was the overwhelming feeling of the Syrian Christians enduring the violence that broke out after the beginning of the uprising, as they were forced to flee their homes, not always because they were Christians, but in search of security like other Syrians. See Bandak, "Reckoning with the Inevitable."

14. Bandak, "States of Exception," and "Performing the Nation."

15. Lisa Wedeen, "Ideology and Humor in Dark Times." On page 843 she writes: "Neoliberal autocracy implies two contradictory logics of rule, cultivating an aspirational consciousness for freedom, upward mobility, and consumer pleasure, on the one hand, while continuing to tether possibilities for advancement to citizen obedience and coercive control, on the other."

For transformations in how literature has reacted to Syrian authoritarianism under Bashar al-Assad, see Weiss, "Who Laughs Last." For more general studies on contemporary Syrian literature, see Chehayed and Toelle, *Al-riwaya al-suriyya al-mu'asira* [The contemporary Syrian novel]; Chehayed and Gonzalez-Quijano, *Al-qissa fi suriya* [The Syrian short story]; and Vauthier, *La création romanesque contemporaine en Syrie de 1967 à nos jours* [Novelistic creation in contemporary Syria from 1967 to our days].

16. For an informative overview of the history of cultural fields in modern Syria, see Boëx, "The End of State Monopoly Over Culture." See also from the same author, "Tahya as-sinama!" [Viva cinema!], "Être cinéaste syrien" [Being a Syrian filmmaker], and "La création cinématographique en Syrie à la lumière du mouvement de révolte" [Cinematographic creation in Syria in light of the revolt movement]. On contemporary Syrian cinema in general, see Salti, *Insights Into Syrian Cinema*.

17. See Wedeen, "Ideology and Humor in Dark Times," 863–71; Joubin, "Resistance Amid Regime Co-optation"; and Salamandra, "Creative Compromise," "Spotlight on the Bashar al-Asad Era," and "Syria's Drama Outpouring."

18. See Della Ratta, "Dramas of the Authoritarian State," and "The 'Whisper Strategy.'" For a text by one of the important Syrian screenwriters mentioning the goal of tanwir and complaining about the impossibility of reaching it with the conservative and populist producers, see this 2008 interview with Najib Nusair, "Najib Nusair."

19. For an analysis of the interaction between these external events and Syrian domestic politics, see Wieland, *A Decade of Lost Chances*, especially chapter 8. On artistic creativity in Syria after the revolution, see Della Ratta, *Shooting a Revolution*.

20. Chronologies of the events in this period can be found in "Hal intaha 'rabi' dimashq'? Sira naqisa [Did the "Damascus Spring" end? An incomplete biography], *Mulhaq al-Nahar*, August 25, 2002; and in Barut and al-Kilani, *Suria bayn 'ahdayn* [Syria between two epochs], 11–14.

21. Ziadeh, *Hiwarat "Muntada al-Hiwar al-watani"* [The dialogues of the "National Dialogue Forum"]; hear him reflect on the Damascus Spring in an interview by

Anas Azraq, *Al-Mun'ataf* [The turn], Syria TV, posted October 9, 2018, https://www
.syria.tv/content/عن-محاولات-الإصلاح-في-سوريا-قبل-الثورة-وكيف-انتهى-ربيع-دمشق. Eid, *Yas'alunak
'an al-mujtama' al-madani* [They ask you about civil society]; and Barut and al-Kilani,
Suria bayn 'ahdayn [Syria between two epochs]. Between June 27, 2018, and October 3, 2018, Syrian opposition writer and activist Wael Sawah wrote a series
of fifteen weekly articles for the Syria TV website, reflecting on the Damascus
Spring as prelude to the 2011 revolution; he called them "Fi muqaddimat al-thawra
al-suriyya" [On the preludes to the Syrian revolution], https://www.syria.tv
/الكتاب/وائل-السّوّاح.

22. See also Ghadbian, "Contesting Authoritarianism." In French, see Burhan
Ghalioun and Farouk Mardam-Bey, eds., "Un printemps syrien," special issue, *Confluences Méditerranée* 44 (Winter 2002–2003), 9–95, comprising essays by Syrian
intellectuals and one Lebanese historian.

23. For an English version of Bashar Al-Assad's inaugural speech, see *Syria Times*,
July 18, 2000.

24. A decade later, Ali Farzat was attacked while coming out of his Damascus
office and left severely injured, with several of his fingers broken. Men from the
regime were suspected. See Nour Ali, "Syrian Forces Beat Up Political Cartoonist
Ali Ferzat," *Guardian*, August 25, 2011, https://www.theguardian.com/world/2011
/aug/25/syria-cartoonist-ali-ferzat-beaten. See also George, *Syria*, 130–32.

25. A list of some of them can be found in Ziadeh, *Hiwarat "Muntada al-Hiwar al-
watani"* [The Dialogues of the "National Dialogue Forum"].

26. For the text of Khaddam's speech and reactions from the attending professors, see Barut and al-Kilani, *Suria bayn 'ahdayn* [Syria between two epochs],
139–45.

27. All three documents are in Barut and al-Kilani, 99, 117, and 146. English
translations are in George, *Syria*, 178–93.

28. The letter can be found in Barut and al-Kilani, *Suria bayn 'ahdayn* [Syria
between two epochs], 123–25.

29. The program can be found in Barut and al-Kilani, 129–38; and in Ziadeh,
Hiwarat "Muntada al-Hiwar al-watani" [The Dialogues of the "National Dialogue
Forum"].

30. This document can be found in Barut and al-Kilani, *Suria bayn 'ahdayn* [Syria
between two epochs], 167–73.

31. On the suppression of the lawyers' protest movements since the late 1970s
and the ordeal of Haytham al-Mallah, see George, *Syria*, 101–20. On the persecution
of the Committees for the Defense of Democratic Freedoms and Human Rights and
the ordeal of Nizar Nayyouf, see 121–24.

32. Ridwan Ziadeh, "Muntada al-hiwar al-watani: Al-takwin al-ijtima'i wa al-
hirak al-siyasi" [The National Dialogue Forum: Social formation and political
action], in *Hiwarat "Muntada al-Hiwar al-watani"* [The dialogues of the "National Dialogue Forum"]. Citations are to the PDF version of the book.

33. It is also in that atmosphere in the late nineties that the philosophy department of Damascus University organized public events, in which prominent speak-
ers from Syria and the Arab world were invited to give talks with some margin of
freedom. Apparently, the events were well attended. The 1995 talks were edited

by Barqawi and Musallam in *Al-'aqlaniyya—al-'almaniyya—"al-sharq awsatiyya"* [Rationalism—secularism—"Middle Easternism"]. Among the contributors were Nassif Nassar from Lebanon, Muhammad Abed al-Jabiri from Morocco, and Ahmad Barqawi from Syria.

34. On this meeting and the development of the civil society movement, see George, *Syria*, 33–46.

35. For that statement, see Ziadeh, *Hiwarat "Muntada al-Hiwar al-watani"* [The dialogues of the "National Dialogue Forum"].

36. Letter published in *al-Hayat*, August 14, 2000. The italics are mine.

37. Abdulrazzaq Eid, "Thaqafat al-khawf" [The culture of fear], in *Yas'alunak 'an al-mujtama' al-madani* [They ask you about civil society], 38–47. A version of the talk was published *in an-Nahar*, March 12, 2001, and in the Egyptian *Akhbar al-adab*, April 1, 2001, with an introduction by Egyptian novelist Gamal Ghitani. Eid's book also includes some of the press coverage of his talk in *Al-hayat*, as well as reactions from various people from the opposition and the regime, including Vice President Khaddam (48–77).

38. Eid, *Yas'alunak 'an al-mujtama' al-madani* [They ask you about civil society], 7–13. Page numbers refer to the PDF version of the book.

39. "Bayan al-99" [Manifesto of the 99], in Eid, 79–82.

40. Eid, 16–28.

41. The most comprehensive scholarly study in Arabic on the concept of civil society was produced by Palestinian thinker Azmi Bishara in *Al-mujtama' al-madani* [Civil society].

42. On Khaddam, see Barut and al-Kilani, *Suria bayn 'ahdayn* [Syria between two epochs], 139–45; on Saqr, see 69–86, 251–53, 267–69, 305–7, 308–10, 311–13; on Salameh, see 302–4, 349–51; on Baath party declarations, see 126–28; and on the regime's anonymous statements, see 109–16, 185–86.

43. See Barut, "Ta'ammulat fi Ihya' al-mujtama' al-madani al-suri wa isti'ab al-nukhba" [Meditations on the revival of civil society and the co-optation of the elite], in Barut and al-Kilani, 205.

44. Barut, 206.

45. "Bayan multaqa ansar al-mujtama' al-madani" [Statement of the supporters of civil society], in Barut and al-Kilani, *Suria bayn 'ahdayn* [Syria between two epochs], 100–8; "Al-wathiqa al-asasiyya li 'lijan ihya' al-mujtama' al-madani'" [The foundational document of the councils of the civil society revival], in Barut and al-Kilani, 117–22; "Mashru' al-wathiqa al-thaniali 'lijan al-mujtama' al-madani'" [Draft of the second document of the councils of the civil society revival], in Barut and al-Kilani, 146–48; "Nahwa 'aqd ijtima'i watani fi suriya: Tawafuqat wataniyya 'amma" [Toward a social contract in Syria: General national agreements], in Barut and al-Kilani, 149–52; Michel Kilo, " 'An al-sulta wa al-dawla wa 'al-mujtama' al-madani'" [On power and the state and civil society], in Barut and al-Kilani, 246–50.

46. Tizini, "Dawlat al-qanun wa al-mu'assasat wa huriyyat al-ta'bir" [The state of law and institutions and freedom of expression], in Barut and al-Kilani, 238–40.

47. Kilo, " 'An al-sulta wa al-dawla wa 'al-mujtama' al-madani'" [On power and the state and civil society], in Barut and al-Kilani, 246–50.

48. Maqdisi, "Bashar al-Asad wa dukhul suriya al-qarn al-hadi wa al-'ishrin" [Bashar al-Assad and the entry of Syria into the twenty-first century], in Barut and al-Kilani, 270–74; and his dialogue with Syrian journalist Ibrahim Hamidi, "Antun Maqdisi," in Barut and al-Kilani, 275–79.

49. Maqdisi, "Bashar al-Asad wa dukhul suriya al-qarn al-hadi wa al-'ishrin" [Bashar al-Assad and the entry of Syria into the twenty-first century], in Barut and al-Kilani, 271.

50. al-Azmeh and Darraj, "Hamish li hiwar majzu'" [Margin for a fragmentary dialogue], in Barut and al-Kilani, 384–89.

51. Ghalioun, "Qam' al-muthaqqafin al-suriyyin yaghluq qanawat al-hiwar wa yatrukuna li mu'adalat al-usuliyya muqabil al-ajhiza al-amniyya" [The repression of the Syrian intellectuals shuts down the channels of dialogue and leaves us to the equation of fundamentalism versus security agencies], in Barut and al-Kilani, 340–48.

52. Barut and al-Kilani, 241.

53. Riad al-Turk, "Je n'irai pas voter pour Bachar el-Assad," interview by Gilles Paris, *Le Monde*, June 28, 2000.

54. Al-Turk, "Min ghayr al-mumkin an tadhall suriya mamlakat al-samt" [It is not possible that Syria remains the kingdom of silence].

55. Al-Turk "Masar al-dmuqratiyya wa afaqiha fi suriya" [The course of democracy in Syria and its horizons], in Barut and al-Kilani, *Suria bayn 'ahdayn* [Syria between two epochs], 499–513. For a glimpse of his talk, see this rare recording: https://www.youtube.com/watch?v=6G1bk1HsSoI.

56. See al-Turk, interviewed by Muhammad Ali Atassi.

57. For more on this point, see Kassab, "The Arab Quest for Freedom and Dignity."

Conclusion

1. See, for instance, Di-Capua, "Nahda."

2. Ferrié, "Réformisme, renaissance et contingence."

3. Al-Tunisi, *Aqwam al-masalek fi ma'rifat ahwal al-mamalik* [The straightest path to knowing the states of kingdoms]. His memoirs were edited by Mohamed-Salah Mzali and Jean Pignon and published as *Khérédine: Homme d'état: Mémoires* (Tunisia: Maison Tunisienne de l'Édition, 1971).

4. Nubar Pacha, *Mémoires de Nubar Pacha* (Beirut: Librairie du Liban, 1983).

5. This is how Ferrié summarizes his thesis:

Or ce qui distingue fondamentalement le réformisme suivant l'Aufklärung du réformisme suivant la *Nahda* est que le premier veut faire du neuf et le second réhabiliter l'ancien. L'un se pense comme un "éclaircissement" du monde, l'autre comme une renaissance: on ne saurait imaginer conceptions plus antagonistes. Il ne s'agit pas, bien sûr, d'entrer dans les détails (si l'on peut dire ainsi): Toqueville a bien montré, par exemple, que la Révolution ne faisait, sur de nombreux points, que suivre les réformes de "l'Ancien régime." Ceci n'est pas contestable, mais la rupture ne se place pas là. La rupture est dans l'affranchissement de la référence à l'ordre divin, au fondement transhistorique (à la transcendance), dans la rhétorique de la justification. ("Réformisme, renaissance et contingence")

6. Gershoni, "The Theory of Crisis and the Crisis in a Theory."

7. Roussillon, *Entre réforme sociale et mouvement national*, 9–35. In German Islamic studies one finds a similar crisis narrative about Taha Husayn as a modernist who allegedly abandons European rationalism and gives in to ideological Islam. See Tilman Nagel, "Abkehr von Europa: Der ägyptische Literat Taha Husain (1889–1973) und die Umformung des Islams in eine Ideologie," *Zeitschrift der deutschen morgenländischen Gesellschaft* 143 (1993): 383–98.

8. See Kassab, conclusion to *Contemporary Arab Thought*.

9. Bamyeh, "Anarchist Method, Liberal Intention, Authoritarian Lesson."

10. Saadallah Wannous, "Al-Juʻ ila al-hiwar" [The hunger for dialogue], *Al-Aʻmal al-kamila* 1:39–44.

Bibliography

Abaza, Mona. *Debates on Islam and Knowledge in Malaysia and Egypt: Shifting Worlds.* New York: Routledge Curzon, 2002.

——. "Egypt: Scattered Thoughts on a Counter-Revolutionary Moment." *OpenDemocracy*, March 19, 2015.

——. "Is Cairene Graffiti Losing Momentum?" *Jadaliyya*, January 25, 2015.

——. "Social Sciences in Egypt: The Swinging Pendulum Between Commodification and Criminalization." In *Facing an Unequal World: Challenges for a Global Sociology.* Vol. 1, *Introduction: Latin America and Africa,* edited by Michael Burawoy, Mau-Kuei Chang, and Michelle Fei-yu Hsieh, 187–212. Taipei: Institute of Sociology, Academia Sinica, Council of the National Association of the International Sociological Association, 2010.

——. "Tanwir and Islamization: Rethinking the Struggle Over Intellectual Inclusion in Egypt." In *Discourses in Contemporary Egypt: Politics and Social Issues,* edited by Enid Hill, 85–117. Cairo: American University of Cairo Press, 2000.

——. "Trafficking with Tanwir (Enlightenment)." *Comparative Studies of South Asia, Africa and the Middle East* 30, no. 1 (2010): 32–46.

——. *Twentieth Century Egyptian Art: The Private Collection of Sherwet Shafei.* Cairo: American University in Cairo Press, 2011.

——. "Walls, Segregating Downtown Cairo and the Mohammed Mahmud Street Graffiti." *Theory, Culture and Society* online (October 9, 2012).

Abdel Latif, Kamal. *Salama Moussa wa ishkaliyyat al-nahda* [Salama Moussa and the problematic of the nahda]. Beirut: Al-Marqaz al-thaqafi al-arabi, 1982.

Abdel Malek, Anouar. "La 'crise des intellectuels'" [The "crisis of the intellectuals"]. In *Égypte: Société militaire,* 191–218. Paris: Éditions du Seuil, 1962. Translated by Charles Lam Markmann as *Egypt: Military Society: The Army Regime, the Left and Social Change Under Nasser.* New York: Vintage, 1968.

Abdel Meguid, Ahmed and Daanish Faruqi. "The Truncated Debate: Egyptian Liberals, Islamists and Ideological Statism." In Fahmy and Faruqi, *Egypt and the Contradictions of Liberalism*, 253–88.

Abdel Rahman, Hasiba. *Al-Sharnaqa* [The cocoon]. No publication information. 1999.

Abdel Raziq, Ali. *Al-Islam wa usul al-hukm* [Islam and the principles of governance]. Cairo: Matba'at Misr, 1925.

Abd Rabou, Ahmed. "'An asatir al-tanwir" [On the myths of tanwir]. *Al-shourouq*, April 12, 2015.

Abou El Fadl, Khaled. "Egypt's Secularized Intelligentsia and the Guardians of Truth." In Fahmy and Faruqi, *Egypt and the Contradictions of Liberalism*, 235–52.

Abu Dehn, Ali. *'Aid min jahannam: Dhikrayat mi Tadmur was akhawatuhu* [A returnee from hell: Memories from Tadmur and its like]. Beirut: Dar al-Jadid, 2012.

Abu Fakhr, Saqr and Sadeq Jalal al-Azm. *Hiwar ma' Sadeq Jalal al-Azm* [Conversation with Sadeq Jalal al-Azm]. Beirut: Al-Mu'assassa al-arabiyya li al-dirasat wa al-nashr, 2000.

Abu-'Uksa, Wael. *Freedom in the Arab World: Concepts and Ideologies in Arabic Thought in the Nineteenth-Century*. Cambridge: Cambridge University Press, 2016.

Abu Zayd, Nasr Hamid. "Al-faza' min al-'ilmaniyya: Fasl al-Din 'an al-dawla" [The fear from secularism: The separation of religion and state]. *Al-Hiwar al-mutamaddin*, July 5, 2010. http://www.ahewar.org/debat/show.art.asp?aid=215277.

——. *Dawa'ir al Khawf: Qira'a fi Khitab al-Mar'a* [The circles of fear: A reading in the discourse on women]. Beirut: Al-Markaz al-Thaqafi al-'Arabi, 2000.

——. "Ishakaliyyat al-'ilaqa bayna al-'aql wa al-wahi" [The problematic between reason and revelation]. Ibn Rushd, October 20, 2011. http://www.ibn-rushd.org/typo3/cms/ar/magazine/11th-issue-winter-20102011/nasr-hamid-abu-zaid/.

——. "Ishkaliyyat al-muthaqqaf wa al-dawla/al-sulta: Al-zawaj al-kathuliki bayn al-muthaqqaf wa al-sulta, istib'ad al-'amma" [The problematic of the intellectual and the state/power: The Catholic marriage between the intellectual and power, the exclusion of the masses]. CivicEgypt, February 17, 2012. http://www.civicegypt.org/?p=19836.

——. "Ladayna du'at tanwir wa laysa sunna' tanwir, wa hunaka farq bayna an tad'u li al-tanwir wa bayna an tassn'ahu" [We have preachers of tanwir, not makers of tanwir, and there is a difference between preaching tanwir and making it]. Interview by Muhammad Hamamsi. *Maaber*. No date. http://www.maaber.org/issue_march12/spotlights3.htm.

——. "Mawqif Imarah min Ali Abd el Raziq: Ghalabat al-idiology 'ala al-ma'rifi" [Imarah's position regarding Ali Abd el Raziq: The prevailing of the ideological over the cognitive]. In *Al-khitab wa al-ta'wil* [The discourse and the interpretation], 89–105. Beirut: Al-markaz al-thaqafi al-'arabi, 2000.

——. *Naqd al-Khitab al-Dini* [The critique of religious discourse]. Cairo: Dar Sina li al-Nashr, 1992; 2nd edition, 1994.

——. "Zaki Naguib Mahmoud, ramz al-tanwir" [Zaki Naguib Mahmoud, the symbol of tanwir]. In *Al-khitab wa al-ta'wil* [The discourse and the interpretation], 67–88. Beirut: Al-markaz al-thaqafi al-'arabi, 2000.

Adwan, Mamdouh. *Al-ghoul: Jamal Basha al-Saffah* (The ghoul: Jamal Pasha the butcher). Damascus: Union of Arab Writers in Syria, 1996.

——. *Difa'an 'an al-junun: Muqaddimat* [In defense of madness: Preliminaries]. Beirut: Dar al-nadim, 1985.

——. *Haywanat al-insan* [The animalization of the human]. 2003. 2nd edition, Damascus: Dar Cadmus, 2004.

al-Ahnaf, Mustapha. "Débats intellectuels et intellectuels en débat." In *L'Égypte au présent: Inventaire d'une société avant révolution*, edited by Vincent Battesti and François Ireton, 1105–51. Paris: Actes Sud, 2011.

——. "L'affaire Haydar Haydar." In "La censure ou comment la contourner." Special issue, *Égypte/Monde arabe* 3 (2000): 167–202.

al-'Awa, Muhammad Salim. "Ta'qib" [Comment]. In *Hasilat al-'aqlaniyya wa al-tanwir fi al-fikr al-arabi al-mu'asir* [The harvest of tanwir in contemporary Arab thought], 118–25. Beirut: Markaz Dirasat al-Wihda al-Arabiyya, 2005.

al-Azm, Sadik J. *Collected Essays*. 3 vols. Vol. 1, *On Fundamentalism*; vol. 2, *Islam: Submission and Disobedience*; and vol. 3, *Is Islam Secularizable? Challenging Political and Religious Taboos*. Berlin: Gerlach Verlag, 2014.

——. *Critique of Religious Thought*. Berlin: Gerlach Verlag, 2014.

——. "An Interview with Sadik al-Azm." *Arab Studies Quarterly* 19, no. 3 (1997): 113–26.

al-Azmeh, Aziz. *Al-'almaniyya min mandhour mukhtalif* [Secularism from a different perspective]. 3rd edition, Beirut: Markaz dirasat al-wihda al-arabiyya, 2008.

al-Azmeh, Aziz and Faysal Darraj. "Hamish li hiwar majzu': Al-mujtama' al-madani am 'iqadh al-siyasa marra ukhra?" [Margin for a fragmentary dialogue: Civil society or awakening politics again?]. In Barut and al-Kilani, *Suria bayn 'ahdayn* [Syria between two epochs], 384–89; first published in *al-Hayat*, June 29, 2001.

al-Bishri, Tariq. *Al-Hiwar al-islami al-'almani* [The Islamic secular dialogue]. 1996. Cairo: Dar al-Shourouq, 2005.

al-Biyari, Ma'n. "Gaber Asfour yakhda' nafsahu mujaddan" [Gaber Asfour deluding himself again]. *Al-Araby al-jadid*, June 20, 2014.

al-Dabbagh, Hiba. *Khams daqa'q wa hasb: Tis' sanawat fi sujun suriyya* [Five minutes only: Nine years in the Syrian prisons]. 1995. Translated by Bayan Khatib as Heba Dabbagh, *Just Five Minutes: Nine Years in the Prisons of Syria*. Ottawa: Library and Archives of Canada, 2007.

Al-Hafiz, Yassin. *al-A'mal al-kamila li Yassin al-Hafiz* [The complete works of Yassin al-Hafiz]. Beirut: Markaz dirasat al-wihda al-arabiyya in Beirut, 2005.

al-Jaba'i, Jad al-Karim. *Hiwar al-'umr* [The life conversation]. Damascus: Dar Huran li al-tiba'a wa al-nashr, 1999.

al-Jabiri, Muhammad Abed. *Arab-Islamic Philosophy: A Contemporary Critique*. Austin: University of Texas Press, 1999.

——. *Bunyat al-'aql al-arabi* [The structure of Arab reason]. Beirut: Dar al-Tali'a, 1986.

al-Juba'i, Jad al-Karim. "Yasin al-Hafiz mu'asiran: Qira'a dhatiyya fi sira mawdu'iyya" [Yasin al-Hafiz as a contemporary: A personal reading of an objective biography]. Arab Center for Research and Policy Studies. https://www.dohainstitute.org/ar/ResearchAndStudies//Pages/art433.aspx.

al-Kawakibi, Abd al-Rahman. *Taba'i' al-istibdad wa Masari' al-isti'bad* [The characteristics of despotism and the deaths of enslavement]. 1902. Reprint, Cairo: GEBO, 1993.

al-Khuli, Ramadan and Abd al-Raziq Isa. "Un bilan controversé: Le point de vue des historiens égyptiens." In Alleaume, "L'expédition de Bonaparte vue d'Égypte," 25–46.

Alleaume, Ghislaine. "Agenda: Les manifestations commémoratives: Colloques, expositions, actualité éditoriale." In Alleaume, "L'expédition de Bonaparte vue d'Égypte," 213–19.

——. "De la renaissance aux Lumières: Autour de quelques productions historiques récentes." "L'Égypte en débats." Égypte/Monde arabe 20 (1994): 67–90.

——. "Des incertitudes de la mémoire aux exigencies de l'histoire." In Alleaume, "L'expédition de Bonaparte vue d'Égypte," 7–12.

——, ed. "L'expédition de Bonaparte vue d'Égypte." Special issue, Égypte/Monde arabe 1 (1999). CEDEJ-Complexe new series.

al-Muhsin, Fatima. Tamthulat al-hadatha fi thaqafat al-'Iraq [Representations of modernity in Iraqi culture]. Baghdad: Manshurat al-Jamal, 2015.

——. Tamathulat al-nahda fi thaqafat al-'iraq al-hadith [Representations of the nahda in the culture of modern Iraq]. Beirut: Dar al-Jamal, 2010.

al-Qimhawi, 'Izzat. "Farouk Hosni akher wazir thaqafa li misr" [Farouk Hosni, last culture minister for Egypt]. Al-Masri al-yawm, July 14, 2014.

Al-Rasheed, Madawi. Muted Modernists: The Struggle Over Divine Politics in Saudi Arabia. London: Hurst, 2015.

al-Sarraj, Bara. Min Tadmur ila Harvard: Rihlat sajin 'adim al-ra'i [From Tadmur to Harvard: Journey of a prisoner without opinion]. Poland: Amazon, no date. http://www.asharqalarabi.org.uk/markaz/k-2-1-2012.pdf.

al-Shayyal, Gamal al-Din. Al-tarikh wa al-mu'arrikhun fi misr fi al-qarn al-tassi' 'ashar [History and historians in Egypt in the nineteenth century]. Cairo: Maktabat al-nahda al-'asriyya, 1958.

al-Sirgani, Khaled. "'Azizi d. Gaber Asfour: 'Yalla 'nkammel lammitna'" (Dear Dr. Gaber Asfour: "Let's continue our gathering"). Al-Masri al-yawm, July 17, 2014.

al-Tamawi, Ahmed Hussein. Al-Hilal: Mi'at 'am min al-tahdith wa al-tanwir, 1892–1992 [Al-Hilal: A hundred years of modernization and enlightenment, 1892–1992]. Cairo: Mu'assasat dar al-hilal, 1992.

al-Tawati, Mustafa, Muhammad ben Ahmuda, and Sadeq Jalal al-Azm. Athar al-thawra al-faransiyya fi fikr al-nahda [The traces of the French Revolution on nahda thought]. Tunis: Al-arabiyya Muhammad Ali al-Hami li al-nashr wa al-tawzi', 1991.

al-Tunisi, Khayr al-Din. Aqwam al-masalek fi ma'rifat ahwal al-mamalik (The straightest path to knowing the states of kingdoms). Tunis: Matba'at al-dawla, 1867. Translated and edited by Leon Carl Brown as The Surest Path: The Political Treatise of a Nineteenth-Century Muslim Statesman. Cambridge: Harvard University Press, 1967.

al-Turk, Riad. Interviewed by Muhammad Ali Atassi. Mulhaq an-Nahar, December 22, 2002. http://www.mafhoum.com/press4/125P58.htm.

——. "Min ghayr al-mumkin an tadhall suriya mamlakat al-samt" [It is not possible that Syria remains the kingdom of silence]. Mulhaq an-Nahar, July 22, 2000. http://www.mokarabat.com/mo12.htm.

——. "Riadh al-Turk: In and Out of Syrian Prison." Interview by Mohammad Ali Atassi. Al-Jadid 10, no. 49 (2004). The original Arabic appeared in al-Quds al-arabi, December 23, 2002.

Antun, Farah. *Ibn Rushd wa falsafatuhu* [Ibn Rushd and his philosophy]. Cairo: al-hay'a al-'amma li al-kitab, 2012.

"Arabic Literature, Criticism and Intellectual Thought from the Nahdah to the Present." Special issue, *Journal of Arabic Literature* 43, nos. 2–3 (2012).

'Asem, Dalia. "Hal yuhawil al-islamiyyun musadarat Taha Husayn ba'd 41 'aman 'ala rahilihi?" [Are the Islamists trying to confiscate Taha Husayn 41 years after his departure?]. *Al-Sharq al-awsat*, November 5, 2014.

Asfour, Gaber. *al-Tanwir yuwajih al-idhlam* [The enlightenment faces obscurantism]. Cairo: Al-hay'a al-masriyya al-'amma li al-kitab, 1993.

——. "Al-thaqafa al-misriyya fi karitha" [Egyptian culture in catastrophe]. *Al-Ahram*, October 25, 2010.

——. *Anwar al-ʿaql* [The lights of reason]. Cairo: Supreme Cultural Council, 1996.

——. *Didd al-taʾassub* [Against intolerance]. Cairo: Maktabat al-Usra, 2000.

——. *Difaʿan ʿan al-tanwir* [In defense of tanwir]. 2nd edition, Cairo: Al-hay'a al-'amma li qusur al-thaqafa, 1993.

——. "Gaber Asfour yakshuf asrar tawzirihi . . . wa istiqalatihi" [Gaber Asfour unveils the secrets of his appointment as minister . . . and of his resignation]. *Al-Hayat*, March 2, 2012.

——. "Gaber Asfour waziran li al-marra al-thaniya: Al-'adala al-ma'rifiyya hadafi" [Gaber Asfour minister for the second time: Cognitive justice is my goal]. Interview by Tareq al-Taher. *Akhbar al-adab*, June 21, 2014.

——. *Hawamish ʿala daftar al-tanwir* [Marginalia on the notebook of tanwir]. Kuwait: Dar Suad al-Sabah, 1994.

——. Interview by Al-Baha' Husayn. *Al-Ahram*, August 8, 2011.

——. Interview by Hamdi Rizk. Al-Balad television, June 19, 2014. Part 1, https://www.youtube.com/watch?v=j6lTW6WXddI. Part 2, https://www.youtube.com/watch?v=kguffftcZFg.

——. "'Like Water and Air.'" Interview by Nevine el-Aref. *Al-Ahram*, July 23, 2014.

——. *Manarat* program, al-Arabiyya television. Posted June 23, 2015. https://www.youtube.com/watch?v=mrmok_eoGRc.

——. *Mihnat al-tanwir* [The crisis of enlightenment]. Cairo: Al-hay'a al-masriyya al-'amma li al-kitab, 1993.

——. *Naqd thaqafat al-takhalluf* [Critique of the culture of backwardness]. Cairo: al-hay'a al-masriyya al'amma li al-kitab, 2009.

——. "Renewing Discourse." Interview by Nevine el-Aref. *Al-Ahram*, February 25, 2015.

——. "Tatwir al-mandhuma al-thaqafiyya li al-dawla" [Developing the cultural system for the state]. *Al-Ahram*, June 11, 2014.

——. "Undhur hawlak fi ghadab" [Look around you in anger]. *Al-Ahram*, September 3, 2007.

——. "Wa madha ʿan al-mustaqbal al-waʿid" [And what about the promising future?]. *Al-Ahram*, January 24, 2011.

Atassi, Mohammad Ali. "The Other Prison." *Al-Jadid* 10, no. 49 (2004). Originally published in *an-Nahar*, cultural supplement, July 11, 2004.

'Attieh, Ahmed Abdel Halim. "Kant wa al-tanwir fi al-fikr al-'arabi" [Kant and tanwir in Arab thought]. In proceedings of the conference dedicated to the memory of Hisham Sharabi's *Al-Tanwir wa al-tasamuh wa tajdid al-fikr al-'arabi* [Tanwir, tolerance, and the renewal of Arab thought], 271–90. Carthage: Al-majma' al-tunisi li al-'ulum wa al-adab wa al-funun, "Bayt el-Hikmah," 2007.

Ayubi, Nazih N. *Over-Stating the Arab State: Politics and Society in the Middle East.* London: Tauris, 1996.

Baldissera, Eros "The Founding Congress of the League of Arab Writers (Damascus 1954) According to the Periodical 'Al-taqafa al-wataniyya.'" *Quaderni di Studi Arabi* 18 (2000): 121–40.

Bamyeh, Mohammed A. "Anarchist Method, Liberal Intention, Authoritarian Lesson: The Arab Spring Between Three Enlightenments." *Constellations* 20, no. 2 (2013): 188–202.

Bandak, Andreas. "Performing the Nation: Syrian Christians on the National Stage." In Salamandra and Stenberg, *Syria from Reform to Revolt*, 110–29.

——. "Reckoning with the Inevitable: Death and Dying Among Syrian Christians During the Uprising." *Ethnos* 80, no. 5 (2015): 671–91.

——. "States of Exception: Effects and Affects of Authoritarianism Among Christian Arabs in Damascus." In *A Comparative Ethnography of Alternative Spaces*, edited by Jens Dahl and Esther Fihl, 197–218. New York: Palgrave, 2013.

Barqawi, Ahmad. "Ma al-tanwir?" [What is enlightenment?]. *Al-Tariq* 3 (May-June 1996): 4–11. Reprinted in his *Muqaddima fi al-tanwir: Al-'ilmaniyya—al-dawla—al-huriyya* [Introduction to enlightenment: Secularism—the state—freedom], 13–31. 2nd edition, Damascus: Dar ma'd, 1998.

Barqawi, Ahmad and Adnan Musallam, eds. *Al-'aqlaniyya—al-'almaniyya—"al-sharq awsatiyya": Abhath al-usbu' al-thaqafi al-thani li qism al-dirasat al-falsafiyya wa al-ijtima'iyya fi al-fatra 22-19 nisan 1995* [Rationalism—secularism—"Middle Easternism": Studies of the second cultural week of philosophy and social studies for the period April 22–29, 1995]. Damascus: University of Damascus, 1995.

Barut, Muhammad Jamal. *Harakat al-tanwir al-arabiyya fi al-qarn al-tasi' 'ashar, halaqat halab: Dirasat wa mukhtarat* [The Arab tanwir movement in the nineteenth century, the Aleppo circle: Studies and selections]. Damascus: Culture Ministry, 1994.

——. "Muthaqqafun dimuqratiyyun yu'idun istikshaf Taha Husayn" [Democratic intellectuals rediscover Taha Husayn]. *Qadaya wa-shahadat* 3 (Winter 1991): 404–12.

——. "Ta'ammulat fi Ihya' al-mujtama' al-madani al-suri wa isti'ab al-nukhba" [Meditations on the revival of civil society and the co-optation of the elite]. In Barut and al-Kilani, *Suria bayn 'ahdayn* [Syria between two epochs], 203–8.

Barut, Muhammad Jamal and Shamsuddin al-Kilani, eds., *Suria bayn 'ahdayn: Qadaya al-marhala al-intiqaliyya* [Syria between two epochs: Issues of the transition phase]. Amman: Dar Sindibad li al-nashr, 2003.

Bashkin, Orit. *The Other Iraq: Pluralism and Culture in Hashemite Iraq.* Stanford: Stanford University Press, 2010.

Batatu, Hanna. "Some Observations on the Social Roots of Syria's Ruling, Military Group and the Causes of Its Dominance." *Middle East Journal* (1981): 331–44.

——. "Syria's Muslim Brethren." *MERIP MER* 110 (November–December 1982): 12–20.

Bauman, Zygmunt. *Legislators and Interpreters: On Modernity, Post-modernity and Intellectuals*. Oxford: Polity, 1987.

Bayraqdar, Faraj. *Al-Khuruj min al-kahf: Yawmiyyat al-sijin wa al-hurriyya* [Exit from the cave: Diary of prison and freedom]. Beirut: Al-Mu'assassa al-arabiyya li al-dirasat wa al-nashr, 2013.

——. *Khiyanat al-lugha wa al-samt: Taghribati fi sujun al-mukhabarat al-suriyya* [The betrayals of language and silence: My alienating exodus into the Syrian Mukhabarat prisons]. Beirut: Dar al-Jadid, 2011.

Beiser, Frederick C. *Enlightenment, Revolution, and Romanticism: The Genesis of Modern German Political Thought, 1790–1800*. Cambridge: Harvard University Press, 1992.

——. *The Fate of Reason: German Philosophy from Kant to Fichte*. Cambridge: Harvard University Press, 1987; reprinted 1993.

Belqziz, Abdel Ilah, ed. *Al-Ma'rifi wa al-idioloji fi dirasat al-fikr al-'arabi al-mu'asir* [The cognitive and the ideological in contemporary Arab thought]. Beirut: Markaz dirasat al-wihda al-arabiyya, 2010.

——. "Al-ma'rifi wa al-idioloji fi dirasat al-fikr al-'arabi al-mu'asir [The cognitive and the ideological in contemporary Arab thought]. In Belqziz, *Al-Ma'rifi wa al-idioloji fi dirasat al-fikr al-'arabi al-mu'asir* [The cognitive and the ideological in contemporary Arab thought], 337–70.

Bishara, Azmi. *Al-mujtama' al-madani: Dirasa naqdiyya (ma' ishara lilmujtama' al-madani al-arabi)* [Civil society: A critical study (with reference to Arab civil society)]. Beirut: Markaz dirasat al-wihda al-arabiyya, 1998.

Boëx, Cécile. "Être cinéaste syrien: Expériences et trajectoires de la création sous contrainte" [Being a Syrian filmmaker: The multiple experiences and trajectories of creation under constraint]. In *Itinéraires esthétiques et scenes culturelles au Proche Orient* [Aesthetic itineraries and cultural scenes in the Near East], edited by Frank Mermier and Nicolas Puig, 175–201. Beirut: Institut Français du Proche Orient (IFPO), 2007.

——. "La création cinématographique en Syrie à la lumière du mouvement de révolte: Nouvelles pratiques, nouveaux récits" [Cinematographic creation in Syria in light of the revolt movement: New practices, new tales]. *Revue des mondes musulmans et de la Méditerranée* 134 (2013): 145–56.

——. "Tahya as-sinama! Produire du sens: Les enjeux politiques de l'expression dans l'espace public" [Viva cinema! Producing meaning: The political stakes of expression in public space]. *Revue des mondes musulmans et de la Méditerranée* 115–16 (December 2006): 231–48.

——. "The End of State Monopoly Over Culture: Toward the Commodification of Cultural and Artistic Production." *Middle East Critique* 20, no. 2 (Summer 2011): 139–55.

Centre d'Études françaises, ed. *Actes du colloque "la réception de Voltaire et Rousseau en Égypte."* Cairo: Centre d'Études françaises, 1990.

Charif, Maher. "Musahama fi al-jadal al-rahin hawl al-tanwir / Salama Moussa namudhajan" [A contribution to the current debate on tanwir / Salama Moussa as an example]. *Al-Tariq* 5 (September 1994): 166–77.

——. *Rihanat al-nahda fi al-fikr al-arabi* [The stakes of the nahda in Arab thought]. Damascus: Dar el-Mada, 2000.

Chehayed, Jamal and Heidi Toelle, eds., *Al-riwaya al-suriyya al-mu'asira: Al-judhur al-thaqafiyya wa al-tiqaniyyat al-riwa'iyya al-jadida* [The contemporary Syrian novel: Cultural roots and new narrative techniques]. Damascus: Institut Français du Proche Orient, 2001.

Chehayed, Jamal and Yves Gonzalez-Quijano, eds., *Al-qissa fi suriya: Asalataha wa tiqaniyyatiha al-sardiyya* [The Syrian short story: Its authenticity and narrative techniques]. Damascus: Institut Français du Proche Orient, 2004.

Cherkaoui, Mohammed D. *What Is Enlightenment? Continuity or Rupture in the Wake of the Arab Uprisings.* Lexington, 2016.

Colla, Elliott. " 'Non, non! Si, si!': Commemorating the French Occupation of Egypt (1798–1801)." *MLN* 118, no. 4 (2003): 1043–69.

——. "State Culture, State Anarchy." *Jadaliyya*, February 5, 2011.

Cooke, Miriam. "The Cell Story: Syrian Prison Stories After Hafiz Asad." *Middle East Critique* 20, no. 2 (Summer 2011): 169–87.

——. *Dancing in Damascus: Creativity, Resilience, and the Syrian Revolution.* London: Routledge, 2016.

——. *Dissident Syria: Making Oppositional Arts Official.* Durham: Duke University Press, 2007.

——. "Ghassan al-Jaba'i: Prison Literature in Syria After 1980." *World Literature Today* 75, no. 2 (Spring 2001): 237–45.

Dab', Mahmud. *Taha Husayn ... laghu al-sayf wa jadd al-shita'* [Taha Husayn . . . The summer play and the winter earnestness]. Cairo: Dar al-Hilal, 2014.

Dakhli, Leyla. *La nahda* (Notice pour le dictionnaire de l'Humanisme arabe), 2012. https://halshs.archives-ouvertes.fr/halshs-00747086/document.

——. *Une génération d'intellectuels arabes: Syrie et Liban (1908–1940).* Paris: Éditions Karthala, 2009.

Dallal, Ahmad S. *Islam Without Europe: Traditions of Reform in Eighteenth-Century Islamic Thought.* Chapel Hill: University of North Carolina Press, 2018.

Darraj, Faysal. *Al-Dhakira al-qawmiyya fi al-riwaya al-arabiyya: Min zaman al-nahda ila zaman al-suqut* [National memory in the Arab novel: From the time of the nahda to the time of the fall]. Beirut: Markaz Dirasat al-Wihda al-Arabiyya, 2008.

——. *Al-Hadatha al-mutaqahqira: Taha Husayn wa-Adonis* [Vanquished modernity: Taha Husayn and Adonis]. Ramallah: Muwatin, al-mu'assassa al-filastiniyya li al-dirasat al-dimuqratiyya, 2005.

——. "Al-kawni wa al-'alami wa al-thaqafa al-wataniyya" [The universal and the worldwide and national culture]. *Qadaya wa-shahadat* 5 (Spring 1992): 7–28.

——. "Al-muthaqqafun wa-suq al-afkar" [The intellectuals and the market of ideas]. *Al-Adab* 45, nos. 1–2 (January–February 1997): 2–7.

——. "Al-sheikh al-taqlidi wa al-muthaqqaf al-hadith" [The traditional sheikh and the modern intellectual]. *Qadaya wa-shahadat* 1 (Winter 1990): 25–66.

——. *Bu's al-thaqafa fi al-mu'assassa al-filastiniyya* [The misery of culture in the Palestinian establishment]. Beirut: Dar al-Adab, 1996.

——. *Dhakirat al-maghlubin: Al-hazima wa al-sahyuniyya fi al-khitab al-thaqafi al-filastini* [The memory of the defeated: The defeat and Zionism in Palestinian cultural discourse]. Beirut: al-Markaz al-Thaqafi al-Arabi, 2010.

——. "Difa'an 'an al-fikr al-'arabi: Fikr al-tanwir bayna al-naqd wa al-tazwir" [In defense of Arab tanwir thought: Tanwir between criticism and vilification]. *Al-Adab* 45, nos. 11–12 (November–December 1997).

——. "Faysal Darraj: Intaha dawr al-muthaqqaf wa tahawwala ila mutafarrij hazin" [Faysal Darraj: The role of the intellectual has ended, and he has become a sad spectator]. *Al-Arab*, April 21, 2015.

——. "Fi ma'na al-tanwir" [On the meaning of tanwir]. In *Hasilat al-'aqlaniyya wa al-tanwir fi al-fikr al-arabi al-mu'asir* [The harvest of tanwir in contemporary Arab thought], 93–117. Beirut: Markaz Dirasat al-Wihda al-Arabiyya, 2005.

——. "Masir al-muthaqqaf bayn al-naqd wa al-hija'" [The fate of the intellectual between critique and derision]. *Al-Adab* 46, nos. 7–8 (July–August 1998): 63–70.

——. *Riwayat al-taqaddum wa ightirab al-mustaqbal: Tahawwulat al-ru'ya fi al-riwaya al-arabiyya* [The story of progress and the estrangement of the future: Transformations of vision in the Arabic novel]. Beirut: Dar al-Adab, 2010.

Della Ratta, Donatella. "Dramas of the Authoritarian State." *MERIP* (February 2012). http://www.merip.org/mero/interventions/dramas-authoritarian-state.

——. *Shooting a Revolution: Visual Media and Warfare in Syria.* Digital Barricades: Interventions in Digital Culture and Politics. London: Pluto, 2018.

——. "The 'Whisper Strategy': How the Syrian Drama Makers Shape Television Fiction in the Context of Authoritarianism and Commodification." In Salamandra and Stenberg, *Syria from Reform to Revolt*, 53–76.

Dib, Thaer. "Mufaraqat Gaber Asfour" [The paradoxes of Gaber Asfour]. *Al-Safir*, February 4, 2011.

Di-Capua, Yoav. "Homeward Bound: Husayn Muruwwah's Integrative Quest for Authenticity." *Journal of Arabic Literature* 44, no. 1 (2013): 21–52.

——. "Nahda: The Arab Project of Enlightenment." In *The Cambridge Companion to Modern Arab Culture*, edited by Dwight F. Reynolds, 54–74. Cambridge: Cambridge University Press, 2015.

——. *No Exit: Arab Existentialism, Jean-Paul Sartre, and Decolonization.* Chicago: University of Chicago Press, 2018.

Donohue, John J. and John L. Esposito, eds., *Islam in Transition: Muslim Perspectives.* New York: Oxford University Press, 1982.

Dudoignon, Stephane A., Komastu Hisao, and Kosugi Yasushi, eds. *Intellectuals in the Modern Islamic World: Transmission, Transformation, Communication.* New York: Routledge, 2006.

Eid, Abdulrazzaq. *Azamat al-tanwir: Shar'anat al-fawat al-hadari* [The crisis of tanwir: The legitimation of civilizational delay]. Damascus: Dar al-Ahali, 1997.

——. "Madkhal li qira'at al-ta'addudiyya fi surya" [Introduction to a reading of pluralism in Syria]. In *Huquq al-Insan wa al-dimuqratiyya fi surya* [Human rights and democracy in Syria]. Paris: EURABE Publications, with the Arab Council for Human Rights and the European Commission, 2001.

——. *Yas'alunak 'an al-mujtma' al-madani: "Rabi' dimashq al-maw'ud"* [They ask you about civil society: The buried Damascus spring]. Cairo: Dar al-Inma' al-Hadari, 2003; Beirut: Dar al-Tanwir, 2003; and Dar al-Farabi, 2004.

el-Ariss, Tarek, ed. *The Arab Renaissance: A Bilingual Anthology of the Nahda.* New York: Modern Language Association of America, 2018.

El-Rouayheb, Khaled. "Was There a Revival of Logical Studies in Eighteenth Century Egypt?" *Die Welt des Islams* 45, no. 1 (2005): 1–19.

——. *Islamic Intellectual History in the Seventeenth Century: Scholarly Currents in the Ottoman Empire and the Maghreb*. Cambridge: Cambridge University Press, 2015.

Elshakry, Marwa. *Reading Darwin in Arabic, 1860–1950*. Chicago: University of Chicago Press, 2013.

El Shakry, Omnia. *The Arabic Freud: Psychoanalysis and Islam in Modern Egypt*. Princeton: Princeton University Press, 2017.

——. "The Arabic Freud: The Unconscious and the Modern Subject." *Modern Intellectual History* 11, no. 1 (April 2014): 89–118.

Enan, Laïla. " 'Si tu le sais, alors c'est une catastrophe. . . .' La commémoration: Pourquoi, pour qui?" In Alleaume, "L'expédition de Bonaparte vue d'Égypte," 13–24.

Encyclopedia of Mediterranean Humanism, s.v. "Tanwīr: Arabic Enlightenment," by Wael Abu-ᶜUksa and Fruma Zachs, accessed January 2016. http://www.encyclopedie -humanisme.com/?Tanw%C4%ABr-240.

Fahmy, Dalia F. and Daanish Faruqi, eds. *Egypt and the Contradictions of Liberalism: Illiberal Intelligentsia and the Future of Egyptian Democracy*. London: Oneworld, 2017.

——. "Egyptian Liberals, From Revolution to Counterrevolution." In Fahmy and Faruqi, *Egypt and the Contradictions of Liberalism*, 1–27.

Fahmy, Khaled. "Dissecting the Modern Egyptian State." *International Journal of Middle East Studies* 47 (2015): 559–62.

Ferrié, Jean-Noël. "Réformisme, renaissance et contingence: La justification de la justice chez Nubar Pacha et Khayr al-Din." In Roussillon, *Entre réforme sociale et mouvement social*, 181–91.

Firat, Alexa. "Cultural Battles on the Literary Field: From the Syrian Writers' Collective to the Last Days of Socialist Realism in Syria." *Middle Eastern Literatures* 18, no. 2 (2015): 153–76.

Frangie, Samer. "Historicism, Socialism and Liberalism After the Defeat: On the Political Thought of Yasin al-Hafiz." *Modern Intellectual History* 12, no. 2 (2015): 325–52.

George, Alan. *Syria: Neither Bread nor Freedom*. London: Zed, 2003.

Gershoni, Israel. "The Theory of Crisis and the Crisis in a Theory: Intellectual History in Twentieth-Century Middle Eastern Studies." In *Middle East Historiographies: Narrating the Twentieth Century*, edited by Israel Gershoni, Amy Singer, and Y. Hakan Erdem, 131–82. Seattle: University of Washington Press, 2006.

Ghadbian, Najib. "Contesting Authoritarianism: Opposition Activism Under Bashar al-Asad, 2000–2010." In *Syria from Reform to Revolt*. Vol. 1, *Political Economy and International Relations*, edited by Raymond Hinnebusch and Tina Zintl, 91–112. Syracuse University Press, 2015.

Ghalioun, Burhan. *Al-Mihna al-arabiyya: Al-dawla didd al-umma* [The Arab crisis: The state against the nation]. Beirut: Markaz dirasat al-wihda al-arabiyya, 1993.

——. *Bayan min ajl al-dimurratiyya* [Manifesto for democracy]. Cairo: Dar Ibn Rush, 1978; 5th edition, Casablanca: al-Markaz al-thaqafi al-arabi, 2006.

——. *Ightiyal al-'aql: Mihnat al-thaqafa al-arabiyya bayn al-salafiyya wa al-tabaᶜiyya* [Assassination of reason: The crisis of Arab culture between Salafism and dependency]. Beirut: Dar al-tanwir, 1985.

——. *Mujatama' al-nukhba* [The elite society]. Beirut: Ma'had al-inma' al-arabi, 1986.
——. "Qam' al-muthaqqafin al-suriyyin yaghluq qanawat al-hiwar wa yatrukuna li mu'adalat al-usuliyya muqabil al-ajhiza al-amniyya" [The repression of the Syrian intellectuals shuts down the channels of dialogue and leaves us to the equation of fundamentalism versus security agencies]. In Barut and al-Kilani, *Suria bayn 'ahdayn* [Syria between two epochs], 340–48; first published in *an-Nahar*, February 28, 2001.
Ghalioun, Burhan and Farouk Mardam-Bey, eds. "Un printemps syrien." Special issue, *Confluences Méditerranée* 44 (Winter 2002–2003): 9–95.
Ghazoul, Ferial. "The Artist vs the Commissar." *al-Ahram*, January 25–31, 2001.
Gonzalez-Quijano, Yves. "La renaissance arabe au XIXe siècle: Médiums, médiations, médiateurs." In *Histoire de la littérature arabe moderne*. Vol. 1, *1800-1945*, edited by Boutros Hallaq and Heidi Toelle, 71–113. Paris: Sindbad Actes Sud, 2007.
——. *Les gens du livre: Édition et champ intellectuel dans l'Égypte républicaine.* Paris: Éditions CNRS, 1998; 2002.
Gran, Peter. *The Islamic Roots of Capitalism: Egypt, 1760-1840.* Austin: Texas University Press, 1979. Translated by Ra'uf 'Abbas as *Judhur al-ra'smaliyya al-islamiyya fi misr* [Roots of Islamic capitalism in Egypt]. Cairo: Dar al-Fikr, 1993.
——. "Une Renaissance récusée: L'Égypte à la fin du XVIIIe siècle." Interview by Ramadan al-Khuli and Abd al-Raziq Isa. *Égypte/Monde arabe* 1 (1999): 55–70.
Haarman, Ulrich. " 'Ein Missgriff des Geschicks': Muslimische und westliche Standpunkte zur Geschichte der islamischen Welt im 18. Jahrhundert" ['A skills' error of judgment': Muslim and European standpoints on the history of the eighteenth-century Islamic world]. In *Geschichtsdiskurs.* Vol 2, *Anfänge modernen historischen Denkens*, edited by Wolfgang Küttler, Jörn Rüsen, and Ernst Schulin, 184–201. Frankfurt: Fischer Taschenbuch, 1994.
Haddad, Bassam. "Enduring Legacies: The Politics of Private Sector Development in Syria." In *Demystifying Syria*, edited by Fred H. Lawson, 29–55. London: Saqi / London Middle East Institute, SOAS, 2009.
Haddad, Lutfi, ed., *Riad al-Turk: Mandela Suryia* [Riad al-Turk: The Mandela of Syria]. Newburgh, IN: Jozoor Cultural Foundation, 2005.
Haddad, Mahmoud. "Arab Religious Nationalism in the Era of Colonialism: Rereading Rashid Rida's Ideas on the Caliphate." *Journal of the American Oriental Society* 117, no. 2 (1997): 253–77.
——. "The Manarists and Modernism: An Attempt to Fuse Religion and Society." In Dudoignon, Hisao, and Yasushi, *Intellectuals in the Modern Islamic World*, 55–73.
Hagen, Gottfried and Tilman Seidensticker. "Reinhard Schulzes Hypothese einer islamischen Aufklärung: Kritik einer historiographischen Kritik" [Reinhard Schulze's hypothesis of an Islamic Enlightenment: Critique of a historiographical critique]. *Zeitschrift des Deutschen Morgenländischen Gesellschaft* 148 (1998): 83–110.
Haj Saleh, Yassin. *Bil Khalas ya shabab! Sittata 'ashara 'aman fi al-sujun al-suriyya* [Hopefully out my friends! Sixteen years in the Syrian prisons]. Beirut: Dar al-Saqi, 2012.
——. "Michel Kilo wa wiladat al-muthaqqaf al-suri" [Michel Kilo and the birth of the Syrian intellectual]. *Al-Safir*, June 3, 2006.

Hamidi, Ibrahim. "Antun Maqdisi: ya'tabir an al-sha'b al-suri la 'ilaqata lahu bima yaktubuhu al-muthaqafun" [Antun Maqdisi considers that the Syrian people are not concerned about the writings of the intellectuals]. In Barut and al-Kilani, *Suria bayn 'ahdayn* [Syria between two epochs], 275–79; first published in *al-Hayat*, Feburary 4, 2001.

Hamzah, Dyala, ed. *The Making of the Arab Intellectual: Empire, Public Sphere and the Colonial Coordinates of Selfhood.* Abingdon, UK: Routledge, 2013.

Hanafi, Hassan. "Al-salafiyya wa al-'almaniyya . . . hal yakhtalifan?" [Salafism and secularism . . . do they differ?]. *Al-Masri al-yawm*, October 23, 2014.

——. "Al-tanwir am al-tathwir?" [Enlightenment or revolutionizing?]. *Al-Masri al-yawm*, April 30, 2014.

——. "Nahnu wa al-tanwir . . . al-huriyya wa al-insan" [We and the enlighten-ment . . . freedom and the human]. *Al-ittihad*, July 19, 2014.

——. "Nahnu wa al-tanwir . . . wa al-wa'i al-tarikhi" [We and the enlightenment . . . and historical awareness]. *Al-ittihad*, August 9, 2014.

——. "Nahnu wa al-tanwir . . . wa iktishaf al-tabi'a" [We and the enlightenment . . . and the discovery of nature]. *Al-ittihad*, July 26, 2014.

——. "Nahnu wa al-tanwir . . . wa thaqafat al-mujtama'" [We and the enlighten-ment . . . and the culture of society]. *Al-ittihad*, August 2, 2014.

——. "Nahnu wa al-tanwir wa al-'aql" [We and the enlightenment and reason]. *Al-Ittihad*, July 12, 2014.

——. "Tanwir aw Tazwir?" [Enlightening or faking?]. *Al-Masri al-yawm*, October 29, 2014.

Hanssen, Jens and Max Weiss, eds. *Arabic Thought Against the Authoritarian Age: Towards an Intellectual History of the Present.* Cambridge: Cambridge University Press, 2018.

——, eds. *Arabic Thought Beyond the Liberal Age: Towards an Intellectual History of the Nahda.* Cambridge: Cambridge University Press, 2016.

——. "Arab Intellectual History Between the Postwar and the Postcolonial." In Hanssen and Weiss, *Arabic Thought Against the Authoritarian Age*, 1–35.

Heikal, Mohamed Hassanein, ed. *Azamat al-muthaqqafin* [The crisis of the intellectu-als]. Cairo: Dar al-udaba' li al-Tiba'a wa al-nashr, 1961.

Heydemann, Steven. "Syria and the Future of Authoritarianism." *Journal of Democracy* 24, no. 4 (October 2013): 59–73.

——. "Upgrading Authoritarianism in the Arab World." Analysis paper 13, Octo-ber 2007. Washington, DC: Saban Center for Middle East Policy, Brookings Institution.

Heydemann, Steven and Reinoud Leenders. "Authoritarian Learning and Authori-tarian Resilience: Regime Responses to the 'Arab Awakening.' " *Globalization* 8, no. 5 (October 2011): 647–53.

——, eds. *Middle East Authoritarianisms: Governance, Contestation, and Regime Resilience in Syria and Iran.* Stanford: Stanford University Press, 2013.

——. "Popular Mobilization in Syria: Opportunity and Threat, and the Social Net-works of the Early Risers." *Mediterranean Politics* 17, no. 2 (July 2012): 139–59.

Hinnebusch, Raymond. *Authoritarian Power and State Formation in Ba'thist Syria: Army, Party and Peasant.* Boulder, CO: Westview, 1990.

——. "Calculated Decompression as a Substitute for Democratization: Syria." In *Political Liberalization and Democratization in the Arab World*. Vol. 2, *Comparative Experiences*, edited by Bahgat Korany, Rex Brynen, and Paul Noble, 223–40. London: Lynne Rienner, 1998.

——. "Syria: From 'Authoritarian Upgrading' to Revolution?" *International Affairs* 88, no. 1 (2012): 95–113.

Holt, Elizabeth M. "Narrating the *Nahda*: The Syrian Protestant College, *al-Muqtataf*, and the Rise of Jurji Zaydan." In *One Hundred and Fifty*, edited by Nadia Maria El-Cheikh, Lina Choueiri, and Bilal Orfali, 273–79. Beirut: American University Press, 2016.

Hourani, Albert. *Arabic Thought in the Liberal Age, 1798-1939*. London: Oxford University Press, 1962; reissued with a new preface by Cambridge University Press, 1983.

Husayn, Taha. *Al-Ayyam* [The days]. Cairo: Markaz al-Ahram, 1992. Translated by E. H. Paxton as *The Days: His Autobiography in Three Parts*. 2nd edition, Cairo: American University of Cairo, 2010.

——. *Fi al-shi'r al-jahili* [On Jahili poetry]. 1926; Cairo: Dar al-nahr li al-nashr wa al-tawzi', 1996.

——. *Mustaqbal al-thaqafa fi Misr* [The future of culture in Egypt]. Cairo: Dar el-ma'aref, 1938.

Hussein Ali, Zahra A. "The Prometheus Myth in the Sculptures of Sami Mohammad and the Plays of Aeschylus and Shelley." *Comparative Literature Studies* 49, no. 1 (2012): 50–83.

Hussein, Louay. *Al-Faqd: Hikayat min dhakira mutakhayyala lisajin haqiqi* [The Loss: Stories of an imaginary memory of a real prisoner]. Damascus: Dar Petra li al-nashr wa al-tawzi', 2006.

——. *Al-Ikhtiyar al-dimuqrati fi suria* [The democratic option in Syria]. Damascus: Dar Petra, 2003.

——. *Hiwarat fi al-wataniyya al-suriyya* [Dialogues on Syrian nationalism]. Damascus: Dar Petra and Beirut: Dar al-Furat, 2003.

Ibrahim, Sonallah. "Sonallah Ibrahim: al-muqawama bi al-qalam" [Sonallah Ibrahim: Resistance with the pen]. Interview by Sherif al-Shafi'i. *Al-Jadeed* 42 (July 2018).

Imarah, Muhammad. *Al-Islam bayn al-tanwir wa al-tazwir* [Islam between tanwir and falsification]. Cairo: Dar al-shourouq, 1995.

——. *Taha Husayn: min al-inbihar bi al-gharb ila al-intisar li al-islam* [Taha Husayn: From infatuation with the West to championing Islam]. Cairo: *Al-Azhar* magazine, 2014.

——. *Salama Moussa: Ijtihad khati' am 'amala hadariyya?* [Salama Moussa: Mistaken effort or civilizational agent?]. Cairo: Dar al-wafa', 1995.

al-Iraqi, Atef. *Al-'aql wa al-tanwir fi al-fikr al-'arabi al-mu'asir* [Reason and enlightenment in contemporary Arab thought]. Cairo: Dar Qaba', 1998.

——. *Al-falsafa al-'arabiyya wa al-tariq ila al-mustaqbal: Ru'ya 'aliyya naqdiyya* [Arab philosophy and the way to the future: A rational and critical vision]. 1998. 6th edition, Cairo: Dar al-rashad, 2009.

——. *Al-faylasuf Ibn Rushd wa mustaqbal al-thaqafa al-'arabiyya: Arb'un 'aman min Dhikrayati ma' fikrihi al-tanwiri* [The philosopher Ibn Rushd and the future of Arab culture: Forty years of my memories with his enlightenment thought]. 2000. 2nd edition, Cairo: Dar al-rashad, 2005.

——. *Ibn Rush mufakkiran 'arabiyyan wa ra'idan li al-ittijah al-'aqli* [Ibn Rushd: Arab thinker and pioneer of the rational orientation]. Cairo: Supreme Council of Culture, 1993.

Ismail, Salwa. "Changing Social Structure, Shifting Alliances and Authoritarianism in Syria." In *Demystifying Syria*, edited by Fred Lawson, 13–28. London: Saqi / London Middle East Institute, SOAS, 2009.

——. "Confronting the Other: Identity, Culture, Politics, and Conservative Islamism in Egypt." *International Journal for Middle Eastern Studies* 30 (1998): 199–225.

——. *Rethinking Islamist Politics: Culture, the State, and Islamism*. London: Tauris, 2003.

——. *The Rule of Violence: Subjectivity, Memory and Government in Syria*. Cambridge: Cambridge University Press, 2018.

Jaba'i, Ghassan. *Asabi' al-mawz: Qisas saghira* [Finger bananas: Small stories]. Damascus: manshurat wizarat al-thaqafa, 1994.

Jacquemond, Richard. *Conscience of the Nation: Writers, State, and Society in Modern Egypt*. Cairo: Cairo University Press, 2008. Originally published in French as *Entre scribes et écrivains: Le champ littéraire dans l'Egypte contemporaine*. Paris: Actes Sud, 2002.

——. "Les limites mouvantes du dicible dans la fiction égyptienne." In "La censure ou comment la contourner." Special issue, *Égypte/Monde arabe* 3 (2000): 63–83.

——. "The Shifting Limits of the Sayable in Contemporary Egyptian Fiction." *MIT Electronic Journal of Middle East Studies* 4 (Fall 2004): 41–52.

Jalabi-Wellnitz, Batoul. *Spectateurs en dialogue: L'énonciation dans le théâtre de Sadallah Wannous de 1967 à 1978*. Damascus: Institut Français du Proche Orient, 2006.

Joubin, Rebecca "Resistance Amid Regime Co-optation on the Syrian Television Series Buq'at Daw', 2001–2012." *Middle East Journal* 68, no. 1 (2014): 9–32.

Jurdi Abisaad, Rula. "Deconstructing the Modular and the Authentic: Husayn Muroeh's Early Islamic History." *Critique: Critical Middle Eastern Studies* 17, no. 3 (2008): 239–59.

Kahf, Mohja. "The Silences of Contemporary Syrian Literature." *World Literature Today* 75, no. 2 (Spring 2001): 224–36.

Kandil, Hazem. "On the Margins of Defeat: A Sociology of Arab Intellectuals Under Authoritarianism." In *The Changing Middle East: A New Look at Regional Dynamics*, edited by Bahgat Korany, 85–118. Cairo: American University Press, 2010.

Karabet, Aram. *Al-rahil ila al-majhul* [Journey to the unknown]. Alexandria: Dar al-jidar, 2009. Translated into French as *Treize ans dans les prisons syriennes: Voyage vers l'inconnu*. Paris: Actes Sud, 2013.

Kassab, Elizabeth Suzanne. "The Arab Quest for Freedom and Dignity: Have Arab Thinkers Been Part of It?" *META*, 2013. http://meta-journal.net/article/view /1038.

——. *Contemporary Arab Thought: Cultural Critique in Comparative Perspective*. New York: Columbia University Press, 2010.

——. "Critics and Rebels: Older Arab Intellectuals Reflect on the Uprisings." "Intellectuals in the Middle East." Special issue, *British Journal of Middle East Studies* (2014): 1–20.

——. "Summoning the Spirit of Taha Husayn's Enlightenment Project: The Nahda Revival of *Qadaqa wa shahadat*." In Hanssen and Weiss, *Arabic Thought Against the Authoritarian Age*, 311–35.

Kepel, Gilles. *Le prophète et Pharaon: Les mouvements islamistes dans l'Égypte contemporaine*. Paris: La Découverte, 1984; 2012 edition with a new preface by the author published by Gallimard. Translated by J. Rothschild as *The Prophet and the Pharaoh*. London: Saqi, 1985.

——. "Les oulémas, l'intelligentsia et les islamistes en Égypte: Système social, ordre transcendental et ordre traduit." In *Revue française de science politique* 35, no. 3 (1985): 424–45.

——. *Muslim Extremism in Egypt: The Prophet and Pharaoh*. University of California Press, 2003.

Khalifa, Khaled. *Fi madih al-karahiyya* [In praise of hatred]. Beirut: Dar Umsiya, 2006. Republished in Beirut by Dar al-adab, 2010. Translated by Leri Price as *In Praise of Hatred*. Black Swan, 2013.

——. *La sakakina fi matabikh hadhihi al-madina* [No knives in this city's kitchens]. Cairo: Dar al-ʻain, 2013. Translated by Leri Price as *No Knives in the Kitchens of This City*. Cairo: American University of Cairo, 2016.

Khalifeh, Mustafa. *Al-Qawqaʻa: Yawmiyyat mutalassis* [The shell: Diary of a voyeur]. Beirut: Dar al-Adab, 2008. Translated into French by Stéphanie Dujols as Moustafa Khalifé, *La Coquille: Prisonnier politique en Syrie*. Paris: Actes Sud, 2012.

Khatib, Line. *Islamic Revivalism in Syria: The Rise and Fall of Baʻthist Secularism*. London: Routledge, 2011.

Khoury, Raif. *Al-adab al-masʼul* [The responsible literature]. 1968. Beirut: Dar al-Adab, 1989.

——, ed. *Al-Fikr al-ʻarabi al-hadith: Athar al-thawra al-faransiyya fi tawjih al-siyasi wa al-ijtimaʻi*. Beirut: Dar al-Makshuf, 1943. Reprinted by Dar al-Saqi in Beirut in 2013. Translated by Ihsan Abbas, revised and edited by Charles Issawi, and published as *Modern Arab Thought: Channels of the French Revolution to the Arab East*. Princeton: Kingston, 1983.

Khuri-Makdisi, Ilham. *The Eastern Mediterranean and the Making of Global Radicalism, 1860–1914*. University of California Press, 2010.

Kienle, Eberhard. *Baʻth Versus Baʻth: The Conflict Between Syria and Iraq*. London: Tauris, 1990.

——, ed. *Contemporary Syria: Liberalization Between Cold War and Peace*. London: Tauris, 1997.

——. *A Grand Delusion: Democracy and Economic Reform in Egypt*. London: Tauris, 2001.

——. "The Return of Politics? Scenarios for Syria's Second *Infitah*." In Kienle, *Contemporary Syria*, 114–31.

Kilo, Michel. " 'An al-sulta wa al-dawla wa ʻal-mujtamaʻ al-madani' " [On power and the state and "civil society"]. *an-Nahar*, February 1, 2001. Reprinted in Barut and al-Kilani, *Suria bayn ʻahdayn* [Syria between two epochs], 246–50.

——. "Al-Muthaqqafun al-suriyyun laysu hizban" [The Syrian intellectuals are not a party]. *an-Nahar*, September 9, 2002.

——. "Limadha taratktu al-iʼtiliaf?" [Why did I leave the coalition?]. *Al-araby al-jadeed*, December 25, 2016.

——. "Muthaqqaf al-taghyir" [The intellectual of change]. *Al-Dawha* 56 (March 2013).

——. "Qisas ukhra min 'alam al-ashbah" [Other stories from the world of ghosts]. *al-Sharq al-awsat*, October 3, 2012.

——. "Tayyeb Tizini aw faylasuf al-'asr!" [Tayyeb Tizini or the epoch's philosopher!]. *An-Nahar*, August 22, 2003.

Kurzman, Charles, ed., *Modernist Islam, 1840–1940: A Sourcebook*. New York: Oxford University Press, 2002.

Labib, Abdelaziz. "Al-ma'rifi wa al-idioloji fi dirasat al-fikr al-gharbi: Al-talaqqi al-arabi lil fikr al-tanwiri al-gharbi: Farah Antun namudhajan" [The cognitive and the ideological in studies of Western thought: The Arab reception of Western Enlightenment thought: The example of Farah Antun]. In Belqziz, *Al-Ma'rifi wa al-idioloji fi dirasat al-fikr al-'arabi al-mu'asir* [The cognitive and the ideological in contemporary Arab thought], 385–419.

——. "Eine Quelle des zeitgenössischen arabischen Denkens: Adib Ishaq (1856–1884) und das Problem der politischen Gemeinschaft" [A source of contemporary Arab thought: Adib Ishaq (1856–1884) and the problem of political community]. *Polylog* 10–11 (2004): 104–12.

——. "Présence de Rousseau dans la Renaissance arabe." In *Jean-Jacques Rousseau, politique et nation*, edited by Musée Jean-Jacques Rousseau, 949–68. Paris: Honoré Champion-Saltkine reprints, 2001.

Laurens, Henry. *L'expédition d'Égypte, 1798–1801*. Paris: Colin, 1989.

Le Caisne, Garance. *Opération César: Au Coeur de la machine de mort syrienne* [Operation Cesar: In the heart of the Syrian killing machine]. Paris: Éditions Stock, 2015.

Leenders, Reinoud. "Prosecuting Political Dissent: Courts and the Resilience of Authoritarianism in Syria." In Kienle, *Contemporary Syria*, 169–99.

Lobmeyer, Hans Günter. "Al-dimuqratiyya hiyya al-hall? The Syrian Opposition at the End of the Asad Era." In Kienle, *Contemporary Syria*, 81–96.

——. "Islamic Ideology and Secular Discourse: The Islamists of Syria." *Orient* 32, no. 3 (1991): 395–418.

Louis, Shady. "Dhulumat al-tanwir al-masri" [The manifold darkness of Egyptian tanwir]. *Al-Modon*, August 20, 2014.

——. "Murad Wahba: Inqadh al-hadara!" [Murad Wahba: Saving civilization!]. *Al-Modon*, January 1 2017.

Luciani, Giacomo, ed. *The Arab State*. London: Routledge, 1990.

Lust-Okar, Ellen. "Reform in Syria: Steering Between the Chinese Model and Regime Change." Washington, DC: Carnegie Papers, Carnegie Endowment for International Peace, 2006.

Mabruk, Muhammad Ibrahim. *Muwajahat al-Muwajaha: Al-munaqasha al-islamiyya lil afkar al-'ilmaniyya wa kutub al-muwajah* [Confrontation of the confrontation: The Islamic discussion of the ideas of secularism and the books of the Muwajaha]. Cairo: Dar thabet li al-nashr wa al-tawzi', 1995.

Mahmoud, Sayyed. "'Al-Kitaba al-ukhra' khadat ma'rakat al-thaqafa al-muhammasha" [Al-Kitaba al-ukhra led the battle for the marginalized culture]. *Al-Hayat*, February 19, 2010.

Maqdisi, Antun. "Bashar al-Asad wa dukhul suriya al-qarn al-hadi wa al-'ishrin" [Bashar al-Assad and the entry of Syria into the twenty-first century]. In Barut and al-Kilani, *Suria bayn 'ahdayn* [Syria between two epochs], 270–74; first published in *as-Safir*, January 22, 2001.

McCallum, Fiona. "Christian Political Participation in the Arab World." *Islam and Christian-Muslim Relations* 23, no. 1 (January 2012): 3–18.

——. "Religious Institutions and Authoritarian States: Church-State Relations in the Middle East." *Third World Quarterly* 33, no. 1 (2012): 109–24.

Mehrez, Samia. *Egypt's Culture Wars: Politics and Practice*. Cairo: American University of Cairo, 2010.

——. "Take Them Out of the Ballgame: Egypt's Cultural Players in Crisis." *Middle East Report* 219 (2001): 12–13.

Mepham, David. "Repression Unbound: Egypt Under Sisi." *Huffington Post*, November 4, 2015.

Moghith, Anwar. "Au nom du peuple: La formation de l'élite en Égypte moderne." *Le Télémaque* 39, no. 1 (2011): 31–36.

——. "Le darwinisme et la sécularisation de la pensée en Égypte." *Rue Descartes* 78, no. 2 (2013): 57–67.

Mosbah, Salah. "Spinoza et le problème du théologico-politique en Tunisie." *Rue Descartes* 61, no. 3 (2008): 42–50.

Moussa, Salama. *Al-yawm wa al-ghad* [Today and tomorrow]. Cairo: Salama Moussa li al-nashr wa al-tawzi', 1928.

Murqus, Elias. *Al-'Aqlaniyya wa al-taqaddum* [Rationality and progress]. Rabat: Al-Majlis al-qawmi li al-thaqafa al-arabiyya, 1992.

——. *Naqd al-'aqlaniyya al-arabiyya* [Critique of Arab rationalism]. Damascus: Dar al-hasad, 1997.

Muruwweh, Husayn. *Al-Naza'at al-maddiyya fi al-falsafa al-arabiyya al-islamiyya* [The material tendencies in Arab-Islamic philosophy]. 4 vols. 1978. 2nd edition, Beirut: Dar al-Farabi, 2008.

Nachar, Karam. " 'An Yasin al-Hafiz al-shab wa zamanihi 'al-thawri' " [On the young Yasin al-Hafiz and his "revolutionary" time]. *Al-jumhuriya* [The republic], November 3, 2014. http://aljumhuriya.net/32545.

Nada, Ahmad. "Nisf Sherif Younis al-akhar" [The other half of Sherif Younis]. *Al-Modon*, March 7, 2016.

Nagel, Tilman. "Autochthone Wurzeln des islamischen Modernismus: Bemerkungen zum Werk des Damaszeners Ibn 'Abdidin (1784–1836)" [The native roots of Islamic modernism: Remarks on the work of the Damascene Ibn 'Abidin (1784–1836)]. *Zeitschrift des Deutschen Morgenländischen Gesellschaft* 146 (1996): 92–111.

Najjar, Fauzi M. "The Debate on Islam and Secularism in Egypt." *Arab Studies Quarterly* 18, no. 2 (1996): 1–21.

——. "Ibn Rush (Averroes) and the Egyptian Enlightenment Movement." *British Journal of Middle Eastern Studies* 31 no. 2 (November 2004): 195–213.

——. "Islamic Fundamentalism and the Intellectuals: The Case of Naguib Mahfouz." *British Journal of Middle Eastern Studies* 25, no. 1 (May 1998): 139–68.

——. "Islamic Fundamentalism and the Intellectuals: The Case of Nasr Hamid Abu Zayd." *British Journal of Middle Eastern Studies* 27, no. 2 (November 2000): 177–200.

Nasser, Amjad. "Limadha ya Gaber Asfour" [Why oh Gaber Asfour]. *Al-Quds al-arabi*, February 1, 2011.

Ne'meh, Talal. *Elias Murqus: Hiwarat ghayr manshura* [Elias Murqus: Unpublished conversations]. Doha: Al-Markaz al-arabi li al-abhath wa dirasat al-siyasat, 2015.

Nusair, Najib. "Najib Nusair: Al-drama al-suriyya tadhhab fi ittijah mu'akis li al-tanwir" [Najib Nusair: Syrian drama goes in a contrary direction to tanwir]. *Al-jaml*, May 21, 2008.

Owen, Roger. *State, Power and Politics in the Making of the Modern Middle East*. London: Routledge, 2004.

Perthes, Volker. "A Look at Syria's Upper Class: The Bourgeoisie and the Ba'th." *MERIP MER* 170 (May–June 1991): 31–37.

——. *The Political Economy of Syria Under Asad*. London: Tauris, 1995.

——. "Stages of Economic and Political Liberalization." In Kienle, *Contemporary Syria*, 44–71.

——. "The Syrian Private Industrial and Commercial Sectors and the State." *International Journal of Middle East Studies* 24 (1992): 207–30.

——. "Syria's Parliamentary Elections: Remodeling Asad's Political Base." *MERIP MER* 174 (January–February 1992): 15–18.

——. *Syria Under Asad*. London: Tauris, 1997.

——. *Syria Under Bashar al-Asad: Modernisation and the Limits of Change*. London: Routledge, International Institute for Strategic Studies, 2004.

Peters, Rudolph. "Reinhard Schulze's Quest for an Islamic Enlightenment." *Die Welt des Islams* 30 (1990): 160–62.

Picard, Elizabeth. "Fin de partis en Syrie." *Revue du monde musulman et de la Méditerranée* nos. 81–82 (1996): 207–29.

Pierret, Thomas. "Merchant Background, Bourgeois Ethics." In Salamandra and Stenberg, *Syria from Reform to Revolt*, 130–46.

Pierret, Thomas. "Sunni Clergy Politics in the Cities of the Ba'thi Syria." In *Demystifying Syria*, edited by Fred Lawson, 70–84. London: Saqi / London Middle East Institute, SOAS, 2009.

Pierret, Thomas. "Syrie: État sans nation ou nation sans état?" [Syria: A state without a nation or a nation without a state?]. In *Vers un nouveau moyen-orient? Études arabes en crise entre logiques de divisions et sociétés civiles* [Toward a new Middle East? Arab studies in crisis between logics of division and civil societies], edited by Anna Bozzo and Pierre-Jean Luizard, 179–92. Rome: Roma TrESPRESS, 2016.

Pierret, Thomas and Kjetil Selvik. "Limits of 'Authoritarian Upgrading' in Syria: Private Welfare, Islamic Charities, and the Rise of the Zayd Movement." *International Journal for Middle East Studies* 41 (2009): 595–614.

Pinto, Paulo G. "God and Nation: The Politics of Islam Under Bashar al-Asad." In *Syria from Reform to Revolt*. Vol. 1, *Political Economy and International Relations*, edited by Raymond Hinnebusch and Tina Zintl, 154–75. Syracuse, NY: Syracuse University Press, 2015.

Qadaya wa-shahadat. Vol. 1 (Spring 1990): rationalism, democracy, and modernity. Vol. 2 (Summer 1991): the nahda, and modernization then and now. Vol. 3 (Winter 1991): nationalism, the culture of difference, and the modernity of others. Vol. 4 (Fall 1991): dependency and *turath*. Vol. 5 (Spring 1992): reason, the nation, and universality. Vol. 6 (Winter 1992): literature, reality, history.

Radtke, Bernd. *Autochtone islamische Aufklärung im 18. Jahrhundert: Theoretische und filologische Bemerkungen: Fortführung einer Debatte* [Native Islamic enlightenment in the eighteenth century: Theoretical and philological remarks: Continuation of a debate]. Utrecht: M. Th. Houtsma Stichting, 2000.

——. "Erleuchterung und Aufklärung: Islamische Mystik und europäischer Rationalismus" [Illumination and enlightenment: Islamic mysticism and European rationalism]. *Die Welt des Islams* 34 (1994): 48–66.

Raymond, André, ed., *La Syrie d'aujourd'hui.* Paris: Éditions du CNRS, 1980.

——. "Les égyptiens et les lumières pendant l'expédition française." In *L'expédition d'Égypte, une entreprise des Lumières, 1798-1801: Actes de colloque*, edited by Patrice Bret, 103–17. Paris: Académie des Sciences, 1999.

Reichmuth, Stephan. "Arabic Literature and Islamic Scholarship in the 17th/18th Centuries: Topics and Biographies: Introduction." *Die Welt des Islams* 43 (2002): 281–88.

Reid, Donald Malcolm. *Cairo University and the Making of Modern Egypt.* Cambridge: Cambridge University Press, 2002.

Roussillon, Alain, ed., *Entre réforme sociale et mouvement national: Identité et modernization en Égypte (1882-1962).* Cairo: CEDEJ–Égypte/Soudan, 1995.

——. "Intellectuels en crise dans l'Égypte contemporaine." In *Intellectuels et militants de l'Islam contemporain*, edited by Gilles Kepel and Yann Richard, 213–58. Paris: Éditions du Seuil, 1990.

——. "Sociologie et société en Égypte: Le contournement des intellectuels par l'état." In *Les intellectuels et le pouvoir: Syrie, Égypte, Tunisie, Algérie*, 93–138. Cairo: Centre d'études et de documentation économique juridique et sociale (CEDEJ), 1986.

Ruiz de Elvira, Laura. "Christian Charities and the Ba'thist Regime in Bashar al-Asad's Syria." In Salamandra and Stenberg, *Syria from Reform to Revolt*, 92–109.

Ruiz de Elvira, Laura and Tina Zintl. "The End of the Ba'thist Social Contract in Bashar al-Asad's Syria: Reading Socio-political Transformations Through Charities and Broader Benevolent Activism." *International Journal for Middle East Studies* 46 (2014): 329–49.

Sadowski, Yahya. "Ba'thist Ethics and the Spirit of State Capitalism: Patronage and the Party in Contemporary Syria." In *Ideology and Power in the Middle East: Studies in Honor of George Lenczowski*, edited by Peter J. Chelkowski and Robert J. Pranger, 160–84. Durham: Duke University Press, 1988.

——. "The Eighth Regional Congress of the Syrian Baath." *MERIP MER* 134 (July-August 1985): 3–8.

——. "Patronage and the Ba'th: Corruption and Control in Contemporary Syria." *Arab Studies Quarterly* 9, no. 4 (Fall 1987): 442–61.

Sakr, Rita. "'We Would Meet Them One Day, and Call Them to Account for Their Oppression': Post-2005 Prison Writings in Syria." In *"Anticipating" the 2011 Uprisings: Revolutionary Literatures and Political Geographies*, 71–99. London: Macmillan, Palgrave Pivot, 2013.

Salam, Khaled Hamza. "Egyptian Culture Minister, Imaginary and Fabricated Battles." *Ikhwanweb*, November 20, 2006. http://www.ikhwanweb.com/article.php?id=3025.

Salamandra, Christa. "Creative Compromise: Syrian Television Makers Between Secularism and Islamism." *Contemporary Islam* 2 (2008): 177–89.

——. "Spotlight on the Bashar al-Asad Era: The Television Drama Outpouring." *Middle East Critique* 20, no. 2 (Summer 2011): 157–67.

——. "Syria's Drama Outpouring: Between Complicity and Critique." In Salamandra and Stenberg, *Syria from Reform to Revolt*, 36–52.

Salamandra, Christa and Leif Stenberg, eds., *Syria from Reform to Revolt*. Vol. 2, *Culture, Society, and Religion*. Syracuse, NY: Syracuse University Press, 2015.

Saleh, Hachem. "Hal akhta'a Gaber Asfour?" [Did Gaber Asfour make a mistake?]. *Al-Sharq al-awsat*, February 10, 2011.

——. *Ma'arek al-tanwiriyyin al-usuliyyin fi Urubba* [The battles of the proponents of enlightenment and the fundamentalists in Europe]. Beirut: Dar al-Saqi and Rabitat al-'aqlaniyyin al-'arab, 2010.

——. *Madkhal il al-tanwir al-urubbi* [Introduction to the European Enlightenment]. Beirut: Dar al-Tali'a li al-tiba'a wa al-nashr and Rabitat al-'aqlaniyyin al-'arab, 2005.

——. *Makhadat al-hadatha al-tanwiriyya: Al-qati'a al-ibistimulujiyya fi al-fikr wa al-hayat* [The processes of enlightenment modernity: The epistemological break in thought and life]. Beirut: Dar al-tali'a li al-tiba'a wa al-nashr, 2008.

Salti, Rasha, ed., *Insights Into Syrian Cinema: Essays and Conversations with Contemporary Filmmakers*. New York: ArteEast and Rattapallax, 2006.

Samu'il, Ibrahim. *Al-Manzil dhu al-madkhal al-wati'* [The house with the low entrance]. Beirut: Al-muassassa al-arabiyya li al-dirasat wa al-nashr, 2002.

——. *Al-nahnahat* [Light coughs]. Damascus: Dar al-Jundi, 1990.

——. *Ra'ihat al-khatw al-thaqil* [The stench of heavy steps]. Damascus: Dar al-Jundi, 1988.

Schulze, Reinhard. "Das islamische achtzehnte Jahrhundert: Versuch einer historiographischen Kritik" [The Islamic eighteenth century: An attempt at a historiographical critique]. *Die Welt des Islams* 30 (1990), 140–59.

——. "Was ist die islamische Aufklärung?" [What is the Islamic enlightenment?]. *Die Welt des Islams* 36, no. 3 (1996): 276–325.

Scott, David. "The Aftermaths of Sovereignty." In *Refashioning Futures: Criticism After Postcoloniality*, 131–57. Princeton: Princeton University Press, 1999.

Seale, Patrick. *The Struggle for Syria: A Study of Post-war Arab Politics, 1945-1958*. Oxford: Oxford University Press, 1965; London: Tauris, 1986.

Seurat, Michel. *L'état de barbarie*. Paris: Éditions du Seuil, 1989. Translated into Arabic by Amal Sara and Mark Bialo as *Al-Dawla al-mutawahhisha*. Beirut: al-Shabaka al-'arabiyya li al-abhath wa al-nashr, 2017.

Shabo, Rateb. *Madha wara' hadhihi al-judran* [What is there behind those walls?]. Beirut: Dar al-Adab, 2015.

Shoair, Mohammed. "Suqut muthaqqaf misri" [The fall of an Egyptian intellectual]. *Al-Akhbar*, February 3, 2011.

Shukri, Ghali. *Diktatoriyyat al-takhalluf al-arabi: Muqaddima fi ta'sil sosyologia al-ma'rifa* [The dictatorship of Arab backwardness: Introduction to the founding of the sociology of knowledge]. Beirut: Dar al-Tali'a, 1986.

——. *Salama Moussa wa azamat al-damir al-arabi* [Salama Moussa and the crisis of Arab conscience]. 4th edition, Beirut: Manshurat Dar al-Afaq al-jadida, 1983.

Sirees, Nihad. *Al-samt wa al-sakhab* [The silence and the roar]. Beirut: Dar al-adab, 2004. Translated by Max Weiss as *The Silence and the Roar*. New York: Other Press, 2013.

Stenberg, Leif. "Muslim Organizations in Bashar's Syria: The Transformation of the Shaykh Ahmad Kuftaro Foundation." In Salamandra and Stenberg, *Syria from Reform to Revolt*, 147–68.

Taher, Baha'. *Abna' Rifa'a: Al-thaqafa wa al-huriyya* [The sons of Rifa'a: Culture and freedom]. 1993. Cairo: Dar al-Shourouq, 2009.

Taleghani, Shareah. "Breaking the Silence of Tadmor Military Prison." "Inside the Inside: Life in Prison." Special issue, *MERIP MER* 275, no. 45 (Summer 2015).

——. "The Cocoons of Language, the Betrayals of Silence: Contemporary Syrian Prison Literature, Human Rights Discourse, and Literary Experimentalism." PhD dissertation. New York University, 2009.

——. "A Memoir Novel of Tadmur Military Prison." Review of *Al-Qawqa'a* [The shell], by Mustafa Khalifeh. *Syrian Studies Association Bulletin* 14, no. 2 (2009). https://ojcs.siue.edu/ojs/index.php/ssa/article/view/374/282.

——. "Vulnerability and Recognition in Syrian Prison Literature." *International Journal of Middle East Studies* 49 (2017): 91–109.

Tizini, Tayyeb. "Al-mufakkir al-suri Tayyeb Tizini: Al-taghayyurat al-'alamiyya ja'alatni u'id al-nadhar fi mashru'i 'an an-turath wa al-thawara" [The Syrian thinker Tayyeb Tizini: World changes made me reconsider my project about tradition and revolution]. *Al-Quds al-arabi*, October 7, 2008.

——. *Bayan fi al-nahda wa al-tanwir al-arabi* [Manifesto on the Arab nahda and tanwir]. Beirut: Dar al-Farabi, 2005.

——. "Dawlat al-qanun wa al-mu'assassat wa huriyyat al-ta'bir: Bidaya qabla kull bidaya" [The state of law and institutions and freedom of expression: A beginning before all beginnings]. In Barut and al-Kilani, *Suria bayn 'ahdayn* [Syria between two epochs], 238–40; first published in *al-Thawra*, November 11, 2000.

——. *Min al-turath ila al-thawra hawl nadhariyya muqtaraha fi qadiyyat al-turath al-arabi* [From tradition to revolution: A suggested theory on the issue of Arab tradition]. Damascus: Dar Ibn Khaldun li al-nashr wa al-tawzi', 1976.

——. *Min thulathiyyat al-fasad ila qadaya al-mujtama' al-madani* [From the trilogy of corruption to the issues of civil society]. Damascus: Dar Jafra li al-dirasat wa al-nashr, 2001.

van Dam, Nikolaos. *The Struggle for Power in Syria: Politics and Society Under Asad and the Ba'th Party*. 1979. London: Tauris, 1997.

Vauthier, Elizabeth. *La création romanesque contemporaine en Syrie de 1967 à nos jours* [Novelistic creation in contemporary Syria from 1967 to our days]. Damascus: Institut Français du Proche Orient, 2007.

Wahba, Mourad. "Al-muthaqqafun sabab nakbat hadha al-balad: La farqa bayna salafi wa wasati wa ikhwani . . . kulluhum wahid" [The intellectuals are the cause of this country's catastrophe: No difference between a salafi, a moderate, or a Muslim Brother . . . they're all the same]. *Al-Ahram*, September 11, 2015.

——. "Al-Sisi wa al-haqiqa al-mutlaqa" [Sisi and the absolute truth]. *Al-Masri al-yawm*, June 22, 2014.

——. *Al-usuliyya wa al-'almaniyya* [Fundamentalism and secularism]. Cairo: Dar al-thaqafa, 1995.

——, ed. *Hiwar hawla Ibn Rushd*. Cairo: Supreme Council of Culture, 1995.

——. "Iqalat al-duktur Ahmad Mujahid" [The dismissal of Ahmad Mujahid]. *Al-Masri al-yawm*, May 20, 2013.

——. *Madkhal ila al-tanwir* [Introduction to tanwir]. Cairo: Dar al-'alam al-thaleth, 1994.

——. *Masar Fikr: Sira dhatiyya* [Thought journey: An autobiography]. Part 1. Cairo: al-hay'a al-'amma li al-kitab, 2011.

——. *Mullak al-haqiqa al-mutlaqa* [The owners of absolute truth]. Cairo: Maktabat al-usra, 1999.

——. "The Paradox of Averroes." *Archiv für Rechts- und Sozialphilosophie / Archives for Philosophy of Law and Social Philosophy* 66, no. 2 (1980): 257–60.

——. *Ruba'iyyat al-dimuqratiyya* [The democracy quartet]. Cairo: al-dar al-misriyya al-sa'udiyya, 2011.

Wahba, Mourad and Mona Abousenna, eds. *Averroes and the Enlightenment*. Amherst, NY: Prometheus, 1996.

——, eds. *Enlightenment and Culture*. Cairo: Goethe Institute, 1990.

Wannous, Saadallah. *Al-A'mal al-kamila* [The complete works]. Beirut: Dar al-Adab, 2004.

——. "Al-thaqafa al-wataniyya wa al-wa'i al-tarikhi" [National culture and historical awareness]. *Qadaya wa-shahadat* 4 (Fall 1991): 5–39.

——. "Bayn al-hadatha wa al-tahdith" [Between modernity and modernization]. *Qadaya wa-shahadat* 2 (Summer 1990): 5–23.

——. "Hiwar ma' Antoun Maqdisi hawl al-hadatha wa al-tahdith" [Dialogue with Antoun Maqdisi on modernity and modernization]. *Qadaya wa-shahadat* 3 (Winter 1991): 5–22.

Waterbury, John. *The Egypt of Nasser and Sadat: The Political Economy of Two Regimes*. Princeton: Princeton University Press, 1983.

Wedeen, Lisa. "Acting 'As if': Symbolic Politics and Social Control in Syria." *Comparative Studies in Society and History* 40, no. 3 (July 1998): 503–23.

——. *Ambiguities of Domination: Politics, Rhetoric, and Symbols in Contemporary Syria*. 1999. Chicago: University of Chicago Press, 2015.

——. "Ideology and Humor in Dark Times: Notes from Syria." *Critical Inquiry* 39 (Summer 2013): 841–73.

——. "New Texts Out Now: Lisa Wedeen, Ideology and Humor in Dark Times: Notes from Syria." Interview. *Jadaliyya*, January 29, 2014.

Weiss, Max. "Who Laughs Last: Literary Transformations of Syria Authoritarianism." In Heydemann and Leenders, *Middle East Authoritarianisms*, 143–65.

Wieland, Carsten. *A Decade of Lost Chances: Repression and Revolution from Damascus Spring to Arab Spring*. Seattle: Cunepress, 2012.

Wild, Stefan, ed. "Islamic Enlightenment in the 18th century?" Special issue, *Die Welt des Islams* 36, no. 3 (1996): 271–75.

Yassin Hassan, Rosa. *Nigativ: Min mudhakkarat al-mu'taqalat al-siyasiyyat* [Negative: From the memoirs of women political detainees]. Cairo: Markaz al-qahira li huquq al-insan, 2008.

Yasushi, Kosugi. *"Al-Manar* Revisited: The 'Lighthouse' of the Islamic Revival." In Dudoignon, Hisao, and Yasushi, *Intellectuals in the Modern Islamic World,* 3–33.

Yazbek, Samar. "Scenario Camera: Antoun Maqdisi wa khadi'at al-ghiyab" [Scenario camera: Antoun Maqdisi and the cheating absence]. *Al-hiwar al-mutamaddin,* April 7, 2005. http://www.ahewar.org/debat/s.asp?aid=34999.

Younis, Sherif. *al-Bahth 'an al-khalas: Azamat al-dawla wa al-islam wa al-hadatha fi misr* [The search for salvation: The crisis of the state, Islam, and modernity in Egypt]. Cairo: Al-hay'a al-misiryya al-'amma li al-kitab, 2014.

——. *al-Zahf al-Muqaddas: Mudhaharat al-tanahhi wa tashakkul 'ibadat Nasser* [The holy march: The demonstrations of the resignation and the formation of Nasser worship]. Cairo: Mirit, 2005; Cairo: Dar al-tanwir, 2012.

——. "Marxisme et patriotisme dans les régimes militaires de libération nationale: Les 'Officiers Libres' et les communistes égyptiens." *Cahiers d'histoire: Revue d'histoire critique* 105–106 (2008): 145–74. www.chrhc.revues.org/543.

——. *Masarat al-thawra: Ru'ya tahliliyya dimuqratiyya jadhriyya* [The courses of the revolution: A radical analytical democratic vision]. Cairo: Dar al-'ayn, 2012.

——. *Nida' al-sha'b: Tarikh naqdi li al-idiyolojiyya al-nasiriyya* [The call of the people: A critical history of Nasserite ideology]. Cairo: Dar al-Shourouq, 2012.

——. *Sayyed Qutb wa al-usuliyya al-islamiyya* [Sayyed Qutb and Islamic fundamentalism]. Cairo: al-hay'a al-misriyya al-'amma li al-kitab, 2014.

——. *Su'al al-huwiyya: Al-huwiyya wa sultat al-muthaqqaf fi ma ba'd al-hadatha* [The question of identity: Identity and the power of the intellectual in postmodernity]. Cairo: Mirit li al-nashr wa al-ma'lumat, 1999.

Zakariyya, Ahmad. "Gaber Asfour . . .'mnawwarati' 'ala rababat al-sulta" [Gaber Asfour . . . pseudo-enlightener on the music of power]. *Al-Araby al-jadid,* July 18, 2014.

Zghayar, Khouloud. "Suria fi mu'taqal al-Baath/al-Asad—Qissat watan" [Syria in the captivity of the Baath/Assad—Story of a homeland]. Parts 1 and 2. *Souria Houria,* March 18 and April 28, 2012.

Ziadeh, Ridwan, ed., *Hiwarat "Muntada al-Hiwar al-watani"* [The dialogues of the "National Dialogue Forum"]. Paris: Éditions Eurabe and the Arab Council for Human Rights, 2004.

Index